Inflection Journal
Volume 09 - Repair
December 2022

Inflection Journal is published annually by the Melbourne School of Design at the University of Melbourne and Melbourne Books.

Editors:
Aurelia Tasha Handoko, Patrick Hayes, Yutong (Kelly) Jin, Bridget McNab and Ioanna Petropoulou

Collaborators:
Yichen Cao, Jarel Cheah, Simran Kaur, Anna-Lena Mueller, Jiqing (Eric) Xie

Academic Advisor:
Dr. AnnMarie Brennan

Academic Advisory Board:
Dr. AnnMarie Brennan
Prof. Alan Pert

The editors would like to thank all those involved in the production of this journal for their generous assistance and support.

Special thanks are due to AnnMarie Brennan, whose continual support, guidance and encouragement has been invaluable.

For editorial enquiries contact:
editorial@inflectionjournal.com

For sales enquiries contact:
info@melbournebooks.com.au

inflectionjournal.com
facebook.com/inflectionjournal
instagram.com/inflectionjournal

ISSN 2199-8094

ISBN 9781877096426

Melbourne Books
Level 9, 100 Collins Street,
Melbourne, VIC 3000,
Australia
www.melbournebooks.com.au
info@melbournebooks.com.au

The opinions expressed in *Inflection* are those of the authors and are not endorsed by the University of Melbourne.

CONGRATULATIONS
INFLECTION JOURNAL
VOLUME 08 - PRESENCE

WINNER OF THE 2022
BATES SMART AWARD FOR
ARCHITECTURE IN MEDIA
(STATE AWARD)

Cover Image:
Kerstin Thompson Architects, Sacred Heart Building/Doorway,
© Derek Swalwell, 2018.

Inside cover:
Kerstin Thompson Architects, Sacred Heart Building/Interior,
© Derek Swalwell, 2018.

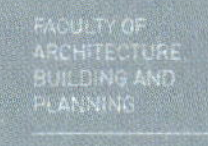

CONTRIBUTORS

Adrian Fernandez
Fernandez is a designer whose interests lie in interrogating the many divides and biases that lie within the architectural profession, through speculative projects and writings. He has participated in talks at Blindside Gallery, MPavilion, Testing Grounds, Black Spark Cultural Centre, and was a part of the Gertrude Emerging Writers program in 2020. Fernandez has written pieces for *Caliper Journal*, *Architect Victoria* and *Dissolution Magazine*, amongst others.

Andrew MacKinnon
MacKinnon is a recent architectural graduate from the University of Melbourne. He currently works at Rebecca Naughtin Architect, a local residential architectural firm, and is interested in design that challenges convention while reducing the built industry's impact on the environment. He is inspired by sustainable urbanisation, urban acupuncture and co-creation for social housing and public spaces.

Ayomi Olasoji
Olasoji is a fourth-year architectural student at Monash University. Underlined by her passion for social change and community directed initiatives, her degree has inspired her investigation into the relationship between architecture, design and context.

Charlie Qiuli Xue
Xue has taught architecture at Shanghai Jiaotong University, the University of Texas, and City University of Hong Kong. He is also extensively involved in design and consultant practice in Hong Kong, the Chinese mainland, and the US. An award-winning architect and writer, he has published 15 books, 40 book chapters, and more than 160 research papers in professional and international peer-reviewed journals including *Cities*, *Habitat International* and *Urban Design Journal*, among others. His book on Hong Kong was awarded by the International Committee of Architectural Critics (CICA) in 2017. His research interests are Chinese architecture, transnational design and high-density environments.

Chris Parkinson
Parkinson is a photographic artist, arts professional and published author who uses photographic processes and practices to remix the visual vocabulary of urban environments across cultures. His PhD at the University of Melbourne researches collective art practices and public cultures in Yogyakarta, Indonesia and Dili, Timor-Leste. Parkinson coordinates and delivers a Street Art elective to undergraduate students at the University. He also co-curates and is a senior editor of PHOTODUST — an Asia Pacific lens-based photo project — and is a Youth Arts Officer with the City of Yarra. He is a member of the University of Melbourne Centre of Visual Art (CoVA) Graduate Academy and the Centre for Projection Art Creative Advisory Committee.

Clare Dieckmann
Dieckmann is the recipient of the 2021 Byera Hadley Traveling Scholarship for her project, *Terracotta: Innovating Australian Rammed Earth Architecture*. Dieckmann's research aims to uncover how robots are innovating sustainable construction methods, making rammed-earth less labour intensive and more widely accessible to the profession. She is currently an architectural graduate practicing with Allen Jack + Cottier Architects, where she aims to make the built environment a more liveable and beautiful place each day.

Dan Cruddace
Cruddace is a senior practice director of BVN Architecture in Sydney, a collaborative firm engaging with civic, institutional and development projects in Australia and internationally. Previously a partner at Sheppard Robson in London, he has worked on a number of high profile schemes in Europe, the Middle East and Australia. Cruddace has particular expertise in the design and delivery of complex residential-led developments, commercial office HQs and high-rise towers. He currently leads BVN's Quay Quarter Tower project.

Daniel Huppatz
Huppatz is an Associate Professor in the Department of Architectural and Industrial Design at Swinburne University of Technology in Melbourne. Huppatz's books include a four-volume edited collection, *Design: Critical and Primary Sources* (Bloomsbury, 2016), *Modern Asian Design* (Bloomsbury, 2018) and *Design: The key Concepts* (Bloomsbury, 2019). He has published extensively in peer-reviewed journals and presented papers at numerous international conferences.

Daniel de Oliveira Vasconcelos
Vasconcelos is a PhD candidate in the Faculty of Architecture, Building and Planning at the University of Melbourne and holds a Master in China Studies from the Yenching Academy of Peking University.

David Mah
Mah is a Senior Lecturer in Urban Design and Architecture at the Melbourne School of Design. Previously, he lectured at the Harvard Graduate School of Design (2010-2017). While at Harvard, Mah was the design research lead for the Health and Places Initiative, a research collaboration between the Harvard Graduate School of Design and the Harvard T.H. Chan School of Public Health, investigating the links between the built environment and health outcomes. He taught design and theory at Cornell University Department of Architecture, and Landscape Urbanism at the Architectural Association in London.

Evan Pavka
Pavka is a writer and editor whose work explores the intersections of power, memory, gender, sexuality and the built environment. He previously held editorial positions at *Azure Magazine*, *Inuit Art Quarterly* and *Canadian Art* and has presented work at the Art Gallery of Ontario, Museum of Contemporary Canadian Art and the KTH Royal Institute of Technology in Stockholm. In addition, his writings have appeared in *Article*, *ArchDaily*, *ANInterior*, *Lunch*, *On Site Review*, *Pidgin*, *The Architect's Newspaper* and *Field Journal*. Pavka is an Assistant Professor at the Wayne University James Pearson Duffy Department of Art and Art History.

Guanghui Ding
Ding is Associate Professor of Architecture at Beijing University of Civil Engineering and Architecture (BUCEA). He is the author of *Constructing a Place of Critical Architecture in China* (Routledge, 2015), co-author of *A History of Design Institutes in China* (Routledge, 2018) and co-editor of *Exporting Chinese Architecture* (Springer, 2022). Ding's research focuses on the history, theory and criticism of modern Chinese architecture. At BUCEA, Ding teaches architecture and urban design studios as well as theory courses critiquing contemporary architecture. Based in Beijing, he practices architecture both independently and collaboratively.

Io Carydi
Carydi is a registered architect and urban designer. With studies in Architecture (NTUA) and Landscape Urbanism (the Architectural Association) and previous working experience with Hargreaves Associates in London, Carydi developed an interest in landscape and environmental systems and their integration with the morphology of urban environments. She has taught as an Adjunct Lecturer in landscape and urban design courses at various universities in Greece and Cyprus and holds her architectural design firm in Athens.

Jeremy Bonwick
Bonwick is a graduate of architecture from the University of Melbourne. He holds a Bachelor of Arts in screenwriting and cinema studies. Bonwick works freelance in design, film and photography in Melbourne. His architectural design work and short films have been exhibited, screened and received recognition and awards around Australia and internationally. His independent architectural thesis project, *(Re)collecting Rural*, was recognised with the Bates Smart Award at its conclusion in 2021.

Joan C. Tronto
Tronto is a Professor of Political Science at the University of Minnesota and Professor Emerita of Political Science at the City University of New York. She received her Bachelor of Arts from Oberlin College and her PhD from Princeton University. In 2014 she was awarded an honorary doctorate by the University for Humanistic Studies in the Netherlands. Tronto has published extensively on the subject of care as a political idea. Her publications include over forty articles and several books, such as *Moral Boundaries: A Political Argument for an Ethic of Care* (Taylor & Francis, 1993).

Kengo Kuma
Kuma established his award-winning practice, Kengo Kuma & Associates (KKAA), in 1990. He is currently a Professor in the Department of Architecture at the University of Tokyo. He holds a PhD from Keio University and is an international and honory fellow of multiple national architectural institutes. Kuma proposes architecture that opens up new relationships between nature, technology and human beings. His major publications include *Makeru Kenchiku* [Architecture of Defeat] (Iwanami Shoten, 2004) and *Shizen na Kenchiku* [Natural Architecture] (Iwanami Shinsho, 2008), among others.

Kirsten Day
Day is an architect and director of Norman Day + Associates. She is a Lecturer in Architecture at the University of Melbourne. Day chairs the Education Committee for the Victorian Chapter of the Australian Institute of Architects and is an examiner for the Architects Registration Board of Victoria. Her publications, workshops, and design studios explore the themes of future scenarios and the impact of change. Day organised the international conference, Future Housing: Global Cities and Regional Problems, at Swinburne University in 2016 with the Architecture Media Politics Society as part of the Housing Critical Futures conference series.

Kristen Wang
Wang is an award-winning designer and graduate of architecture, based in Melbourne. She holds a Bachelor of Architecture (Honours) from the University of Kent in the United Kingdom and a Master of Architecture from the University of Melbourne. Wang has worked in architectural studios such as Bandesign Architect (Japan) and taught digital fabrication and technical skills at the University of Melbourne. In 2018, Wang opened her own design studio with a focus on materiality, functionality, sustainability and aesthetics.

Leire Asensio-Villoria
Asensio-Villoria is currently a Senior Lecturer at the Melbourne School of Design. Previously, she has taught at the Harvard Graduate School of Design, the Architectural Association in London and Cornell University College of Architecture, Art and Planning. While at Harvard, Asensio-Villoria was part of the leadership team for the Waste to Energy Group and was a design research lead for the Health and Places Initiative, a research collaboration between the Harvard Graduate School of Design and the Harvard T.H. Chan School of Public Health, studying the links between the built environment and health outcomes.

Malkit Shoshan
Shoshan is the founder and director of FAST: Foundation for Achieving Seamless Territory, an architectural think tank that uses research, advocacy and design to investigate the relationship between architecture, urban planning and human rights in conflict and post-conflict areas. Born in Israel and based in the US, Shoshan is an award-winning author and map maker of several books, including *Atlas of Conflict: Israel-Palestine* (Uitgeverij 010, 2010) and the new book, *BLUE: Architecture of UN Peacekeeping Missions* (Actar, 2022). She lectures in urban planning and design at the Harvard Graduate School of Design.

Orkun Kasap
Kasap is a senior assistant at Construction Heritage and Preservation at ETH Zurich. He studied architecture and urban planning in Turkey, Denmark and Switzerland. After receiving his Master of Architecture from ETH Zurich in 2014, he worked at Gramazio Kohler Research, ETH Zurich and at the National Center of Competence in Research (NCCR) Digital Fabrication as a project coordinator until June 2019. He has also worked in various architectural offices and participated in architectural competitions in Turkey and Switzerland.

Silke Langenberg
Langenberg is Full Professor for Construction Heritage and Preservation at ETH Zurich. Her chair is in the Institute for Preservation and Construction History as well as the Institute for Technology in Architecture. From 2014 until 2020, she was Professor for Design in Existing Contexts, Preservation, and Building Research at the Munich University of Applied Sciences. She studied architecture and holds a PhD in engineering sciences. Her research focuses on the rationalisation of building processes as well as the development, repair, and long-term conservation of serially, industrially, and digitally manufactured constructions.

Yingting Chen
Chen is a PhD candidate in Architecture at City University of Hong Kong. She has five years of practice experience in the US and China working on urban design, landscape, and architecture projects. Her research interest lies in the human-nature relationship, the impact of design on health and wellbeing, and transnational design exchange and cooperation. She is a contributing author in *Exporting Chinese Architecture: History, Issues and 'One Belt One Road'* (C. Q. Xue, & G. Ding (eds.), Springer, 2022) as well as four research papers in professional and international peer-reviewed journals including, *The Journal of Architecture*, *Journal of Urban Design* and *International Journal of Architecture*.

Yutaka Terasaki
Terasaki is a partner at Kengo Kuma and Associates and a director of the firm's Shanghai office since 2020. A graduate of Tokyo University of Science, Teraski has worked in multiple architectural practices in both Japan and China. He played a key role in the design of Shipyard1862.

CONTENTS

HEALING SCARS / MAKE DO AND MEND

EDITORIAL

Aurelia Tasha Handoko, Patrick Hayes, Yutong (Kelly) Jin, Bridget McNab and Ioanna Petropoulou

Inflection *acknowledges the Traditional Custodians of the land on which we work and are published, the Wurundjeri People of the Kulin Nation. We pay our respects to their Elders past, present and emerging and acknowledge First Nations people as our first storytellers and architects.*

Repair is a loaded word. On the surface it is seemingly benevolent and optimistic. Indeed, to repair is to acknowledge that something broken requires fixing. However, its application is subjective. To some, repairing suggests a return to halcyon days of a former time, a retroactive process of "making [something] great again." To others, repair is anti-utopian, a rejection of tabula rasa principles, a challenge to accept the damage of our time and create something new with the broken pieces.

The Abbotsford convent, this volume's cover image, is no less charged. Founded by The Sisters of the Good Shepherd in 1863 and repurposed as an artist retreat at the forefront of Melbourne's creative scene, the precinct grapples with traumatic history as the former site of a women's asylum and Magdalene laundry – a site characterised by abandonment, exploitation and brutality. In light of this, Kerstin Thompson Architects' renovation of the convent's Sacred Heart Building makes a poignant statement by embracing its old, stripped and flaking walls. This approach reveals important questions: How do we heal our environment while acknowledging the scars of the past? And, to what extent should we repair?

In her article, *Notes on the Architecture of UN Peacekeeping Missions,* Malkit Shoshan investigates UN peacekeeping bases as an infrastructure of societal repair on similarly contentious ground: post-conflict Mali. While on the surface the UN's infrastructure of repair appears benevolent, Shoshan reveals that the material presence of temporary reparative interventions and actions remain indefinitely, often to the detriment of the surrounding natural environment and existing culture. Here, healing scars creates new wounds.

Repairing damage equally has implications of concealed history. In Australia, repairing colonial infrastructure masks the fact that 200 years of European built heritage has been to the detriment of the country's Indigenous cultural landscapes. Beneath the University of Melbourne's colonial heritage grounds, natural creek systems carrying short-finned eels once valued by local Wurundjeri people are now invisible to the eye, rerouted into subterranean storm drains.[1] The layers and complexity of history may be extinguished in choosing to restore historic buildings. As such, we ask how we can repair without erasing, simplifying, or hiding the complexity of the past.

Rejuvenating former industrial areas into natural landscapes and deluxe developments, a common theme of many adaptive reuse projects, hides an uncomfortable truth: the built industry has historically exacted significant environmental harm. Indeed, this volume's theme was originally inspired by the repair of other violent 'scars' on the landscape: the Latrobe Valley's open-cut mines in Victoria, one of the world's largest known brown coal deposits. Aligned with COP26's goal of limiting coal mining and fossil fuel usage, the Victorian Government is in the process of retiring the Latrobe Valley's mines. Ironically, the Rehabilitation Strategy by Engie and Arup proposes flooding the pits to create a series of artificial lakes, erasing the industrial scars only to make a pseudo-return to nature while exacerbating the environmental damage to the region.[2] Reflecting on the words of landscape designer Gilles Clement, as curators and stewards of the "global garden" that is Earth, we asked our contributors to question how architects and practitioners can repair anthropocenic environmental damage without inducing further harm.

In his article, *Rhizomatic Rejuvenation*, Andrew MacKinnon imagines a long-term design strategy for the Latrobe Valley in stark opposition to the current official solution. His work sings the complexities of repair. The adapted thesis proposes five humble architectural gestures, generated over long periods of time, that individually reflect the deeply complex histories and stories of the site. Industrial influence is rife in the use of existing structures and materials; consultation with the First Nations people, the Gunaikurnai people is advocated for in each development stage with shared governance of the site; and phytoremediation is a priority and exists in the architectural program as well as an ongoing maintenance. Here, the repair is more than architecture, it acknowledges that buildings are part of systems: social, global, ecological and economical. Their existence either supports or questions the ever-consuming and ever-growing state of the world. When do we stop buying and building anew and look to repair what exists?

The 2021 Pritzker Prize winners, Anne Lacaton and Jean-Philip Vassal ask the same question through their work.[3] When designing, their first task is to stop and think, and to decide whether to intervene. The simplicity of this question unravels our current fixation on the capitalist notion of continuous newness and an ignorance towards what is and was. In this issue, Evan Pavka's piece celebrates this dichotomy through an exploration of rubble. *Record of Rubble* investigates the stories that contemporary ruins present; the historical memories of what exists and how these begin to dictate their own places. Focusing on Detroit, the industrial rubble is unpacked as political, social and economic mirrors of the city. Here, history is ubiquitous and acknowledged to the detail it deserves, directly speaking to the richness of the repair process.

Similarly, in Kengo Kuma's *Shipyard1862*, the architects eschew the glamour of renovation to instead adopt a bear bones and sombre approach to their intervention. Hiding contemporary technology such as new HVAC and acoustic systems inside existing rusting pipes, the building presents an honest materiality that allows visitors to thoughtfully connect with the building's past, its former inhabitants and its legacy.

The current trend of material overconsumption and waste necessitates repair through recycled and renewable sources. We act as though resources are endless, yet material abundance is an illusion. According to a recent study updating the 1972 The Limits to Growth research, if the world maintains its current economic and population growth rates, the complete absence of natural materials will be seen within 20 years.[4] In response, BVN Architects' Quay Quarter Tower serves as an optimistic precedent, revolutionising material reuse on a grand scale. Inheriting a mid–century skyscraper in central Sydney, the architects and developers made the daring decision to forego the wrecking ball and instead, appropriate the existing concrete structure, expanding and recladding the building in a contemporary skin. The form and appearance of the existing building is hardly recognisable; the new tower cantilevers and curves where the old was boxy and banal yet, BVN's project illustrates that opportunities to reuse and repair lie beyond skin deep. The new building may be a glamorous reincarnation but in retaining the existing concrete structure it has profoundly reduced its material carbon footprint. The project proves that architecture can move into its next state of being by adapting rather than eliminating the existing.

Faced with the wicked crises of our world, from historic injustices and global inequalities to the rapidly warming climate, repair may seem a naive and Sisyphean task. However, as all of the pieces in this issue describe, to repair is a chance to reflect, to hone in on and recalibrate our vision for our built and natural environment. This volume does not hide the fact that repairing is a tedious, sometimes unsuccessful and counteractive process. Nevertheless, Joan Tronto's words serve as an optimistic comfort, as she advocates for architects to "care." We suggest that repairing is a method of caring, a chance to think critically about our profession, practices and methods.

While repair is an acknowledgement of a broken system, it is also a means of salvaging and embracing what is important.

01 Zach Hope, "One eel of a story: the slippery truth of a fishy underground migration," *Age*, February 6, 2021.

02 Miki Perkins, "Latrobe Valley mine 'pit lakes' risk river health in drying climate: reports", *Sydney Morning Herald*, December 10, 2020.

03 Samanata Kumar, "Anne Lacaton and Jean-Phillipe Vassal - Winners of 2021 Pritzker Prize." Rethinking the Future, published August 7, 2022, https://www.re-thinkingthefuture.com/architectural-news/a3729-anne-lacaton-and-jean-philippe-vassal-winners-of-2021-pritzker-prize/

04 Gaya Herrington, "Update to limits to growth: Comparing the World3 model with empirical data," *Journal of Industrial Ecology* (Yale University), vol. 25 (3), 614-626.

RECORD OF RUBBLE

Evan Pavka

Rubble speaks if you listen. Fragments of concrete, piles of brick, fissures in sidewalks are as indicative of material flows as they are of larger systems of management, mismanagement and disenfranchisement. Whether broken deliberately or by entropy, they are detached from a greater whole but remain constantly in reference to it. As opposed to simply connecting back to their counterpart, these objects also reference the immaterial logic embedded in their form. In this sense, rubble is indicative of both the past and potential futures. Contemplating rubble — its fractures, striations, markings and more — opens a form of temporal awareness, exposing the fragility of current structures and the possibility of other relations to place and space.

In the architectural imaginary, ruins and fragments have been coveted if not fetishised since at least the 18th century. These fractured or weathered elements embody traces of the past while offering space for projection, to conceptually complete the gaps and absences with speculative futures. As historian Jonathan Hill notes, ruins and fragments are "richly suggestive because they are incomplete" and therefore "imply potential as well as loss."[1] Rubble, therefore, is a platform. It's a place to start.

Rubble dots the nearly 6,750 kilometres of sidewalks that stitch together the over 6,200 square kilometres comprising the greater metropolitan area of Detroit, Michigan. Often romanticised as an urban sprawl of derelict and decrepit buildings that evoke the extreme limits of governmental corruption, racial disparity and late capitalism, the city was once analysed by geographer Ronald Horvath as exemplary of the idea of "machine space." For Horvath, this was "territory devoted primarily to the use of machines" and where "machines have priority over people."[2] Nothing captured the nature of machine space more than the extensive infrastructure — from roads to highways to parking lots — devoted to the automobile.

Both the automobile and its corresponding space are inseparable from Detroit and directly connected to the rubble that fills it. Broken curbs and fractured bollards are produced directly by these machines. Cleared from the street, they encroach into the area dedicated to human occupants. In other instances, the slow deterioration of infrastructure is connected to the independence the vehicle affords. In the mid-twentieth century, urban renewal projects razed neighbourhoods like Black Bottom for a new residential district by Mies van der Rohe in addition to the Interstate 375 highway. In the late 1990s, legislation was altered so that city workers such as police officers or firefighters no longer had to reside in the city that employed them.[3] Due to the extensive network of highways, such employees could easily live in the suburban areas north of 8 Mile — the de facto border of the city proper and the larger metropolitan area — while conveniently commuting downtown. This loss of revenue from property taxes contributed to further austerity measures that cut public services and maintenance to predominantly Black areas. Sidewalks became the purview of individual residents as an extension of their property, abdicating the city from responsibility for upkeep. As the median yearly income of residents remains just over $30,000 USD according to census records from 2016 to 2020, there are limited resources to fix such deteriorating infrastructure. Thus fractures, heaves and overgrowth are common features in the pedestrian paths stitching together residential areas.

Fracturing surfaces contested histories of movement contained beneath the infrastructural skins of concrete and asphalt. Along Cass Avenue, fissures in the paving near Stimson Street show metal tracks belonging to a lost transit system, revealing the slow violence against equitable, accessible transit in favour of the personal vehicle. Between 1929 and 1931, the Grant Trunk Western Railroad implemented a public route linking Detroit to Pontiac, the most northern suburb of the metro area. It joined the nearly 1,600 street cars that knit the expansive city together. By the mid-1940s, a fleet of busses, street cars and a commuter rail formed a robust system of public transit. A two-month transit strike in the early 1950s significantly impacted use and by 1956 streetcar service was shuttered. Exacerbated further by population and employment decline, fiscal mismanagement and the echoes of the 1967 riots, the Detroit-Pontiac route closed in 1983 with no other plans for infrastructure of that size though Gerald Ford had offered the region $600 million USD to construct a new rail system. The urban heritage of these post-war complications date back to at least 1920, where plans to construct a subway system were halted due to single "no" vote by a council member. A public vote in 1933 showed significant support from Detroit residents yet no subterranean system was recommended to the federal government by the state.[5] In 2017, years after all former streetcar tracks had been covered or removed, the city completed the QLine: a 5.3-kilometre-long rail running along Woodward Avenue. The irony of the eradication of an expansive system only for a shadow to return decades later is not lost. Like geological strata, layers of ineffective and predatory bureaucracy that created class-based and racial divisions in the city through the accessibility of public or personal transportation are embodied in (if not inseparable from) the debris.

Paradoxically, the automobile was largely responsible for Detroit's industrialisation and the deindustrialisation that followed. The proliferation of employment opportunities at the "Big Three" (Chrysler, General Motors and Ford) was slowly shuttered due to the same automation that had catapulted these very industries. Coupled with the relocation of factories and outsourcing to cheaper labour markets, the flight of industries and residents was close behind. By July 2013, the city officially filed for bankruptcy. Though a product of decades of disinvestment, depopulation and decline, the already tenuous conditions were exacerbated by the financial crisis of 2008, leading to an estimated deficit of 18 to 20 billion USD. The technology of the car — its association with individual freedom — privileged a particular way of seeing the city that continues to have specific spatial ramifications.

Rubble, too, records the nuances of the economic shifts that followed. In the wake of the crisis, scrapping emerged as a viable industry. Everything from the steel on pedestrian bridges to sewer lids to the wiring in long-abandoned residences was salvaged and scavenged.[4] The architectural violence of the activity left much detritus in its wake.

Above: Cast concrete from load bearing block. 2022. Image by author.

Above: Painted concrete from the surface of an underpass, asphalt from a carpark pavement and concrete from a broken pathway. 2022. Image by author.

Opposite: Brick from chipped facade of Film Exchange Building and weathered concrete from unidentified urban element. 2022. Image by author.

Amid the ongoing gentrification of the downtown and midtown areas, rubble remains ever-present as if contesting the use of the contemporary city as a temporary playground for those on the urban periphery. For the past decade, Quicken Loans founder Dan Gilbert and real estate arm Bedrock have purchased numerous vacant, palatial structures in the central core. This affordable property yielded cheap office space, which spurred the need for additional commercial enterprises to cater to employees. The larger result of this process of acquisition and renovation was a veritable destination for suburban workers who flood the area by day — filling nearly every surface parking lot — and flee by night. But a city is not a theme park, even if treated as such. Broken remains, recalling the fractured and fragmented pasts behind recent development, expose the infrastructural wear caused by this form of occupation and the ongoing pattern of disregard for the city's maintenance and care.

While significantly contributing to these architectural fractures, spatial logic of the automobile also demonstrates the emergence of a new temporal period. Folding out from, proceeding and perhaps even engulfing the Anthropocene (a period where human activity has significantly impacted the planet's geography and ecosystems), the Autocene is a geological epoch where all of the Earth's systems have been influenced by machines.[6] The fallacy of levelled neighbourhoods, distributed communities built on the foundation of the nuclear family and access to resources defined by access to the car are all products of the sprawling spatial logic of highways and roads that prioritise the machine rather than the human inhabitant. The layers of paving that lines this automotive space adds additional skins to the Earth. Rubble then serves an important archeological function. Hunks of concrete, asphalt, brick and cast cement are evidence of the Autocene; artefacts of the new geology of machine infrastructure.

In this shifting geological time, such urban and architectural remnants reflect a particular strategy of inhabiting brokenness. Occasionally, one will pass by an abandoned house and notice the small light illuminating the interior. Elsewhere, vacant commercial buildings are adorned with prolific murals that seem to suggest their former use. Even in the long-dormant and crumbling Fisher Body Plant 21, which once exclusively provided automotive bodies for General Motors, traces of occupation can be found: the coals from recently made fires, empty water bottles, makeshift bridges between openings in the foundations and swatches from torn sleeping bags. Larger myths of the city and its urban blight ignore these textures of quotidian and everyday activities that move through vacant or disregarded spaces. Life unfolds amidst ruins and rubble as if Joseph Gandy's fictional 1798 watercolour depicting four figures finding refuge around a fire in the speculative, overgrown husk of Sir John Soane's scheme for the Bank of England had manifested.

If the city, as the Italian architect Aldo Rossi once argued, is the locus of historical memory, what role does this debris play?[7] These urban relics can only be discovered by countering the very logic of machine space. By walking the Motor City, resisting the circulation of the automobile, one encounters an unfolding terrain of rubble. In each splinter and fragment, histories of neglect, disinvestment and structural inaptitude coalesce. Strewn throughout the streets, these artefacts can be seen as small everyday monuments — little acts of memory and testaments to the sedimentary layers of political, social and economic forces that have shaped and continue to shape Detroit.

Joining the strata of the planet's surface, segments of brick, asphalt and concrete relay the material impacts of broken and ineffective systems in desperate need of repair. Patterns of disinvestment, structural racism and displacement by urban renewal projects as well as other forces are embedded in their contours and fractures. However, this rubble does not signal or produce repair. Rather, rubble remains on the street for a particular reason. Cracks, fractures and fragments make visible a long, complicated history of disrepair. Here, such breaking is not forgetting but, instead, remembering. Breaking also makes room for imagining other relations, other spaces, other cities, other communities. In their chipped edges, peeling surfaces and more, there is room to speculate and project a more equitable future among all the ruins of the past — one that centres on the collective rather than the machine. The embrace of brokenness, too, offers fleeting but important territory to remember the generations who — out of desire or necessity — have found ways to flourish amidst the rubble.

01 Jonathan Hill, *Weather Architecture* (New York: Routledge, 2012), 90.

02 Ronald J. Horvath, "Machine Space," *Geographical Review* 65, no.2 (1974): 168.

03 For a more sustained analysis of the contested histories of Detroit see Thomas J. Sugrue, *The Origins of the Urban Crisis: Race and Inequality in Postwar Detroit* (New York: Princeton University Press, 2014).

04 John Eligon, "Ruin and Renewal: Crackdown in a Detroit Stripped of Metal Parts," *The New York Times*, March 16, 2015, 1.

05 See Harry Dalheimer, *Public Transportation in Detroit* (Detroit: Wayne University Press, 1951); Michigan Legislature, *Transit History of the Detroit* (Lansing: Michigan State Legislature, 2009), 1-7.

06 Stephanie Sherman, "The Autocene: Towards a Post-Automotive Future," *Strelka Mag*, 25 January 2022, https://strelkamag.com/en/article/the-autocene.

07 Aldo Rossi, *The Architecture of the City* (Cambridge: MIT Press, 1986), 16.

NOTES ON THE ARCHITECTURE OF UN PEACEKEEPING MISSIONS

Malkit Shoshan

In 2016, Malkit Shoshan travelled to Mali to visit and investigate United Nations peacekeeping bases. As part of her ongoing research into architecture in conflict and post-conflict areas, the field reseach was exhibited at the Dutch Pavilion at the 2016 Venice Architecture Biennale and is the subject of her 2022 book Blue: Architecture of UN Peacekeeping Missions. *Including analysis of UN peacekeeping practices and policy as well as first person observations, this essay highlights the expanding material footprint of UN missions with a focus on the UN mission in Mali.*

Background

Peacekeeping operations in Africa cannot be disassociated from a long history of violence and oppression. Beginning with the first European expeditions to Africa in the 15th century, which laid the foundations for European domination and exploitation, modern global practices of resource extraction (materials and bodies), trade systems, supply chains and modular construction techniques continue the legacy of European colonisation. These early expeditions of religious and scientific explorers are at the root of many of the conflicts that have shaped people's lives, nature and large ecological systems across Africa and the world. These are the conflicts that the next generation of international missions are meant to address under the auspices of the international community and the UN. The first UN mission to Israel-Palestine was followed by 56 others, many of which were situated in areas of former European colonies.

Above: Super Camp at Gao. 2016.
Photo courtesy of the author.

As of 2020, United Nations peacekeeping missions were taking place in 13 countries; seven of them were in Africa. Their material footprints cover large territories, with a physical presence in over 150 African cities and rural areas. These missions are deployed in some of the world's most impoverished areas, where issues of perpetual armed violence, extraction, dispossession and extreme climate conditions converge. Their spatiality is deeply embedded in the legacy and history of modernity and the nation-state – its institutions, bureaucracy and governance structure. Since 2000, with the end of the Cold War and the beginning of globalisation, the impact and footprint of peacekeeping missions have grown markedly. Their expansion can be linked to global processes of militarisation, financing and procurement methods dependent on centralised and ever-growing global supply chains. Their spatial and environmental impact is reflected in this exponential growth

and raise questions about the effectiveness and legitimacy of international, financial, spatial and cultural structures society puts in place to support communities across the world in times of crisis.

Missions Today

The United Nations Peacekeeping website describes the organisation as "a unique global partnership."[1] It states:

> [UN peacekeeping] brings together the General Assembly, the Security Council, the Secretariat, troop and police contributors and the host governments in a combined effort to maintain international peace and security. Its strength lies in the legitimacy of the UN Charter and in the wide range of contributing countries that participate and provide precious resources.[2]

In 2020, the United Nations' 13 peacekeeping operations worldwide cost US $6.5 billion in spending and deployed a total of 95,110 personnel in the field.[3] In 2016, peacekeeping operations covered an area of over a million square kilometres, having a large-scale presence in hundreds of cities, villages and rural areas across the world. Mission bases, camps, supercamps, airfields, headquarters and logistics hubs were planned, constructed and deployed by the UN within and adjacent to populated areas, becoming long-term features within local environments. This vast spatial manifestation comprised about 270 sites with a yearly construction, real estate and heating and cooling budget totalling $448,287,372.[4]

UN peace operations are often deployed in the world's most impoverished and imperilled urban and rural environments. In 2016, UN peace operations were present in more than 170 municipalities in Africa, with a combined population of 31 million. These areas are inhabited precariously, often poorly planned and situated in zones exposed to various hazards, making them vulnerable to droughts, floods and violence. Such pressures intensify with the effects of climate emergency and rapid population growth. In rural areas, too, peace operations are present in environments threatened by desertification, over-exploitation of natural resources and climate variability.

Despite the multidimensional challenges for peace and security, peace operations are driven by narrow political and security considerations and siloed mandates. Mission personnel often have little familiarity with or regard for the local context and are poorly trained in responding to such complex challenges. Furthermore, peacekeeping operations increasingly intervene in conflict settings that are highly violent and remote.[5] This results in a growing dependency on external supply chains, fortification and militarisation of mission bases, which expands their material footprint, isolates peacekeepers from the local context and, increases their environmental waste and carbon emissions. Although UN missions are designed to function as autonomous infrastructures and perceived as self-sustaining operations guided by the principle of "Do No Harm," they share ground with the surrounding communities. They are connected to local water resources by drilling wells and pumping water from aquifers; they consume resources from the local markets, inflating commodity prices and the massive amounts of materials, equipment and goods that they bring into mission areas generate long-term pollution and altogether contribute to global environmental degradation.[6]

The Beginning of a UN Peacekeeping Mission: MINUSMA

The peacekeeping mission in Mali was authorised in April 2013 with a mandate to support a peace agreement between the Malian government and the Tuareg.[7] The mission was asked to support Mali's interim authorities in the stabilisation of the country and the implementation of the transitional roadmap. Their duties included backing the redeployment of the reformed Malian Defence and Security Forces, protecting civilians and countering asymmetric attacks in defence of their mandate. By unanimously adopting resolution 2164 of 25 June 2014, the Security Council further decided that the mission should focus on tasks such as stabilisation and safeguarding civilians, supporting national political dialogue and reconciliation and assisting in the re-establishment of State authority, the rebuilding of the security sector and the promotion and protection of human rights in that country.[8]

The United Nations Multidimensional Integrated Stabilisation Mission in Mali (MINUSMA) resolution indicated that the mission would comprise up to 11,200 military personnel, including reserve battalions capable of deploying rapidly within the country when required and 1,440 police personnel (comprising formed police units and individual police officers). Most of the military, police and civilian substantive and support components were expected to operate primarily in the north with a possible logistics base in Gao or Sevare. A light presence, including civilians, military and police elements would be based in Bamako. Currently, 15,209 uniformed personnel are deployed to support MINUSMA.[9] Since 2013, the UN has built dozens of compounds and super camps in 14 cities across Mali.[10] Two large UN bases located in Gao house an estimated 4,000 UN peacekeepers from eight different countries: Germany, the Netherlands, Cambodia, Bangladesh, China, Senegal, Egypt and Burkina Faso.

Spatial Footprint

Since its inception in 2013, MINUSMA's troop-contributing countries (TCC), UN agencies and their sub-contractors have designed and built dozens of camps, super camps, headquarters, logistics hubs and airfields inside and adjacent to 14 cities across Mali in support of the mission.[11] Although these spaces are mostly located within existing inhabited areas, as stipulated by the host government, the mission has rarely taken into account its multidimensional impacts on the local population and the environment when it comes to planning, procurement, construction and deployment processes. The following description and analysis of MINUSMA corresponds to the beginning phase of the mission, from 2013 to 2018. It is based on workshops, field observations and conversations with local inhabitants, policymakers, diplomats, military engineers, activists, human rights lawyers, designers, anthropologists and others. The study focuses on cases from the Malian capital of Bamako and the city of Gao in the northern part of the country.

The field research in Mali took place during the early phases of the mission construction, revealing the spatial processes and various stages of a UN base's construction, the engineering logics and in-situ implementation. The research was conducted in March 2016 in Bamako and Gao and was hosted by the Dutch ministries of Foreign Affairs and Defence. The observations from the field study contributed to a series of events at the UN, reports, policy papers and follow-up research.

The Construction of a UN Peacekeeping Base

The UN base is the most emblematic spatial output of a peacekeeping mission. It is the site where all the UN protocols, guidelines and bureaucracy — mitigated by financial, technological, environmental and political factors — are distilled into material form. Its spatial production is complex; it follows strict guidelines, protocols and a hierarchical command chain. The *United Nations Peacekeeping Missions Military Engineer Unit Manual* describes the base, in technical terms, as a site that provides the peacekeepers with basic human needs in a secure and safe environment. The bases are designed to operate as self-sustained islands: "when the UN Military Engineer Unit arrives in the Mission area, it is responsible for meeting all its own needs for rations, water, petrol, oil, etc. for up to 90 days."[12]

UN construction engineering is grouped into vertical and horizontal elements. Vertical construction capabilities include

Opposite: Satelite image of Super Camp Castor. Gao. Image © Maxar Technologies, 2020.

building rigid/semi-rigid and prefabricated structures, rehabilitating and repairing existing structures, well drilling and surveying. Horizontal construction encompasses the construction and maintenance of roads and bridges, airfields and helipads. Rigid/semi-rigid or prefabricated structures (such as purpose-built container-type modular units) ensure the mission infrastructure has an adequate shelter for operational, administrative and accommodation purposes on a continuous and extended basis. The structures must have sufficient strength to protect from local weather conditions. Given the construction's enduring intent, sub-tasks may include site planning, building foundations, mainframe construction work, internal finishing and utility work.[13]

These multidimensional tasks result in a rapid spatial production that often has a vaster footprint than the surrounding inhabited areas. Although missions and bases are considered temporary, self-sufficient systems, they have enduring consequences on their surrounding socio-economic, cultural and natural ecosystems.

Midgard Transit Camp, Bamako

The following passages are excerpts from the author's personal observations upon arrival at the UN base in Mali:

On the night of 13 March 2016, I landed at Modibo Keita International Airport in Bamako with a Dutch delegation. Although Bamako is home to 2.5 million inhabitants and has a population growth rate of 3.5%, at night, the city is surprisingly dark; it was almost invisible at the time of our arrival. The delegation and I stepped out of the Air France plane into the fierce African heat. As we walked down the airstair, a group of officers from the UN mission's Movement Control Unit (MOVCON) approached us and escorted us swiftly through the packed airport, assuring us a smooth and expedited path through immigration. They wore Dutch military uniforms with a desert camouflage pattern and bright-yellow vests bearing the letters MOVCON. We were under their supervision from the moment we got off the plane until we left the country. They quickly grabbed our luggage and walked us to white UN van that was waiting for us in the airport parking lot. The local driver greeted us in French, carefully stacked our bags in the back of the car and drove us away. It was hard to see anything beyond the beaming front lights of the vehicle. The local scenery was hidden in the darkness of night.

We headed toward Midgard, a small transit camp operated by the Dutch and Swedish peacekeepers. Although it was located just to the other side of the airport runway, the car ride took us about half an hour because the road was secured and surveilled by the Malian army. The car zigzagged its way through checkpoints and physical roadblocks; our MOVOCON guides explained away each obstacle as a necessary security measure connected to past incidents. As we drove down the pitch-dark road, our escorts pointed out their landmarks: the UN super camp, the Malian base, the Bangladeshi base, a police station. By the time we left Mali, we had become very familiar with this foreign landscape and the newly installed security infrastructure. Each of the bases was enclosed with barbed wire; they appeared, one bubble after another, all together forming secure corridors for international movement. The checkpoints, camps, guard posts and fences were all constructed in the past two years.

When we arrived at the transit camp, Camp Midgard, the vehicle stopped, greeted the patrol unit and guards and then passed through the gate. The head of the camp arrived to welcome us, briefly pointed out our tents and showed us the location of showers and lavatories. We received a security briefing, our schedule for the next morning and were then accompanied to our tents. The tents sat on a hard concrete platform. They had electricity, light and an air conditioning unit attached high up on the tent fabric as if it were a wall. Six beds were ordered in two rows, ready for people in transit. Each metal-frame bed had a clean mattress and a mosquito-net around it shaped like a mini tent. Next to the bed, there was a small locker with sealed plastic water bottles. The tent felt solid, like a concrete room.

Tents

According to the *United Nations Peacekeeping Missions Military Engineer Unit Manual:*

> Tentage must include flooring and the ability to heat and cool as appropriate; and netting at doors, windows and the inner/outer fly of tents. Double-layered tents with metal pipe frames are recommended due to conditions in the field. It is also recommended to mount the tents on cement or wooden foundations to ensure their stability. Deployable accommodations noted in the paragraph above are excluded from this requirement.[14]

In the book *African Nomadic Architecture: Space, Place and Gender,* Labelle Prussin refers to the tent as architecture, despite its temporary nature. According to her, to understand the architecture of the tent, we must examine the correlation between the nature of desert life and the technology of transportation. The shape, size and construction method of a tent are contingent on means of mobility. She distinguishes the indigenous African tent from the missionary tent; while the first is considered home and a complex space of social reproduction and family life, the second, in her view, can be referenced as a political or religious institutional symbol that can be traced back to the Roman military, the Crusaders, the explorers of the Age of Reason and the missionaries of modernity. Following Prussin, the typology of the Midgard tents is, too, a political and institutional symbol.

Prussin's research is situated at the intersection of history, ethnography and gender studies. She offers another differentiation between indigenous and institutional tents: the former are designed and built by women; the latter by men. Whereas women were the architects of the nomadic built environment, men were the designers of military bases. These discrepancies can be read in the form, tactility and production processes of each.

Prussin draws another connection between modernist architecture and the institutional tent in an allusion to "a primitive temple" referenced by Le Corbusier. His book *Towards a New Architecture* celebrates the achievement of the engineer: "The Engineer's Aesthetic and Architecture – two things that march together and follow one from the other – the one at its full height, the other in an unhappy state of retrogression."[15] As he continues to develop the logic of measures, he dedicates a section to regulating lines as an invisible architectural element. The tent is used in his narrative as an object that connects the past and the future of architecture as an engineering project. In his theories of measure and modular design, the primitive temple – created by "he who builds a shelter for his god" – constitutes the model of perfect proportions.

In Bamako, the military engineers attributed the name of their base to divine spirits too. In Norse mythology, Midgard – also called Manna-Heim ("Home of Man") – is Middle Earth, the abode of humankind, made from the body of the first being, the giant Aurgelmir (Ymir). According to legend, the gods killed Aurgelmir, rolled his body into the central void of the universe and began fashioning the Midgard. Aurgelmir's flesh became the land, his blood the oceans, his bones the mountains, his teeth the cliffs, his hair the trees and his brains (blown over the earth) became the clouds. Aurgelmir's skull was held up by four dwarfs: Nordri, Sudri, Austri and Vestri (the four points of the compass) and became the dome of the heavens. The sun, moon and stars were made of scattered sparks that were caught in the skull. Midgard is situated halfway between Niflheim on the north, the land of ice and Muspelheim to the south, the region of fire. Midgard is joined with Asgard, the abode of the deities, by Bifrost, the rainbow bridge.[16]

It was interesting to realise how mythology offered an escape from the material world and a spirit for this carefully engineered space. Across the base, various symbolic ornaments were placed to celebrate the Swedish gods; perhaps like in Le Corbusier's tale, two stories became one, both a product of the imagination. The first was the temple, a shelter that man designed for his god; the second was the narrative of the ancient tent, attributed, too, to the skills of men. In contrast, Prussin's careful research associated the design of the nomadic tent and camp (which inspired the Roman soldiers in antiquity) with women. Women were the sole architects of the nomadic built environment; they chose the site, designed the camp and constructed and decorated its tents.

Holes in the Ground

The *Military Engineer Unit Manual states:*

> Earthworks and site preparation are the reshaping of land by cutting, levelling, filling and compacting earth to the desired shape using earth moving equipment. Earthworks and site preparation are fundamental to other engineer projects as they provide the basis upon which roads and bridges are built or upgraded, foundations and drainage are created for new projects and berms put into place for force protection.[17]

The ground in Midgard was covered with a thick layer of gravel. The tiny grey stones separated the base from the local soil. At the time of our visit, parts of the camp were still under construction. Holes in the ground revealed the striking red colour of the local soil, as well as depth of the base's infrastructure, including water tubes, electricity wires, sewage and telecommunication cables. However, on top of the gravel, a setup of containers and tents made the UN base appear foreign and ephemeral.

Containers

The *Manual on Policies and Procedures concerning the Reimbursement and Control of Contingent-Owned Equipment of Troop/Police Contibutors Participating in Peacekeeping Missions* states:

> Containers are mobile shelters used for a specific purpose or service. There are three basic types of containers: truck-mounted, trailer-mounted and sea containers. Truck-mounted containers can be dismounted and operated separately from the vehicle. Trailer-mounted containers need not be dismounted but are not reimbursed as trailers in the vehicle category. Sea containers must be maintained to international standards (i.e., certified for shipping) in order to be eligible for reimbursement.[18]

CHINA SHIPPING

One of the most indicative objects of a UN mission is the container. Ashley Carse wrote famously about the container:

> [N]o object distils an era, but it would be hard to beat the intermodal shipping container to make sense of the past half-century of economic globalisation. By linking shipping, rail and trucking networks, the container has been central to developments in logistics that have dramatically reduced the cost of moving goods over great distances. There is, to date, no environmental history of the so-called container revolution, but one might reasonably extend the well-known story summarised above to argue that this humble connective technology lubricated the operation and expansion of the vast sociotechnical infrastructure that formatted the Anthropocene – well before we knew it as such. Indeed, it is difficult to imagine a post-1950 Great Acceleration marked by rapid population growth, expanding consumption and urbanisation apart from the economic geographies of the container.[19]

UN agencies and mission-contributing forces from around the world are heavily dependent on the connective technology of the container. Each UN mission site reserves a large area for gathering shipping containers; as the mission ages, the accumulated number of containers increases exponentially and they pile up into an odd and sad-looking landscape of material decay.

Containers are central to the logistic planning and deployment of missions; they are brought into newly occupied UN areas from around the world. At the beginning of each mission, containers are packed with construction machinery such as bulldozers, forklifts, trenchers and excavators, loaders and telescopic handlers and all sorts of cranes. Others are filled with modular construction elements to be assembled on site, such as dry and wet walls, windows, various roofing systems, kitchens, showers, latrines, sinks, toilets, solar panels, air conditioners and pipes. There are container units that assemble medical facilities: from operating rooms to dental clinics, pharmacies and labs. UN bases are designed in advance by UN engineers, mostly in Europe-based logistic hubs situated in Brindisi, Italy and Valencia, Spain. These two centres incorporate the training and logistics nucleus of the UN missions' apparatus. During training sessions, engineers use abstract computerised simulators – a sort of UN SimCity of plug and play components obtained from a database administered by the logistics and financial team. The bases are shaped remotely on a variety of scales. Whether in response to sustainability factors, climate variation, or any number of risk factors. New and old indicators are spatialised, designed and tested on a UN simulator in Europe and then applied physically in the actual context.

At the end of a mission, the UN base is deconstructed and sorted into small pieces. All the elements that have been shipped to sustain the mission and its forces are collected into a liquidation and disposal site. Mountains of latrines, sinks, screws, water coolers, desks, office chairs, toilets, toilet seats, computers, printers, pipes and so on are crushed into tiny pieces. Some are stuffed back into the old containers or simply vanish. The base elements are carried away from the mission area and the critical eye of potential environmental activists or UNEP agents. My first visit to such a liquidation site was in Liberia, although, in Mali, large piles of waste had already accumulated at the edge of UN bases in the mission's early construction phase. In Gao, plastic, wood and steel crates that had efficiently stored machines, furniture and ammunition in shipping containers had been set aside, gathered densely into vertical structures that formed a skyline of empty boxes. Next to the empty packaging material, an otherworldly landscape of detritus included a tired line-up of vehicles of all sizes that had rapidly deteriorated due to over-use or because they had been rendered inoperable by the desert wind, blowing thick dust and sand into their engines. Containers are at the heart of the sociotechnical administration of missions. They enable their accelerating large scale and are the foundation of the rapidly spreading new typology: the super camps.

The introduction to the book *Arts of Living on a Damaged Planet* by Anna Tsing describes the tangled relationship between the past, present and future of our planet and human actions:

> Every landscape is haunted by past ways of life. We see this clearly in the presence of plants whose animal seed-dispersers are no longer with us. Some plants have seeds so big that only big animals can carry them to new places to germinate. When these animals became extinct, their plants could continue without them, but they have been unable to disperse their seeds very well. Their

Top left: Generators at Camp Castor. Gao. 2016. All photos courtesy of the author.

Top right: Tents inside tents at Camp Midgard. Bamako. 2016.

Bottom left: $US 50,000 tents at Camp Midgard. 2016.

Bottom right: The other side of Midgard's fence. 2016.

distribution is curtailed; their population dwindles. This is an example of what we are calling haunting.[20]

Whether they are containers or UN bases, human-designed systems and materials contribute to the emergence of new lives, ecologies and futures. The consequences of our past decisions and actions remain with us indefinitely. Even after a liquidation, a mission exacerbates pollution, which persists in the landscapes we inhabit and occupy.

Containers – perhaps like the big animals – transport and scatter not only a material footprint; they carry ideas and values that remain in spaces and places long after missions have gone. In host communities, the containers themselves can be found at distances foreign to them, dispersed along the narrow streets of desert cities like Gao. In a human habitat cultivated organically over millennia from sand, clay, fabric and leather, a container might appear obsolete, an alien intervention, poor and dilapidated, modern and merciless.

Conclusion

Beyond making visible and exposing the daily and institutional reality of UN peacekeeping missions, this emphasises the importance to ask how entrenched institutional bureaucracies can be challenged to use inclusive engagement and empowerment models in order to reallocate resources in a more just and sustainable manner and respond to a history of violence.

The UN was founded after the world wars to prevent the devastation of life and the environment along three pillars: peace and security, human rights and development, which are intrinsically connected. Under the peace and security pillar, the UN peacekeeping department is an international apparatus dominated by the exclusive veto power of five nations (US, UK, France, Russia and China) and at the same time expected to sustain peace across the world.

With presence in hundreds of cities worldwide, it is the largest agency of the UN in terms of its budgetary needs and expenditure. Peacekeeping missions are excessively wasteful, designed as single purpose infrastructure and dependent on extractive global supply chains. They profoundly impact local livelihood and the environment. The environmental impact of the peacekeeping department is responsible for more than half of the carbon emission of the entire UN and equal to the annual emission of the city of London.

On their quotidian operation, UN peacekeeping missions are taking place in the most impoverished and perilled urban and rural environments that are not only at the frontline of perpetual armed conflicts, but at the forefront of the climate crisis. These spaces are subjected, historically and presently, to multiple forms of violence, including environmental racism.

As such, this study, more than anything else, emphasises the urgency to challenge our institutions and power structures and direct our creativity and resources toward reimagining a transformative societal and cultural change based on the values of environmental and social justice and radical care.

01 "What is Peacekeeping," UN Peacekeeping, accessed August 2020, https://peacekeeping.un.org/en/what-is-peacekeeping.

02 Ibid.

03 UN Peacekeeping, *Peace-keeping Operations Fact Sheet* (UN, 2017), peacekeeping.un.org/sites/default/files/pk_fact_sheet_dec_17.pdf.

04 "Statistics," UN Procurement Division, accessed August 2020, https://un.org/Depts/ptd/statistics/2016.

05 Lucile Maertens and Malkit Shoshan, *Greening Peacekeeping: The Environmental Impact of UN Peace Operations* (New York: International Peace Institute, 2018). https://www.ipinst.org/wp-content/uploads/2018/04/1804_Greening-Peacekeeping.pdf.

06 This data was collected through interviews and observations as part of an independent research project. The spatial, socioeconomic and urban aspects and the case study on Mali draw on broad practical and analytical expertise in architecture, urbanism, anthropology, landscaping, economics, military engineering and policy gathered through workshops, field research and design exercises. See also: Malkit Shoshan and Jane Szita, "Reimagining the Peace-keeping Mission: Legacy Scenarios for Camp Castor," Het Nieuwe Instituut, January 2015, https://droneshoneycombs.hetnieuweinstituut.nl/sites/default/files/workshop_report._gao_legacy.pdf; Malkit Shoshan, "BLUE: Architecture of UN Peacekeeping Missions," *Archis* 48,(2016): pp 1-48.

07 "Mali: UN officials welcome accord between Government and Tuareg rebels," *UN News*, June 2013, https://news.un.org/en/story/2013/06/442632).

08 Information Management Unit, DPPA-DPO, *MINUSMA Fact Sheet* (UN Peacekeeping, 2017), https://peacekeeping.un.org/en/mission/minusma.

09 "MINUSMA Background - United Nations Multidimensional Integrated Stabilization Mission in Mali," United Nations, published 2017, www.un.org/en/peacekeeping/missions/minusma/background.

10 United Nations Department of Field Support Cartographic Section, MINUSMA JUNE 2022 [Map], 2022, scale not given, in: "Situation in Mali: report of the secretary General," June 2022. UN Secretary General, 2022.

11 "UN Geospatial Information," United Nations,accessed August 2022, www.un.org/Depts/Cartographic/english/htmain.htm.

12 Department of Peacekeeping Operations and the Department of Field Support, *United Nations Peacekeeping Missions Military Engineer Unit Manual*, (United Nations, September 2015), 31

13 Ibid., 31.

14 Ibid., 32.

15 Le Corbusier and Frederick Etchells, *Towards a New Architecture* (New York: Dover Publications, 1986), 11.

16 "Muspelheim", Encyclopedia Britannica, accessed August 2022, www.britannica.com/topic/Muspelheim.

17 Department of Peacekeeping Operations and the Department of Field Support, *The UN Peacekeeping Military Engineer Unit Manual*, 20.

18 2017 Working Group on Contingent-Owned Equipment, *Manual on Policies and Procedures concerning the Reimbursement and Control of Contingent-Owned Equipment of Troop/Police Contributors Participating in Peace-keeping Missions A/72/288* (New York: United Nations, August 2017), 33.

19 Ashley Carse, "Dredge," in *Anthropocene Unseen: A Lexicon*, eds. Cymene Howe and Anand Pandian, (Santa Barbara: Punctum Books, 2020), 121-125.

20 Anna Tsing, et al., *Arts of Living on a Damaged Planet: Ghosts and Monsters of the Anthropocene*, (Minneapolis: University of Minnesota Press, 2017), 2.

UN Flag. Gao. 2016. Photo Courtesy of the author.

THE SEARCH FOR MEMORY IN A SEA OF ROOTLESSNESS

REPAIRING XI'AN

Daniel de Oliveira Vasconcelos

Our historical memory is intangible and it is nearly impossible for us to cleanly divorce our own perceptions of history from the semi-orchestrated construction of our national narrative.
–Zheng Wang, NEVER FORGET NATIONAL HUMILIATION

Walking through a not so crowded street of downtown Xi'an, we notice a small restaurant, simple and local, which in that moment had only a single customer. We decide to enter and talk to the couple running the place. While her husband chats with the lone, seemingly frequent costumer, Ms. Li smiles at us and waits intriguingly.[1] Questioned if she could talk to us about her life in Xi'an, she very naturally responds in Xi'anhua – the city's local dialect. We then apologetically ask if she could speak in Mandarin since none of us had any clue of what she was saying. Sounding genuine and honest, she asserts she's comfortable with her life and proud to be a Xi'an citizen. "My hometown is my hometown," she confesses. Asked why, she replies: "Here is the capital of ten dynasties." She decidedly acknowledges that the environment around her is in constant change and she's in content with it, but stresses that certain historic sites, like the Bell Tower and the City Wall, must never be destroyed, comparing their importance to Beijing's Forbidden City.

Certainly, Xi'an is today a modern city of 12 million people that still struggles to maintain its identity to its past. In many aspects, the city is different from other Chinese metropolises. From the Muslim Street to historic monuments here and there, it is inevitable to think that its history dates back to the founding of the People's Republic of China (PRC) in 1949. However, crossing beyond the gates of the City Wall, the impression is that we also pass through a time portal: tall residential buildings spread everywhere, futuristic shopping malls are lured in front of you and large avenues give space for endless traffic. Here, the "socialism with Chinese characteristics" gains its modern form. But Xi'an is a city of contrasts between its past and present, a powerful engine that creates new identities and new contradictions. How do people make sense of a city that is continually repairing itself?

Once considered the start and terminus of the Silk Road, Communist Xi'an is now a place where fragments of the past are engulfed by zones of intensive development. In this rapid-change scenario, the city's landmarks are repaired, identities are reshaped, the public memory is recreated. More than ever, the government intervenes in order to revive history. The general sense is that the effort to repair lies in forging public memories and stories to bring legitimacy to its rule more than preserving history. If in the first decades of the PRC the political orientation was to obliterate the archaic past, nowadays this same past is one of Communist Party of China (CPC)'s main sources to create a natural continuity between China's traditional culture and its modernity. Amid this, there are people bargaining to use and shape their own urban environment.

Xi'an, as other great, long-standing cities all over the world, has been reborn uncountable times. But Xi'an is also unique. A quick stroll around its streets leaves the impression that it is in the process of birth, where a novel, comprehensive public memory is made. Where is Ms. Li amid this urban turmoil?

Development and conservation in Xi'an: filling the void

Ms. Li wasn't wrong: Xi'an was indeed the capital of ten different dynasties.[2] Its history dates back to ancient China, when the unification of the Empire into the Middle Kingdom would still wait some centuries to arrive. Later, China's first Emperor, Qin Shihuang, would build its imperial capital just some miles northeast and succeeding Emperors from several dynasties would consider Xi'an – sometimes named as Chang'an – as a geographical and 'geopolitical' core of their times. Nevertheless, it is during the Tang dynasty (618-907) that Xi'an is considered to have reached its heyday. An enormous walled city of approximately 84 squares kilometers sheltered nearly one million people.[3] A cosmopolitan, mercantile centre, Xi'an embraced the commercial flows brought through the Silk Road from places as far as Eastern Europe.

However, the city wall that today can be seen around the city centre – and virtually almost every other historic site, with the two Goose Pagodas being one of few exceptions – is not a Tang achievement, but a Ming (1368-1644) endeavor. The downfall of the Tang dynasty was accompanied by the total destruction of Xi'an, which would only recover part of its importance in the Ming dynasty. Xi'an was thus rebuilt many times and this process would not cease in the twentieth century.[4] In this historical cycle of destruction and rebuilding, the geography of the city altered significantly.

Opposite: The city beyond the Wall. The city wall was built during the Ming Dynasty and repaired many times since then. Protected by the wall, the city within its limits boasted key historical landmarks and sheltered the majority of the city's population until early 20th century. After 1978, the enormous rural-urban migration stimulated sprawl with high-rise buildings to accommodate the ever-growing population. Image by author.

Landscapes were modified to support urban development; innumerous amounts of monuments, relics and ancient buildings vanished; and a negligent stance by the government contributed to a geographical transition that disregarded the importance of Xi'an's material heritage.

Even the most imposing structures, which Ms. Li believed had endured for centuries, are no more than 'representations' of the past, due to their constant alterations – both materially and symbolically. As Wang Yaping, a Chinese expert in urban development, argues in his study about planning and conservation in Xi'an, "historical settings of important structures such as the City Wall, the Bell Tower and the Drum Tower were altered significantly."[5] They all lost their original meaning, partially to give birth to new narratives that are related to the present political context. Journalist Ian Johnson considers this to be an overall phenomenon that applies to multiple Chinese cities. He concludes:

> Walking the streets of China's cities, driving its country roads and visiting its centres of attraction can be disorienting. On the one hand, we know this is a country where a rich civilisation existed for millennia, yet we are overwhelmed by a sense of rootlessness. China's cities do not look old. In many cities there exist cultural sites and tiny pockets of antiquity amid oceans of concrete. When we do meet the past in the form of an ancient temple or narrow alleyway, a bit of investigation shows much of it to have been recreated. If you go back to the Five Pagoda Temple today, you will find a completely renovated temple, not a brick or tile out of place. The factory has been torn down and replaced by a park, a wall and a ticket booth. We might be on the site of something old, but the historical substance is so diluted that it feels as if it has disappeared.[6]

Why does this happen and what is the role of government in stipulating what is to be preserved? Surely, many city planners stressed their concern over the years "that heavy construction amid the villages, flood plains and ancient ruins between Xi'an and Xianyang will perpetuate Xi'an's urban sprawl while eating away at some of the area's richest farmland and most delicate environmental and cultural resources."[7] However, the preponderant political orientation was that of fast development, dubbed as the "high-density and high-rise approach."[8] This is even clearer when we assess in detail the several plans that touched upon the topic of historical preservation in Xi'an. The raised consensus in all these plans is that only fragments of the past were to be preserved.

According to Wang, "the plan shifted away from preservation of the entire old town and toward a policy of protecting a few areas."[9] This conveyed the idea that Xi'an's historical patrimony could not be a liability to the city's economic growth and they would only preserve sites that supported the grand narrative of the glorious past, or those which were symbols of the city's intended identity. The demolition of the majority of traditional houses demonstrates the government's intention to manipulate what people would experience in terms of historical heritage. Instead of 'ugly,' less representative parts of the past, people would experience what was preserved and reconstructed to be framed within the official history of China as a great nation.

This has served many purposes: the rewiring of China's history could boost city branding in a time of rising mass tourism, bring new investments, and forge modern identities for a city of global aspiration. According to this planning ideal, massive infrastructure was needed to accommodate the growing population and the deluge of tourists. However, as a regional hub, Xi'an also demanded economic dynamism. Urban renewal would thus give some landmarks totemic status – such as the Terracotta Army – while others, deemed less representative of the glorious past, were left to decay, and quickly vanished to give way to new buildings, roads, shopping malls and high-tech development zones. Therefore, one could argue that Xi'an is no longer a historic town, since only a few heritage sites and buildings exist along the vastness of the city sprawl.[10] Despite this unauthentic hodgepodge of modern and historic buildings, why were there 150 million tourist visits in Xi'an in 2016 and why do its citizens seem proud to live in a place where "you can breathe the past?"[11] The answer can reasonably be found in the forging of stories that reinterpret the past and in the making of public memory through landmark repairs, which give materiality to the historical narrative and unravel new meanings to historic sites.

Identity, memory and urban morphology in Xi'an

Why did Ms. Li passionately advocate for the preservation of these most famous historic structures and why was she proud to confess her acknowledgment of the city's importance as "the capital of ten dynasties?" In order to understand her point of view, it is necessary to grapple with how public memory functions and the role of historic sites and monuments in the process of forging a historical narrative that fits the needs of present, fresh generations residing in Xi'an.

As historian Paul Cohen summarises, "stories form a vital part of the community's cultural endowment."[12] Societies tend to rewrite history through different stories, trying to identify contents of the past that can be translated into and correlated to the present. This can be achieved by material and immaterial transformations of reality, such as re-building or reforming ancient monuments, demolishing facilities, re-creating narratives and rewriting books. In this process, popular memories, conceived as "what people in general believe took place in the past," are re-shaped. Because of that, as Bernard Bailyn puts it,

Above (left): Xi'an on the map. Xi'an (red dot) is the capital of Shaanxi province, situated in China's central plain. Source: OpenStreetMap.

Above (middle): Image Courtesy of Arthur Araujo.

Others: Image Courtesy of author.

> [Memory] is not a critical, skeptical reconstruction of what happened. It is the spontaneous, unquestioned experience of the past, it is absolute, not tentative or distant and it is expressed in signs and signals, symbols, images and mnemonic clues of all sorts. It shapes our awareness whether we know it or not and it is ultimately emotional, not intellectual.[13,14]

This process is more prominent in China, where the government's tight grip on memory and history tends to reveal its need for controlling people's access to the past in order to legitimise its present rule. It is apparent how the Chinese government "seeks to craft the appearance of memories, to create in them a sense of permanence and normalcy."[15] For instance, Ms. Li's belief – and shared by many others - that Xi'an has a glorious past reveals how a recently forged narrative is also disguised as a 'natural law' for the city's memory. This is intimately connected to the reconstructing of the City Wall and reforming of the Bell and Drum towers, an effort that makes them "imbued with a powerful sense of historical authenticity and affective vividness."[16]

The importance of these monuments and archaeological findings to the crystallisation of a public memory is evident in Hu Ying's study of Qiu Jin, a famous Chinese martyr. Qiu Jin was buried nine times, in different social and political contexts and each event represented a minor or substantial rereading of the past. The author concludes that "the making of public memory such as Qiu Jin's is by necessity an exercise of state power."[17] It happens because such material manifestations – monuments, buildings, replicas – "carry meaning into the future so as to help sustain memory and cultural traditions."[18] In the Chinese case, official history and popular memory are intertwined, where the forms of collective remembrance of the past and the government's rewriting of history feed one another.

Perhaps the most revealing example is Xi'an's Terracotta soldiers and horses, discovered by chance in 1974 along with Emperor Qin Shihuang's tomb. Since its archaeological exploration, Xi'an gained new status as a provincial capital that holds national importance. References to these discoveries can be found in virtually every street within the City Wall – we could obviously see one from Ms. Li's front door. Indeed, there is a symbolic aspect, related to the "sense of permanence," that this two thousand years-old historical patrimony contributed to the city's public memory. It is, allegedly, the uncontested proof that the city carries a quasi-immutable position as a first-rate city, which imbues its citizens with pride and, ultimately, satisfaction with their lives.

History and memory are different facets of how to conceive our past. In China, both history and memory are composed by a "highly rhetorical process," which does not necessarily delegitimise the historical narrative, but is a process that involves, as Bailyn explained, emotions more than reason.[19] Public memory tends to attach to fragments of history that convey the ideas and images that resemble the present and to which ordinary people identify. The fast development of Xi'an in the last decades, notwithstanding its enormous impact on the preservation of historic monuments and buildings, required a story of the past that could be found in just a few historic sites and archaeological findings – which the government transformed into a 'real' public memory through restoration. In this process, Ms. Li consumed a "story that makes sense," and converted it into a genuine sentiment regarding this 'memory' of the past. Like her, millions of migrants that came to Xi'an looking for opportunities to work and a better life became part of a collective experience of identity-searching. After all, what could pull people together as 'Xi'an ren' (or native of Xi'an) if not their past? The concrete city of Xi'an needed a soul.

Inhabitants not only absorbed public memory through the consumption of the urban environment; they contested, adapted and pursued their own interests through instrumenting memory originally forged to conform them. Studies by Zhu and Qian et al. show, for instance, that heritage discourses and conservation policies were faced by ordinary citizens with 'passive bargains' and 'tolerated illegalities,' which, in the end, contributed to the changing morphology of historic places.[20,21] It is rational that Ms. Li adheres to the narrative of the glorious, ancient city: she is selling not only noodles, but an experience of dining near the place where past Emperors commanded the whole Chinese civilisation.

These 'passive bargains' and other (not so passive) popular manifestations are reflected in the built environment. It is a perceived fact that fast development coupled with the conservation policy to only protect a few areas would result in the destruction of sites and relocation of people. Many families from historic neighbourhoods decided to adopt 'self-initiate' rehabilitation and retrofitting as a strategy to increase land value and when the time comes, they will be able to demand a greater compensation from the government.[22] In other households, renovation was intended to conserve the original architecture to look as 'neat' as the protected historic landmark. As examples elsewhere in China abound – such as Tianzifang, Shanghai – renovated historic neighbourhoods are also rapidly gentrified due to the large influx of tourism and high-income residents.[23]

Whether it indeed involved more emotions than reason, as Bailyn argued, the resulting behavior by ordinary people, like Ms. Li, was the instrumentalisation of public memory. Ms. Li was able to appropriate the top-down policies shaping public memory in Xi'an and leverage the changes in the built environment to make sense of her place.

Repairing of histories and identities

But public memory, instrumentalised or not, creates its own sets of dilemmas. Ian Johnson characterises Chinese cities as 'ghost towns.' For him, the "country's urban centres are built on an obliterated past," where the reinvention of this past – or public memory – is more vivid than the factual past itself.[24] In its more than two thousand years of history, not much has endured – especially anything that may bring about inconvenient memories. For this reason, amid skyscrapers and shopping malls, there can be found only a few monuments and historic sites that recapitulate glimpses of a glorious past. On the other hand, however, its recent past is made by the ordinary people that inhabit this urban environment.

As Wang contends, "the case study of Xi'an has shown that some of the earlier mistakes made by Western planners in implementing urban renewal were repeated in Chinese cities in the 1990s."[25] For him, "although it is impossible to restore the historic landscape in Xi'an, the lessons are important for the protection of many small historic towns and villages in China which have remained undisturbed to date."[26] But these 'mistakes' made by the government were, in fact, an integral part of the engine that fabricates public memories; they were based on the political and ideological orientation of what is important to preserve – though sometimes contested by the locals, who fought over the permanence of sites chosen to be destroyed – in order to support the public memory they want to create. As Ying observes, "gaps and lapses in the record of public memory [… are] as important as the actual monuments because they reveal the precise point of erasure in historical narrative."[27]

This, of course, is not new in China – or anywhere else. According to Johnson, "each succeeding dynasty wrote its predecessor's history and the dominant political ideology – what is now generically called Confucianism – was based on the concept that ideals for ruling were to be found in the past, with the virtuous ruler emulating them."[28] If Confucianism has any remnants in today's Chinese politics, it is related to CPC's search for legitimacy by both re-creating the past and adapting it to its development needs. Thus, repairing the city landmarks and historical sites serves a greater purpose of collective subject-making. In between, there are people, like Ms. Li, who absorb and consume – but also shape – this forged memory.

At the same time, history and memory are processes that no single agent acting independently can shape. Ms. Li's restaurant – though at first it seems to appear prosaic alongside the great landmarks of Xi'an – is also imbued with (public) memory. It's been there for decades, surviving successive waves of urban renovation and retrofitting, organically reinventing itself. An ordinary place within an ordinary city. And here, perhaps, more people than we are able to grasp found their roots to the city. The unique flavor of Ms. Li's noodles is almost undetachable from the street corner where the mom-and-pop shop dwells. In this sense, the past is not only something that was forged hundreds of years ago, but also the one that citizens unconsciously and collectively shape. This organic process of public memory-shaping is probably the true source of people's loyalty to the city: the ever-changing urban environment leaves intact a few historic landmarks, for sure, but also other few, ordinary places that remind them of their roots.

At the end of our talk, Ms. Li teaches us how to say 'excellent' in Xi'anhua, a word she used quite often to describe her city. It is almost impossible to distinguish what is public memory from what is her personal belief. Regardless of how she came up with this assumption, it ultimately revealed a latent need to fill the void left by the city's fast development. Repairing strategic places, such as the City Wall and the Bell Tower, may prove to be an effective way to avoid this feeling of rootlessness in a modern city in the making – though not without raising reticence about their authenticity and sustainability through time. However, repairing strategic sites did not suffice: people also tended to find their memory and agency in what developed organically over the decades, through a complex mix of sheer adherence, contestation, bargaining and subversion. In Xi'an, like elsewhere, the bulldozers of modernity could not – yet – obliterate ordinary places that produce meaning to city dwellers.

01 The name is fictitious to preserve her anonymity.
02 Valerie Hansen, "The Cosmopolitan Terminus of the Silk Road,"in *Silk Road: A New History* (Oxford: 2012).
03 Stephen Turnbull, *Chinese Walled Cities 221 BC - AD 1644* (Osprey Publishing, 2009).
04 Mark Edward Lewis, *China's Cosmopolitan Empire* (Harvard, 2009).
05 Ya Ping Wang, "Planning and Conservation in Historic Chinese Cities: The Case of Xi'an," in *The Town Planning Review*, Vol. 71, No. 3 (Jul, 2000), 318.
06 Ian Johnson, "China's memory manipulations,"in *The Guardian*, 8 June 2016.
07 Kyle Jaros, "Forging a Metropolis: State-led Urban Development in Xi'an, China." Available at: (http://wcfia.harvard.edu/publications/centerpiece/fall2013/feature_jaros)
08 Wang, "Planning and Conservation in Historic Chinese Cities: The Case of Xi'an", 311-332.
09 Ibid., 327.
10 Ibid., 328.
11 Yiying Fan, "Xi'an,Home of the Terra-Cotta Army, Is Fed Up with Tourism". *Sixth Tone*, 14 Aug 2017.
12 Cohen Paul, *A. History and Popular Memory: The Power of Story in Moments of Crisis* (Columbia University PresS,2014), 193.
13 Ibid., XIII.
14 Ibid., 210.
15 Kendall R Philips, *Framing Public Memory* (The University of Alabama Press,2004), 8.
16 Hu Ying, "Qiu Jin's Nine Burials: The Making of Historical Monuments and Public Memory"in *Modern Chinese Literature and Culture*, Vol. 19, No. 01 (Spring, 2007), 142.
17 Ibid., 141.
18 Ying, "Qiu Jin's Nine Burials: The Making of Historical Monuments and Public Memory", 142.
19 Kendall R Philips,*Framing Public Memory* (The University of Alabama Press,2004), 2.
20 Yujie Zhu, "Uses of the past: negotiating heritage in Xi'an,"in *International Journal of Heritage Studies*, vol. 24, issue 2, 2018, 181-192.
21 Zhu Qian and Hongyan Li, "Urban morphology and local citizens in China's historic neighborhoods: A case study of the Stele Forest Neighborhood in Xi'an,"in *Cities*, vol. 71, 2017, 97-109.
22 Ibid., 103.
23 F Padovani,"Tianzifang: The Dilemma of Urban Renovation at the Turn of the XXI Century,"in *Urbanities*, 9(1), 2019, 3-20.
24 Johnson,"China's memory manipulations."
25 Wang, "Planning and Conservation in Historic Chinese Cities: The Case of Xi'an," , 330.
26 Ibid., 330.
27 Ying, "Qiu Jin's Nine Burials: The Making of Historical Monuments and Public Memory."in *Modern Chinese Literature and Culture*, Vol. 19, No. 01 (Spring, 2007), 142.
28 Ian Johnson, "China's memory manipulations,"in *The Guardian*, 8 June 2016.

Author's email: deoliveirava@unimelb.edu.au

FROM 'THINGS' TO BUILDINGS

REPAIR AS A DIDACTIC INSTRUMENT FOR SUFFICIENCY IN ARCHITECTURE

Orkun Kasap & Silke Langenberg

The climate emergency and the growing scarcity of resources have made it evident that there is a problem with how we make, use and dispose of the objects that make up our built environment. The correlation between these human activities and their negative impact on society, the economy and the environment is now widely recognised.[1] Recent international conventions such as the Paris Agreement also state that sustainable consumption and production patterns are essential in addressing climate change.[2] In this context, the concepts of 'repair,' 'repairability' and 'durability' are critical to achieving a truly sustainable economy and reducing resource consumption.[3] However, despite countless initiatives, campaigns and actions by political bodies such as the European Commission to establish a "right to repair" towards facilitating the development of a circular economy, the vast majority of consumer products are still planned and made to become obsolete too quickly.[4,5,6] Policies and initiatives focusing on the efficiency of products and buildings in terms of energy consumption often encourage and subsidise consumers to replace their fully functioning phones, computers, appliances and even their homes with new ones that require less operating energy. This attitude not only accelerates the loss and consumption of resources but also disregards the inherent qualities of existing objects — particularly their reparability and durability — which significantly extends their lifespan.

Figure 1: This chess table was severely worn-out. The board was replaced, and the board pieces conserved under a glass plate in the drawer below. The table was restored to its original condition, with some decorative pieces modelled after the originals. The missing chess pieces were replaced with 3D printed ones. This project demonstrates different measures applied to an object, aiming to conserve as much of the original substance as possible while ensuring the object is fully usable again.

Keywords: Conservation, Restoration, Preservation.
Student: Veronika Müller

Figure 2: The plastic handles of this mocha pot had melted, the lid was missing, and the surface was damaged due to extensive use; common reasons for replacing such an object. Instead, the defective parts were redesigned and replaced with high-quality handmade parts out of wood that are more ergonomic than the original design. The surface was also restored, removing all rust and burn stains. The result improves the object's usability and significantly prolongs its lifespan.

Keywords: Restoration, Repair, Upgrade.
Student: Jökull Jonsson

Similarly, in architecture, repair considerations hardly influence buildings and their plans.[7] Recent declarations by professional associations argue for the use of durable, repairable, recyclable and separable materials and constructions in new buildings.[8] Various initiatives plead for prioritising the maintenance of our building stock and repairing existing buildings, as opposed to replacing them with new ones.[9] In practice, however, incentives for such measures and the necessary awareness are lacking; current building standards and codes oblige architects, contractors and clients to resort to cheaper, complex composites glued together and virtually impossible to repair, disassemble or recycle. As a result of such reduced repairability of individual components, the life cycles of buildings are becoming shorter and the cycle of demolition and replacement is accelerating.[10] There is also insufficient recognition of the fundamental fact that it is better to preserve, repair or upgrade what already exists than to recycle building materials or demolish buildings to repurpose their parts elsewhere. To make matters more confusing, different concepts of preservation and circular economy, such as reuse, repair, refit, recycle and upcycle, are used as easily replaceable terms; however, each has distinct implications for architecture.

Our course "Repair" at ETH Zurich engages architecture students with the established themes of preservation and the topic of repairability at a fundamental level through conceptual thinking and the following act of repair. Initiated in 2014 by Silke Langenberg at Munich University of Applied Sciences, the pioneering course combines traditional approaches from monument preservation to novel ones of the repair and FAB movement to consciously address the young generation of architects and designers to awaken their enthusiasm for repair.[11,12] During the course, students are asked to identify objects with material, cultural, historical, personal or design values that are either broken, have defects or problematic constructions that tend to cause problems or break repeatedly. The scale and complexity of the objects range from personal electronics such as headphones, to larger furniture, to building parts. After an initial discussion on the objects and their different qualities, students develop and present their approach to repairing them based on acknowledged concepts of preservation: Should they conserve the object or parts of it as found? Restore it to its former state with careful and appropriate interventions to recover its value? Consider reconstruction if parts of the object are damaged or missing? Or should they transform the object, giving it a new or additional purpose to enhance its value? The resulting discussion allows the students to reflect on different concepts of preservation and their implications and trains them for the complex decision-making processes which they face in practice

Figure 3: These headphones were known to break repeatedly at the same location due to poor material quality and a weak joint. Replacing the connection element with a higher-quality part handmade from brass fixes an inbuilt structural flaw and imbues a standard product with additional character and value through repair.

Keywords: Repair, Upgrade.

Student: Benedikt Dietz

Figure 4: The toaster no longer worked as the heating wire had burned out at a weak point. One of the support plates made of mica was also broken. The heating wire was repaired where possible to retain the toaster's original visual qualities. After replacing the cable and the support plate, the toaster became fully functional.

Keywords: Repair, Refit.

Student: Mike Zweidler

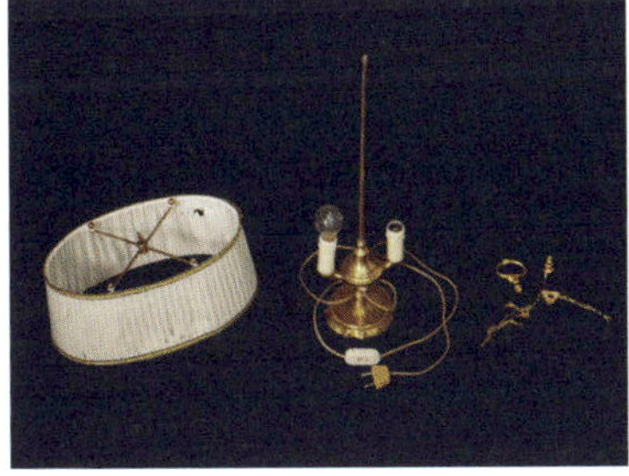

Figure 5: This copper-coloured lamp with a thin textile shade was found in a second-hand shop. The rust on the lamp's metal body was removed with standard treatment. As it was too difficult to repair or replace the textile lampshade, it was replaced with a 3d-printed PLA element, modelled after the original. Several tests were conducted to ensure that the configuration and thickness of the PLA would produce a similar lighting effect to the textile.

Keywords: Restoration, Repair, Upgrade.

Student: Ying Zhai

while working with both existing and new objects (Fig. 1 to 4). This exercise urges students to recognise how difficult — or even impossible — it is to repair something that has not been designed to do so. Ultimately, for both consumer goods and for buildings, the constructive and material preconditions that enable subsequent repairs must be established at the design and manufacturing stages to extend their lifespan.

In a second step, students independently repair the objects based on their developed concept, with appropriate expert advice and support using both traditional manual techniques and novel manufacturing methods such as 3D-printing.[13, 14] The latter is especially relevant to maintaining and repairing objects with complex parts, manufactured industrially in large quantities (Fig. 5). However, repairing the industrially-produced façade elements with conventional refurbishment methods might require their complete replacement and result in the loss of valuable original building substance. Digital fabrication allows for producing custom-fit replacement parts for such objects without industrial production constraints; such logic can also apply to buildings. In our ongoing research at ETH Zurich, we investigate the possibilities of digital fabrication, particularly in additive manufacturing for the repair of existing constructions.[15] Buildings with non-standard structural or façade elements that were once manufactured industrially using machines and processes no longer readily available are excellent candidates for applying such processes. The façade of the ETH Zurich's CLA Building is one such example, as it shows characteristics of the High-Tech Architecture movement with non-standard and complex structural elements, designed and industrially explicitly manufactured for this building (Fig. 6). Repairing the industrially-produced façade elements with conventional refurbishment methods might require their complete replacement and result in the loss of valuable original building substance. This approach enables the targeted, local and rapid repair, remanufacturing and, where

possible, the performative upgrade of individual damaged elements as opposed to the complete replacement of an entire structure or façade system. It allows for the preservation of as much material as possible, saving valuable embedded and fresh resources and maintaining original parts and constructions as a legacy of past building processes and the building culture.

The perpetual acts of repair instil a genuine form of sustainability and sufficiency in architecture that relies on the further use of building materials, local know-how and production. However, the extent to which it is possible to repair an object or a building depends heavily on its repairability. To design an object so that it can be repaired, one must anticipate the act of repair itself. This means making sure that the design is comprehensible to the people who later need to work on it and that it is possible to open, disassemble and reassemble the parts multiple times. In addition, the design must be carefully documented and the tacit knowledge associated with making the object must be disclosed. This may sound difficult given the number, variety and complexity of the things and buildings made around the world. However, novel computational tools such as augmented reality and digital twins, growing access to digital modelling and fabrication tools and the ability to archive and share any type and amount of data regardless of time and space compel us to rethink the limits of repair. To develop genuinely sustainable patterns of production and consumption, we must both learn from the past and explore innovative using new tools and methods to engage with our built environment.

Figure 6 (opposite): The ETH Zurich's CLA Building (Facade). Photograph by Matthias Brenner (left). Façade mock-up, © Fosco, Fosco-Oppenheim, Vogt (right).

All photography pages 28-29 courtesy of Authors.

01 The United Nations Sustainable Development Goals (SDGs) provide guidelines for improving the current state of the planet in the near future. The SDG number 12 on "Responsible Production and Consumption Patterns" focuses on our current reliance on the extraction of fresh resources and demonstrates the relationship of current production and consumption habits with sustainable development. See: https://sdgs.un.org.

02 The Paris Agreement is an international treaty on climate change adopted by 196 nations at COP 21 in Paris. Despite references in the agreement to sustainable consumption and production, its meaning and application remains vague and needs to be further defined by parties to the agreement. See: https://unfccc.int/process-and-meetings/the-paris-agreement/the-paris-agreement/key-aspects-of-the-paris-agreement

03 The European Green Deal emphasises on the importance of "longer lasting products that can be repaired, recycled and re-used" towards improving the well-being and health of citizens and future generations." See: European Comission, "A European Green Deal," https://ec.europa.eu/info/strategy/priorities-2019-2024/european-green-deal_en.

04 In Europe, there are also many do-it-yourself initiatives which offer both the social setting and the infrastructure for repair. A good overview for German-speaking countries can be found on the website of "Netzwerk Reparatur-Initiativen." See: https://www.reparatur-initiativen.de.

05 Several environmental and NGOs such as Greenpeace have been campaigning for the "right to repair" to extend the lifecycle of consumer products and against waste accumulation. See: Greenpeace Switzerland, "REPARIEREN: DER WEG AUS DER WEGWERFGESELLSCHAFT," https://www.greenpeace.ch/de/erkunden/reparieren-der-weg-aus-der-wegwerfgesellschaft/.

06 European Parliament, "Right to Repair," (Briefing Summary, January 12, 2022), https://www.europarl.europa.eu/thinktank/en/document/EPRS_BRI(2022)698869.

07 Silke Langenberg, "Das Konzept "Ersatz"? Probleme bei der Reparatur industriell gefertigter Bauteile," in Günter Bayerl, Georg Stöger (eds.), *Reparieren – oder die Lebensdauer der Gebrauchsgüter*, vol. 3, Berlin 2012 (Cottbusser Studien zur Geschichte von Technik, Arbeit und Umwelt 79), 255-272.

08 The recent position paper by the Swiss Society of Engineers and Architects (sia) on climate change mitigation and energy calls on its members to "choose materials of appropriate quality, that are repairable, recyclable and separable."

09 The ongoing campaign "Klimaoffensive Baukultur" in Switzerland asks all agents in the building sector to embrace the principles of circular economy, to build fewer new buildings, to reuse and repair existing building elements, and to use durable materials and constructions. See: https://klimaoffensive.ch.

10 Uta Hassler (ed.), *Towards a Sustainable Development of the Built Environment* (Zürich: 2011).

11 Neil Gershenfeld, *Fab: The Coming Revolution on Your Desktop – from Personal Computers to Personal Fabrication* (New York: 2007).

12 For a review of all student work from the course offered at the University of Applied Sciences Munich from 2014 to 2018, see: Silke Langenberg, *Repair: Encouragement to Think and Make* (Berlin: 2018).

13 The art foundery Sitterwerk in St.Gallen, Switzerland is a unique workshop that produces and restores plastic works of art on behalf of artists, galleries and museums. The associates Foundation Sitterwerk also offers an extensive material archive and library in related areas. See: https://www.kunstgiesserei.ch and https://www.sitterwerk.ch.

14 Girsberger, "Remanufacturing," https://girsberger.com/de/loesungen/remanufacturing/.

15 The research project "High-Tech for High-Tech" led by Matthias Brenner at the Chair of Construction Heritage and Preservation in collaboration with the Digital Building Technologies at ETH Zurich explores the application of additive manufacturing methods and processes towards the repair and maintenance of the High-Tech Architecture of the 1980s.

COMMERCIALISATION VS CONSERVATION

ARCHITECTURAL HERITAGE PRESERVATION IN HONG KONG

Yingting Chen and Charlie Qiuli Xue

Economic development and heritage conservation is a common dilemma in world cities, which is even more pronounced for a dense metropolis like Hong Kong. As an intersection of Chinese and Western cultures, Hong Kong has retained more than 1,000 historic buildings since its opening as a commercial port in 1840. In terms of aesthetic, Hong Kong's heritage buildings may not be as valuable as those in European countries or even in other Chinese cities. However, these buildings reflect unique moments in the city's evolving lifestyle and living conditions, becoming tangible evidence of Hong Kong's urban transformation over the last 200 years. Unfortunately, in the incentive of privatisation, marketisation, and financialisation, heritage conservation and development needs are constantly challenged.

While emphasising historical and cultural values, it is inevitable to address the need for development and associated costs. What buildings deserve conservation? How to conserve? How can modern values be brought into play without concealing history in order to achieve sustainability? Hong Kong has been struggling with these challenges for the past 50 years. This process has yielded positive and negative lessons which are certainly worth discussing.

We wonder how the quest of preserving historic buildings as carriers of collective memory has developed under the dominant influence of commercialisation in Hong Kong. To delve deeper, three conserved buildings — the Comix Home Base, the Central Market, and the State Theatre — are selected as typical cases to demonstrate and compare the effects of conservation. Hong Kong is known for its extremely high land price and the contest between profit-making and cultural conservation. The authors highlight the conservation method of integrating the collective memory of heritage into current community life. This paper sheds light on these conflicts and attempts to suggest a possible direction to help achieve balanced development.

The 1960s–1970s: the "Culture of Disappearance" Caused by Capitalist Market Forces

The beginning of conservation was signaled by the enactment of the Antiquities and Monuments Ordinance in 1976, and the establishment of the Antiquities Advisory Board (AAB) and the Antiquities and Monuments Office (AMO) in the same year.[1,2,3] At that time, Hong Kong's manufacturing and financial industry boom led to the massive demolition of old buildings and the construction of new high-rise buildings.

By the end of the 1970s, the ruthless destruction of the Hong Kong Club at the heart of Central aroused widespread public concern and calls for the preservation of "collective memory."[4] The four-story building had a typical Victorian style with a central front entrance consisting of a projecting stone arch foyer and balcony, flanked by towers. Along with the Statue Square, it formed a landmark of Hong Kong's distinctive City of Victoria, which was deeply engraved in the hearts of Hong Kong people. However, the club's General Committee was suffering from a deficit for years and could not afford HK$40 million for repairs. The building was eventually demolished and rebuilt in 1981 at Hong Kong Land's expense, in exchange for the first 25 years of rent on the upper 17 floors to be leased for commercial purposes (Fig. 1).[5] The story ended with a victory for the economic value of capital.

Examples like the Hong Kong Club happened over and over again. In the context of a rapidly expanding population, soaring land values and scarce buildable land in urban areas, heritage conservation, and new development projects are constantly in contradiction and conflict. The demolition of these well-recognised buildings is deplorable and typical of the "culture of disappearance" created by capitalist market forces.[6,7]

Fig. 1 : The old (1897) buildings of the Hong Kong Club. (left)Image courtesy of National Archives-Kew Collection. (right)Image by author.

The 1980s–1990s: the Awakening of "Seeking Roots" by Preserving "Collective Memory"
To break the deadlock, in 1982, the Hong Kong-British Joint Declaration established the system of "temporary monuments" to announce some buildings as declared monuments. The governor of Hong Kong, David Wilson, who served from April 1987 to July 1992, was also particularly keen on heritage conservation. Benefiting from this, in 1988, the Land Development Corporation (the predecessor of the Urban Renewal Authority) was established to renovate some contemporary historic buildings in relatively good conditions. At the same time, the Environmental Impact Assessment Ordinance was formally implemented to assess the environmental impact of designated projects.[8,9]

At that time, the sense of insecurity of Hong Kong people kept increasing in a rapidly developing social environment with endless changes. The return of Hong Kong to China in 1997 led to the dissolution of colonial status, and the establishment of the Chinese government promoted the rethinking of local consciousness and made the thirst for "seeking roots" even more eager.[10,11]

2000–2009: From Heated Confrontation to Joint Forces of Government, NPOs and the Public
Since the late 20th century, architectural heritage has received increasing attention. However, due to the overwhelming desire for local identity, some structures without prominent architectural values had also become objects of an intense public appeal for protection. In 2006 and 2007, a bottom-up movement calling for the Star Ferry Pier and the Queen's Pier's preservation thoroughly stimulated public awareness of finding citizens' own roots — who we are and where we are from — and led to a series of new policies, including the adding of the Commissioner for Heritage's Office (CHO) in the Development Bureau (DEVB) to manage the heritage assessment and public participation (Fig. 2). [12,13,14]

Subsequently, the notable "Revitalising Historic Buildings Through Partnership Scheme" was launched in the 2007–2008 Policy Address to provide financial assistance to non-profit making organisations (NPOs).[15,16] The partnership scheme was intended to display the civic forces in maintaining the heritage buildings while responding to the increasing demand of people in this respect. However, most organisations could hardly sustain the operation. They returned the buildings to the government halfway through the contract. Therefore, the preservation and running of heritage buildings had to resort to capitalist forces.

By then, the institutional and legal system of Hong Kong's heritage architectural conservation was established (Fig.3). The Development Bureau (DEVB) and Antiquities and Monuments Office (AMO) are the main government agencies, coordinating with the Antiquities Advisory Board (AAB), the Urban Renewal Authority (URA), the Architectural Services Department (ArchSD), and the Planning Department (PlanD). Studies on historic buildings are usually carried out by the AAB before decisions are taken by the AMO, determining the declared monuments and the grading of historic buildings. The AMO obtains assistance from other government departments, such as the Leisure and Cultural Services Department (LCSD), the Land Administration Office (LAO) and the Environmental Protection Agency (EPA), etc., to preserve historic buildings according to their granted grade.[17,18,19] The heritage conservation of Hong Kong has entered a new era of tripartite conservation mode of government, NPOs, and the public.

After 2010: Reconciling Antagonism between Private Profits and Public Values
In 2012, the Ho Tung Garden was demolished after the private owner and the government failed to reach an agreement on compensation claims. The antagonism between the private nature of property rights and the public nature of cultural

values was once again brought to the fore. In 2013, the Chief Executive clearly stated in his Policy Address that "There is a need to review the policy on the conservation of private historic buildings."[20]

Three main strategies were developed to reconcile the increasingly acute public-private conflict. The first strategy was to increase compensation for private owners and incentivise their conservation activities through urban planning. For example, in 2009, the height restriction at Pok Fu Lam was partially removed to conserve the Jessville mansion; in 2012, the King Yin Lei mansion was successfully preserved by donating the adjacent plot to the private owner.[21,22]

The second strategy was to enhance public participation and promote the reconstruction of social values. In the absence of an optimal solution on private-public conflict, strengthening public participation helps to some degree. That was, by establishing the new social value of "private historic building conservation is a public undertaking," conservation is given a nonprofit character that matters more than market value. The 2016 Policy Address provided stronger support for architectural conservation by establishing a HK$500 million Fund to support and promote public education, community engagement, and academic activities (Fig. 3).[23] The DEVB also requires all new projects involving monuments or historic buildings to undergo heritage impact assessment and formulate mitigation measures with guaranteed public participation.[24,25]

Fig. 2 (above) : Public defense of the Queen's Pier, Hong Kong, 2007. Image by author.

Fig. 3 (opposite): A workshop on the conservation and revitalisation of the Wan Chai Market hosted by the Hong Kong Institute of Architects. Image by author.

The third strategy was to re-examine the meaning and true values of conservation projects. Some programs that have worked well are once again being questioned, such as 1881 Heritage, a high-end shopping and hospitality landmark converted from the Old Marine Police Headquarters by Cheung Kong Holdings (Fig. 4). It highlights the sharp contradiction between the public service of historical buildings and the profit-seeking nature of development. Under the dominant influence of commercialisation, it is a fact that the conservation of historic buildings is becoming more and more "commodified." Even if the physical building components are intact, the cultural and historical features are qualitatively changed. When history is erased, simplified or even distorted, despite business opportunities, do the original intention and value of conservation still exist? Do heritage conservation and economic development have to be stuck in an "either/or" tug of war? In the following, we will analyse and discuss these issues through three typical cases.

No.7 Mallory Street: A Tower of Babel in Idealism — Architectural Elements and their Historical Value

As the first conservation project of the URA, the 2,400m^2 site comprises ten pre-war tenement buildings. Constructed by the Hong Kong Land Corporation in the 1910s, the ten buildings are arranged back-to-back in pairs along Burrows Street and Mallory Street in Wan Chai and are graded as Grade II historic buildings. Their value is mainly reflected in three aspects. Firstly, as the most common sample of Tong Lau, the ten buildings also have exotic components such as terraces, French doors and windows, iron railings, and wooden staircases due to the influence of colonial history. Secondly, these buildings were designed and built in accordance with the first Medical Sanitation and Building Ordinance promulgated in 1903 after the great plague in 1894.[26,27] Thirdly, the mushrooming of these low-cost,

quick-to-build tenement buildings was in response to the housing needs of immigrants from the mainland during the 1930s to the 1960s. To alleviate the pressure of rent, a single tenement unit was often shared by three to eight families, giving rise to such social roles as "landlord" and "landlady," characterising Hong Kong's local rental relationship and social hierarchy. [28] These tenement buildings witnessed the historical transformation of Hong Kong from a fishing and farming economy to a commercialised society dominated by manufacturing. As a symbol of social and economic development, the architecture records the lifestyle changes of the working class and the emerging social relationship in Hong Kong.

The 1970s and 1990s were Hong Kong's "golden years of animation." Wan Chai, where the ten tenement buildings are located and known as the cradle of Hong Kong comics, created memories and generations of iconic artists and comic classics such as Old Master Q, Fung Wan, and McDull, whose development spanned the toy and movie industries. In 2005, the Hong Kong Arts Center won the bidding for operation through the "Revitalising Historic Buildings Through Partnership Scheme." Inspired by the booming market of the comic industry, Connie Lam, Director-General of the Hong Kong Arts Center, operated the site as "the Comix Home Base," with the intention of providing a creative platform for local and overseas animation artists to promote Hong Kong's comic arts and rejuvenating the local memories.[29]

The renovation project was completed in 2013 by Aedas. Six intact tenement buildings have been preserved, while four on Burrows Street were demolished due to structural deficiencies. The unique architectural features, such as the Chinese pitched tile roofs, French doors and windows, iron railings, wooden staircases, and brick walls, are retained and carefully repaired. The roof restoration adopts a pioneering "upper tube, lower tile (上筒下瓦)" technique. This design not only preserves the historic characteristics of the tiled roof, but the built-in steel frame structure and insulation materials also greatly improve its sturdiness and stability to comply with the current building regulations.

The ground floor retains street stalls dating back to 1952, including a luxury coffee and tea house established in the 1980s, two boutique stores opened in 1985 and 2009, and a traditional bakery selling pastries, cookies, and sweets. The storefronts are kept the same as they were in the old times, with double-sided doors.[30, 31] The interior repairs preserve the traditional Cantonese architectural features of the 1930s. The walls are finished with red brick dust ground from the original bricks to maintain a consistent tone. The hall includes a wide exhibition space and a kitchen to showcase the original structures.[32]

The second floor is an adaptive reuse of a Hong Kong-style café, while the third floor is occupied by Hong Kong Comics and Animation Federation (HKCAF, moved out in 2018), comic salons, and art studios.[33,34] A $300m^2$ public courtyard was created to host comic events and activities, paved with black and white bricks to illustrate the boundaries of the original building. The position of the partition walls of the original building is marked by red brick paving with built-in light strips, which serve as night lighting and symbolise steel reinforcement in the preserved walls.[35] The actual partition walls are made of metal frames with potted plants, providing vertical greenery with a permeable visual experience. An aerial walkway connecting Burrows Street and Mallory Street is added on the fourth and fifth floors to allow visitors to watch activities in the courtyard from above. Standing models of comic characters were placed on the cantilevered terraces,

the most recognisable components of the aerial walkway, to highlight the theme of the venue.

Yet the dream of reviving local comics is far too wishful thinking. Due to the single theme, the remote location from MTR station, and the lack of effective publicity, many exhibitions and activities are only attended by industry members. Hong Kong, known as the cultural desert, also suffers from a lack of cultural and market support. The rise of the internet in the late 1990s provided easy access to more dynamic and diverse comic products from foreign countries, and the limited themes of local creations were no longer attractive. The lack of regulation for copyright took a heavier toll on the sales of local comics. Hong Kong's comics industry rapidly declined in the mid-1990s and is still struggling today. With only about 550,000 visitors in three years since its opening, the Comix Home Base finally closed in 2018. The URA then renamed it '7 Mallory Street,' abandoned the single theme, and tried to expand its clientele by introducing a variety of art and cultural activities such as yoga, community forum, and concerts.[36] Only introducing additional events and activities did the site regain a bit of a revival.[37]

The failure of Comix Home Base proves that the idealism of deliberately imposing an imported idea on a historical building is the Tower of Babel that is destined to collapse. The conservation of historical buildings cannot be sustained without the support of the market and the engagement of the community. Lee Man-long, a member of the Wan Chai District Council, said that the Comix Home Base was neither attractive nor needed in the neighbourhood.[38] Responding to market needs, achieving public sharing, and benefiting social groups in the community is the only sustainable way out.

The Central Market: The Recall of Past Memories with Active Public Participation

The existing fourth-generation Central Market is a Grade III historic building with a gross floor area of 4,150m^2. It was built in 1939 and designed by Alfred Water Hodges, a British architect of the Public Works Department. As one of the few pre-war indoor street markets, it symbolises the continuity of Guangdong street market culture in Hong Kong.[39] After the 1840s, street vendors were relocated progressively to indoor markets to avoid environmental nuisance and traffic obstruction, but the term "street market" was retained. Although supermarkets and shopping malls are becoming more common in Hong Kong today, going to "street markets" to buy daily necessities, especially fresh ingredients, is still integral to everyday life.[40]

The old Central Market (1939) was composed of a four-story cubic block and a trapezoidal sunken atrium with a public restroom on the south side. The three-story market space is the core, with affiliated penthouses on the fourth floor (Fig. 5). The design and construction represent the most advanced British sanitary system, design concept, and construction techniques at that time, demonstrating distinctive characteristics of the times and political significance.[41] As one of the earliest modern indoor market buildings, the concise streamlined and geometrical design was derived from the late Art Deco, and is a typical example of the Bauhaus functionalism applied in Hong Kong public buildings.[42]

In 2009, in response to the Policy Address, the URA was commissioned to undertake a conservation project for the Central Market. Over 10,000 residents were actively involved throughout the project, including two rounds of surveys in 2010 and 2011 and an exhibition of four proposals from April to May 2011 with public forums to facilitate in-depth discussion. Experts and professionals participated after each round of the survey, as well as a series of workshops and symposiums to identify the design scheme and resolve technical issues.[43]

In November 2011, AGC Design's proposal "Urban Floating Oasis" was approved but simplified in order to expedite the construction schedule.[44] According to Zhu Juanying, author of the *Memoir Our Central Market*, "Central is now so expensive in terms of land price, but there was once a place where small businesses were allowed to support livings in a fair and open way, which was an expression of independence and freedom." With this in mind, the Chinachem Group operates the new Central Market as a "playground for all," hoping that it will continue to nurture the rich neighbourhood

relationships and foster the growth of local brands and start-ups as it did before.[45]

At the district level, the current Central Market has been integrated with other historic buildings and conservation projects in Central for positioning and planning. Since the launch of the Central-Mid-Levels Escalator and Walkway System in 1993, the Central Market has served as the starting point and linked the footbridge system of Central's major commercial centres, such as the International Finance Centre (IFC) and Exchange Square. The Central Market is also incorporated and accessible to several historical attractions, such as the Tai Kwun, the Sun Yat-sen Historical Trail, and the Dr. Sun Yat-sen Museum. [46,47]

At the street level, the original volume, outline, and style of the building are maintained. On the basis of conforming to the original pattern, the accessibility of the site is improved and a wider and safer pedestrian environment is created around the building. The atrium on the ground floor provides 745 m^2 of mixed-use public space with direct access to Des Voeux Road, Queen's Road, and Jubilee Street. The open space in front of the southwest main entrance is created as a 255m^2 urban plaza with hard paving, seating, and landscaped greenery (Fig. 6).[48]

At the architectural level, the basic principle is "to respond to community needs with minimal intervention," and "to preserve the iconic architectural components as much as possible to restore the street memories of the past."[49] At the beginning of the project, the Architectural Heritage Research Center of the Chinese University of Hong Kong was commissioned to conduct a detailed study of the architecture.[50] Five characteristic components of the market space, including the atrium, the front facade, the terrazzo staircase, five types of stalls, and the overall style of column network, were determined to be preserved and applied in the new design scheme.[51,52]

Fig.4 (opposite left & middle): Former Marine Police Headquarters (1884) and the 1881 Heritage (2009). Image courtesy of 1881 Heritage(Left) and Charlie Q.L. Xue(Middle).

Fig.5 (opposite right): The original fourth-generation Central Market (1939). Image by author.

Fig.6 (left): The Central Market after repair (2021). Image by author.

Fig.7 (middle & right) The State Theater and its golden age in 1950s-1980s. Image courtesy of creative common (middle) and author (right).

The repair of the facade continues the original modernism, with the window size, featured eaves, and the round corners restored to what they were in 1939. The original concrete walls are replaced by frosted glass, and transparent glass is installed in the linear openings to achieve a clear distinction between the "old" and the "new."[53] However, some interior alterations "significantly destroy the character and quality of the original space and structure."[54] First, the interior boundary on the east side is pushed inwards by one span to expand the open atrium, interrupting the original circular ("回") spatial composition of the ground floor; second, the partition walls for stalls on the north and south sides are replaced with full-height ones, weakening the spatial characteristics of symmetry on both sides and permeability in the middle; third, all but 13 typical stalls (three for pork stalls and two for each of the remaining types) are removed, destroying the original rhythm and hierarchy of the space.[55, 56]

From an architectural perspective, the original space and structure have not been preserved to the ideal extent due to insufficient recognition of the architectural value by stakeholders during the conservation process of the Central Market. The current result, however, is a balance between conservation and development achieved with the multidisciplinary collaboration among stakeholders. The occupancy rate of the Central Market in the first phase of the trial operation exceeded 95%, with more than 3 million visitors in two and a half months.[57] Given the balance of multiple interests and its current popularity, the Central Market can be considered a relatively successful story of revitalising street life through architectural heritage preservation.

While the initial success still has to stand the test of time, this case demonstrates three noteworthy features. Firstly, conservation programs could benefit from the support of financially strong developers (like Chinachem Group), which can contribute to the dynamics, vitality, and sustainability of historic buildings. Secondly, well-organised public participation can be powerful and effective and deserves careful consideration and response. Thirdly, public support for historic buildings is not based on the degree of retention or innovation, but on whether it is responding to market demand and meeting the most pressing interests of the public. The new Central Market integrates leisure, entertainment, catering, and cultural functions, serving businesses, office workers, residents, and tourists of the whole Central and Mid-levels districts. It adapts to the modern development needs, yet provides a positive treatment of the remains from the colonial period and promotes social and cultural progress of the community.

The State Theatre: Unprecedented Conservation with Endorsement from Private Developer

Located in King's Road, North Point, the State Theatre Building was completed in the 1950s, covering an area of 3,360 m^2, and was awarded as a Grade I historic building in 2016. As the oldest stand-alone theatre on Hong Kong Island for more than 60 years, the building witnessed the eastward urban expansion and westernisation of North Point. In the 1950s-1980s, the theatre became an international landmark for cultural performances. The world-top music and dance troupes, such as Shouchiku Kageki Dan (SKD) from Japan and E. SHA from Taiwan (where Teresa Teng served), all chose to perform here, bringing the best of world culture, art, movie, opera, and dance to the public.[58]

Designed by architects George W. Grey and S.F. Liu, the theatre building reflected the simplicity of modernism. The curved front facade was occupied by a large relief sculpture entitled "Cicada fan Dong Zhuo" by the famous painter Mei YuTian, which integrated Chinese, Southeast Asian, and Western art and culture. The most distinctive feature was a series of parabolic roof trusses, which realised a column-free interior space and enhanced the audio-visual quality, making it one of the top theatres in the world at that time (Fig. 7).[59]

The use of the State Theatre building has undergone a transition from a theatre to a commercial and residential site, and finally became a billiards centre in 2000. Since its public auction in 2015, this iconic building has evoked the interest of large developers due to its excellent location and massive volume. Taking note of this circumstance, Walk in Hong Kong (WHK) submitted a heritage assessment report on the old theatre, highlighting its unique historical, architectural, and social significance. On 23 March 2016, Docomomo released a "heritage crisis alert," stating that the theatre was a modern landmark and its unique roof structure was "the only one of its kind in the world" that should be preserved intact. The WHK, Conservancy Association, and Docomomo issued a joint statement urging to rate the State Theatre as a Grade I historical building.[60]

Unfortunately, on April 18, the AMO rated the building as Grade III, citing "excessive internal alterations resulting in the lower historical value of authenticity." The news aroused great concern. The WHK immediately invited professionals to review the alternation records and inspected on site to confirm the structural integrity, enabling the AMO to admit that they did not fully understand the changes made to the State Theatre and their decision was made by "an estimate."[61] Meanwhile, mass media further informs the public about the value of the State Theatre, the grading dispute, and the perfunctory bureaucracy of the AAC which deviated from professionalism and public sentiment. With unremitting efforts, on 8 December 2016, the AAB voted to overturn the grading suggestion of the AAC, and the State Theatre was officially awarded Grade I historic Building status.[62]
After five years of intense competition, the New World Development (NWD) acquired the ownership for HK$4.776 billion in 2020 (the largest auction case ever in HK).[63] Adrian Cheng, the CEO of New World Development, described the theatre as "one of the last standing cultural icons of Hong Kong with historical significance in promoting the performing arts and film." He pledged to preserve the essence of the building and "build a cultural oasis that serves the community and preservation campaign."[64]

In October 2020, the NWD hired award-winning British architecture firms Purcell and WilkinsonEyre with extensive experience in heritage renovation, and AGC Hong Kong Limited who participated in preserving Lui Seng Chun museum, to develop a conservation plan. "With the focus of bringing back the architectural merits, artisanship, and cinematic culture, the conservation project will include the revitalisation of the roof structure…while the cinematic functions will also be restored, returning State Theatre into its original glamour as a thriving cultural events venue once again."[65,66]

In order to stimulate public interest and enthusiasm for this conservation project, from 11 April to 16 May 2021, the NWD held a month-long interactive exhibition titled "Discover the State Theatre in All of Us" ahead of the start of construction. The event displayed a collection of old theatre tickets, theatre seats, staff uniforms, and other items related to the State Theatre collected by the NWD three years ago. A vintage box office was set up at the entrance, where staff handed out replica tickets and introduced the history of the theatre to visitors.[67,68]

The preservation of the State Theatre and the unprecedented endorsement from the private developer are mainly due to three factors. Firstly, the early attention, professional assessment, and effective response from social conservation organisations. Active social intervention from the very beginning of the auction of the theatre prevented the vandalism and made it a declared Grade I historical building in just one year. Secondly, powerful publicity. Social organisations and media disclosed information to the public timely, and pressure of public appeal strongly influenced the government and developers to act. Thirdly, a new understanding of the relationship between heritage conservation and development interests. Introducing developers to conserve heritage projects can not only save money and effort for the government but also bring these old assets back to the development track and radiate new vitality. Heritage conservation seems to gradually become important leverage and inspiration for development.

Conclusion

Back to the original questions: what deserves conservation? A valuable heritage building should be representative, creative and advanced in architectural design, structural technique, and construction technology. Meanwhile, it should also carry and represent the humanistic spirit, social customs, and economic and cultural development of that particular era, or record important historical events, and accommodate important activities and figures.

How to conserve? The case of Hong Kong demonstrates that the complexity of heritage conservation stems from the diverse and contradictory needs of stakeholders. Conservation solutions based solely on profit maximisation are unacceptable to the government and the public, while practice regardless of economic benefits and capital trends tends to be unsustainable. However, as long as a beneficial balance among stakeholders can be achieved, heritage conservation and economic benefits can be compatible. Moreover, the public is not always positive about preserving historical buildings. The ultimate determinant of conservation success is whether it responds to market demand and meets the public's most pressing interests.

How can modern values be brought into play without concealing history? Development, conservation, economy and culture should be understood from a macro, long-term perspective. In contrast to opposing each other, conservation is development, while economics and culture are mutually supportive. A developed perception of conservation is not simply to renovate historic buildings according to one single modern need, or insert narrowly defined "cultural elements" as a gimmick to make profits by attracting consumers with medium and high incomes. What truly matters is to preserve and nurture the rationale of good spatial design, rich lifestyle, and social values that the old building once carried. And on this basis, to renew and expand a variety of cultural and economic potential of the heritage, and improve the quality of life for the community.

Hong Kong's conservation system and practices are not perfect. There are still remaining problems such as lack of land in urban areas, shortage of funding, defective grading mechanism, and insufficient participation of professionals and the public. However, its people-oriented philosophy, the voice of social organisations and the public, and the government's active response to explore diversified and multi-path conservation modes are unique contributions to the world experience of cultural heritage conservation and revitalisation. We expect that, advancing into the future, valuable heritage sites will no longer be unceremoniously razed to make way for shiny new skyscrapers, but as a long-term investment that carries a rich history and collective memory, benefiting us today and leaving behind an irreplaceable treasure for generations to come.

01 Antiquities and Monuments Office, "About Us," https://www.amo.gov.hk/tc/home/index.html (accessed January 30, 2022).

02 Antiquities Advisory Board, "About Us," https://www.aab.gov.hk/en/home/index.html (accessed January 30. 2022).

03 Fuhe Zhang 張複合,"Conservation and Utilization of Historic Buildings in Hong Kong 香港歷史建築的保護利用,"in *World Architecture 世界建築*, no.03(1986): 62-67.

04 Zhongwei Lin 林中偉, *Architectural conservation and local culture 建築保育與本土文化* (Hong Kong: Chung Hwa Book Company Limit 香港: 中華書局有限公司, 2015).

05 The News Lens 關鍵評論網, "The Old Hong Kong Club Building - A Failed Conservation Movement 40 Years Ago 舊香港會大樓--40年前一場失敗的保育運動," https://www.thenewslens.com/article/146754 (accessed Feb 8, 2022).

06 Ackbar Abbas, Hong Kong: culture and politics of disappearance (Hong Kong: Hong Kong University Press, 1997).

07 Qiuli Xue 薛求理, "Architectural Heritages of the Peoples' Republic of China 新中國建築遺產芻議,"in *Heritage Architecture 建築遺產*, no.03, (2019): 62-67. doi:10.19673/j.cnki.ha.2019.03.002.

08 Antiquities and Monuments Office, "About Us."

09 Lin 林中偉, *Architectural conservation and local*

culture 建築保育與本土文化.

10 Ibid.

11 Hongtai Zhen and Shaolun Huang 鄭宏泰 & 黃紹倫, "Identity of Chinese in Hong Kong: Changes before and after 1997 香港華人的身份認同: 九七前後的轉變," *The 21st Century 二十一世紀*, vol.73, no.10 (2002): 71-80.

12 Lin 林中偉, *Architectural conservation and local culture 建築保育與本土文化*.

13 Subin Xu and Nobuo Aoki 徐蘇斌 & 青木信夫, "Observation and Reflection on Cultural Heritage Conservation in Hong Kong under the Background of 'One Country, Two Systems'" "'一國兩制' 背景下香港文化遺產保育之觀察與思考," Design Community 住區, no.04 (2017): 22-31. doi:CNKI:SUN:ZUQU.0.2017-04-006.

14 Xue 薛求理, "Architectural Heritages of the Peoples' Republic of China 新中國建築遺產芻議," 62-67.

15 Lin 林中偉, *Architectural conservation and local culture 建築保育與本土文化*.

16 Yicong Qi, Xinguo Zhang and Yue Wu 齊一聰,張興國 & 吳悅, "The Enlightenment of the Revitalization of Hong Kong Heritage Architecture to the Mainland 基於香港文物建築的活化對中國內地的啟示," *Chinese Landscape Architecture 中國園林*, no.03 (2015): 110-114. doi:CNKI:SUN:ZGYL.0.2015-03-024.

17 Hong Kong Idea Center, "Report of Heritage Study," https://www.ideascentre.hk/wordpress/wp-content/uploads/2009/02/Report-of-Heritage-Study-final-SC.pdf (accessed February 8, 2022).

18 Wei Chen and Lianjie Luo 陳蔚 & 羅連傑, "The Experience and Enlightenment on 'Conservation and Revitalization' of Contemporary Historic buildings in Hong Kong 當代香港歷史建築'保育與活化'的經驗與啟示," *Journal of Human Settlements in West China 西部人居環境學刊*, no.03 (2015): 38-43. doi:10.13791/j.cnki.hsfwest.20150308.

19 Jie Zhang, Cheng Hua and Ruijie Du 張佳,華晨 & 杜睿傑, "The Cause and Response of Different Outcomes in Private Historic Building Conservation in Hong Kong: Based on Three Typical Cases 香港私人歷史建築保育中不同結局的原因及應對——基於三個典型案例," *Urban Planning International 國際城市規劃*, no.06 (2015): 85-92.

20 The Antiquities Advisory Board, "Looking forward, Valuing the Past: Heritage Conservation Policy," https://www.ideascentre.hk/wordpress/wp-content/uploads/2009/02/Report-of-Heritage-Study-final-SC.pdf (accessed February 10, 2022).

21 Xu and Aoki 徐蘇斌 & 青木信夫, "Observation and Reflection on Cultural Heritage Conservation in Hong Kong under the Background of 'One Country, Two Systems' '一國兩制' 背景下香港文化遺產保育之觀察與思考," 22-31.

22 Zhang 張佳et al., "The Cause and Response of Different Outcomes in Private Historic Building Conservation in Hong Kong 香港私人歷史建築保育中不同結局的原因及應對," 85-92.

23 GovHK News, "Appointments to new Advisory Committee on Built Heritage Conservation announced," https://www.info.gov.hk/gia/general/201604/22/P201604220670.htm (accessed February 8, 2022).

24 Antiquities Advisory Board, "About Us."

25 Zhang 張佳et al., "The Cause and Response of Different Outcomes in Private Historic Building Conservation in Hong Kong 香港私人歷史建築保育中不同結局的原因及應對," 85-92.

26 Ruizhi Wang, 王睿智, "How did Hong Kong fight the epidemic in the past? 昔日香港如何抗疫？" https://www.hkchronicles.org.

27 Zhuoying Zhong, 鐘卓盈, "The Green House is transformed into the Comix Home Base, and the building tells the history in detail 灣仔綠屋化身動漫基地 由建築細說歷史," https://ps.hket.com/article/214809 (accessed February 12, 2022).

28 Yanyu Cui and Xuan Guo 崔燕宇 & 郭璇, "Analysis on conservation and revitalization techniques of historical buildings of Hong Kong Comix Home Base 香港動漫基地歷史建筑保育活化技術淺析," *Packaging World 包裝世界*, no.02 (2016): 64-67. doi:10.13337/j.cnki.packaging.world.2016.02.016.

29 Jingwei Huang 黃靜薇, "The Comix Home Base is suspected to end due to the loss of capital after 5-year operation, and will "go back" to the Hong Kong Arts Center 灣仔動漫基地營運5年，疑因蝕本結束，日後「回歸」香港藝術中心," https://www.hk01.com/%E7%A4%BE%E6%9C%83%E6%96%B0%E8%81%9E/227509/%E7%81%A3%E4%BB%94%E5%8B%95%E6%BC%AB%E5%9F%BA%E5%9C%B0%E7%87%9F%E9%81%8B5%E5%B9%B4-%E7%96%91%E5%9B%A0%E8%9D%95%E6%9C%AC%E7%B5%90%E6%9D%9F-%E6%97%A5%E5%BE%8C-%E5%9B%9E%E6%AD%B8-%E9%A6%99%E6%B8%AF%E8%97%9D%E8%A1%93%E4%B8%AD%E5%BF%83 (accessed February 12, 2022).

30 Cui and Guo 崔燕宇 & 郭璇, "Analysis on conservation and revitalization techniques of historical buildings of Hong Kong Comix Home Base 香港動漫基地歷史建筑保育活化技術淺析," 64-67.

31 URA (Urban Renewal Authority) and HKAC (Hong Kong Arts Centre) 市區重建局及香港藝術中心, *Cultural Heritage · Cohesive Community: Art community in historical buildings - the Comix Home Base 文化傳承·凝聚社區 : 歷史建築中的藝術社區——動漫基地* (Hong Kong: Urban Renewal Authority 香港: 市區重建局, 2014).

32 Cui and Guo 崔燕宇 & 郭璇, "Analysis on conservation and revitalization techniques of historical buildings of Hong Kong Comix Home Base 香港動漫基地歷史建筑保育活化技術淺析," 64-67.

33 Ibid.

34 URA and HKAC, *Cultural Heritage · Cohesive Community 文化傳承·凝聚社區*.

35 Cui and Guo 崔燕宇 & 郭璇, "Analysis on conservation and revitalization techniques of historical buildings of Hong Kong Comix Home Base 香港動漫基地歷史建筑保育活化技術淺析," 64-67.

36 No.7 Mallery Street, "About M7," https://mallory.ura-vb.org.hk/ (accessed February 12, 2022).

37 Xiujun Ruan 阮秀君, "24 hours live in the Green House - event design director: no time limitation 24小時活用灣仔綠屋——活動設計總監：不需限晝夜," https://www.hk01.com/%E7%A4%BE%E5%8D%80%E5%B0%88%E9%A1%8C/277569/24%E5%B0%8F%E6%99%82%E6%B4%BB%E7%94%A8%E7%81%A3%E4%BB%94%E7%B6%A0%E5%B1%8B-%E6%B4%BB%E5%8B%95%E8%A8%AD%E8%A8%88%E7%B8%BD%E7%9B%A3-%E4%B8%8D%E9%9C%80%E9%99%90%E6%99%9D%E5%A4%9C (accessed February 12, 2022).

38 Ibid.

39 STNN 星島環球網, "German Consul General in Hong Kong wants to save the Bauhaus-style Central Market 德國駐港總領事欲搶救包豪斯風格中環街市," https://web.archive.org/web/20080220012442/http://www.singtaonet.com/global/hk_macau/t20060406_184078.html (accessed February 22, 2022).

40 Weibin Liu 刘卫斌, "The Death and Revival of Hong Kong's 'Street Markets' 香港 '街市' 的死去与活来," *World Architecture Review 世界建筑导报*, no.1

(2013): 22-23.

41 Meiying Jiang 江美瑩, "An Analysis of the Space's Originality Presentation of Conservation and Revitalization of Central Market in Hong Kong 香港中環街市保育與活化實踐的原意呈現探析," Master Thesis, (Shenzhen University 深圳大學, 2020). https://kns.cnki.net/KCMS/detail/detail.aspx?dbname=CMFD202102&filename=1020367661.nh

42 STNN 星島環球網, "German Consul General in Hong Kong wants to save the Bauhaus-style Central Market 德國駐港總領事欲搶救包豪斯風格中環街市".

43 Central Market, "Central Market Revitalization," https://www.centralmarket.hk/en/revitalization/undefined (accessed February 12, 2022).

44 HKET, "The Central Market closed for 18 years and reopened, the old stalls become shopping mall-style restaurants and stores 中環街市閪閉18年活化重開, 舊攤檔變商場式食肆小店," https://topick.hket.com/

45 Yuanlong Yuan 袁源隆, "Interview with old householders and customers of the Central Market, retrieving memories of the past 尋訪中環街市上一代檔戶顧客, 重塑昔日回憶," https://www.mpweekly.com/culture/%e6%88%91%e5%80%91%e7%9a%84%e4%b8%ad%e7%92%b0%e8%a1%97%e5%b8%82-%e6%9c%b1%e9%9b%8b%e7%a9%8e-%e6%89%93%e6%9b%b8%e9%87%98-189830 (accessed February 12, 2022).

46 Jiang 江美瑩, "An Analysis of the Space's Originality Presentation of Conservation and Revitalization of Central Market in Hong Kong 香港中環街市保育與活化實踐的原意呈現探析".

47 Liu 刘卫斌, "The Death and Revival of Hong Kong's 'Street Markets' 香港 '街市' 的死去与活来," 22-23.

48 Jiang 江美瑩, "An Analysis of the Space's Originality Presentation of Conservation and Revitalization of Central Market in Hong Kong 香港中環街市保育與活化實踐的原意呈現探析".

49 Man Han, Jiawei Wu and Daqing Gu 韓曼, 吳佳維 & 顧大慶, "Space-Structure as the Primary Consideration for the Conservation and Revitalization of Modernist Architecture: Lessons Learnt from the Hong Kong Central Market Project 空間-結構作為現代主義建筑遺產保育和活化的重要考量:香港中環街市項目的經驗教訓," Time + Architecture 時代建筑, no.05 (2021): 165-171. doi:10.13717/j.cnki.ta.2021.05.025.

50 Daqing Gu, Tinfwei Bai and Peiling Hu 顧大慶,柏庭衛 & 胡佩玲, "The Great Form Has No Shape: The Case Study of Hong Kong Modern Architecture: the Central Market 大象無形: 香港現代建筑個案研究之中環街市," *Time + Architecture 時代建筑*, no.03 (2015): 128-136. doi:10.13717/j.cnki.ta.2015.03.022.

51 Ibid.

52 Han 韓曼 et al., "Space-Structure as the Primary Consideration for the Conservation and Revitalization of Modernist Architecture 空間-結構作為現代主義建筑遺產保育和活化的重要考量," 165-171.

53 Jiang 江美瑩, "An Analysis of the Space's Originality Presentation of Conservation and Revitalization of Central Market in Hong Kong 香港中環街市保育與活化實踐的原意呈現探析".

54 Han 韓曼 et al., "Space-Structure as the Primary Consideration for the Conservation and Revitalization of Modernist Architecture 空間-結構作為現代主義建筑遺產保育和活化的重要考量," 165-171.

55 Ibid.

56 Jiang 江美瑩, "An Analysis of the Space's Originality Presentation of Conservation and Revitalization of Central Market in Hong Kong 香港中環街市保育與活化實踐的原意呈現探析".

57 Hong Kong Economic Journal 信報財經新聞, "Three million people visited the central market in two and a half months 中環街市兩個半月人流300萬," https://www1.hkej.com/dailynews/property/

58 Walk In Hong Kong 活現香港, "State Theater Statement of Significance 舊皇都戲院文物價值評估報告," https://web.archive.org/web/20180126131916/http://walkin.hk/wp-content/uploads/2016/04/Heritage_Value_Assessment_Former_State_Theatre.pdf (accessed February 13, 2022).

59 Ibid.

60 Walk In Hong Kong 活現香港, "Joint statement by Walk in Hong Kong, The Conservancy Association and Docomomo HK to the Antiquities Advisory Board 活現香港、長春社、Docomomo HK 聯合聲明促請古諮會將舊皇都戲院至少評為一級歷史建築," https://walkin.hk/joint-statement-state-theatre/ (accessed February 13, 2022).

61 Mingpao Daily News 明报, "A Closer Look at the Imperial Theater 街知巷聞: 深入內部逐處比對 皇都戲院現形記," https://news.mingpao.com/pns/%e5%89%af%e5%88%8a/article/20160717/s00005/1468692102109/%e8%a1%97%e7%9f%a5%e5%b7%b7%e8%81%9e-%e6%b7%b1%e5%85%a5%e5%85%a7%e9%83%a8%e9%80%90%e8%99%95%e6%af%94%e5%b0%8d-%e7%9a%87%e9%83%bd%e6%88%b2%e9%99%a2%e7%8f%be%e5%bd%a2%e8%a8%98 (accessed May 22, 2022).

62 Guandian Property and Co. 觀點地產網, "The story of the State Theater and the conservation of heritage properties on Hong Kong Island 皇都戲院舊事與港島文物物業保育一二事," http://m.caijing.com.cn/api/show?contentid=4703942. (accessed February 13, 2022).

63 Ibid.

64 Lai, "State Theatre is saved - but the real test for Hong Kong's heritage conservation is still to come," https://hongkongfp.com/2020/10/17/state-theatre-is-saved-but-the-real-test-for-hong-kongs-heritage-conservation-has-yet-to-come/ (accessed May 21, 2022).

65 Purcell, "Project information of the State Theater, Hong Kong," https://www.purcellap.com/projects/the-state-theatre-hong-kong (accessed May 22, 2022).

66 iMoney 智富, "Conservation and redevelopment: New World announced the conservation of the Grade I historic buildings-Royal City Theater, and the preservation of the 'parabolic roof trusses' to continue the function of the theater 保育重建: 新世界宣佈保育一級歷史建築皇都戲院,保留'飛拱'延續戲院功能." https://inews.hket.com/article/2771783 (accessed February 13, 2022).

67 Culture for Tomorrow, "Discover the State Theater for All of Us," https://www.culturefortomorrow.org/events/discover-the-state-theatre-in-all-of-us/ (accessed May 22, 2022).

68 Jiaming Zhang 張嘉敏, "New World Presents Royal City Theatre Experience, Exhibits Old Ticket Replica Chairs, Recreates the Atmosphere of the Past 新世界辦皇都戲院體驗活動: 展出舊戲票仿製櫈, 重現昔日氣氛," *HK 01 香港01*, https://www.hk01.com/sns/article/607180 (accessed May 22, 2022).

ROBO-REPAIR

THE ROBOTIC MAINTENANCE OF ATOMIC ARCHITECTURE

Clare Dieckmann

On the Sellafield Nuclear Site, automated robots search for radioactive contamination amongst a vast tangle of pipework, tanks and machinery. Amongst the power plant's extensive network of machines, the robots gather information using sensors and scanners, sending data to human receivers at a location free from contamination. While remote-controlled, the robots act to extend the reach of a team of scientists who are tasked with removing contamination leaking from breaches in Sellafield's corroded pipework and aging machinery.[1] Salty air blowing in from the nearby sea works to corrode the protective layer of infrastructure that shields the reactors and weakens their structure. If Sellafield's aging infrastructure were to collapse, the leaked amounts of radiation could cause irreversible damage to the environment. As part of the maintenance effort to prevent this, remote-controlled robots work to maintain and repair Sellafield's architecture until its buildings can be dismantled and the site can be slowly decommissioned. These yellow robots are welcome participants accompanying humans in their ongoing efforts to repair Sellafield by processing the nuclear power plant's radioactive uranium into a more stable form.

Designed by engineering and robotics company Boston Dynamics, *Spot* is a yellow quadruped robot that can climb stairs and access unpredictable terrain.[2] Due to *Spot*'s quadruped design, it can inspect uncertain and dangerous

territory characteristic of Sellafield's radioactive environment inaccessible to other wheeled robots and drones. To equip *Spot* particularly for Sellafield, physical attachments including 360-degree cameras and payloads are added to the robot's body, giving *Spot* enhanced sensory capabilities. *Spot*'s attachable kit-of-parts can collect data specific to the radiation released on the Sellafield site. Equipment fitted to *Spot* enables it to scan, inspect, map and collect data needed to characterise areas as hazardous and desperate for repair. This type of high-tech equipment leads to highly accurate detection capabilities, surpassing manual detection methods. Allowing *Spot* out from the confines of the Boston Dynamics laboratory and onto dangerous sites has shifted this type of avant-garde technology out from the lab and into the real world, where the technology can be applied.

The decommissioning of Sellafield's architecture has become the testing ground for autonomous robotic technology. By introducing *Spot* onto the Sellafield site, hazards and risks are detected by robots rather than humans, modernising the repair process. The addition of autonomous robots with machine intelligence is pioneering the robotic repair of architectural spaces. Designers must now ask themselves how the robotic repair of architecture affects their building's longevity and how non-human machines might interact with manual maintenance methods. The collaboration between *Spot* and people reflects a novel partnership between humans and non-humans. This advanced type of hybrid repair indicates a unique style of maintenance that demands a new kind of tailored technology to accommodate their companionship. Architects are ready to innovate

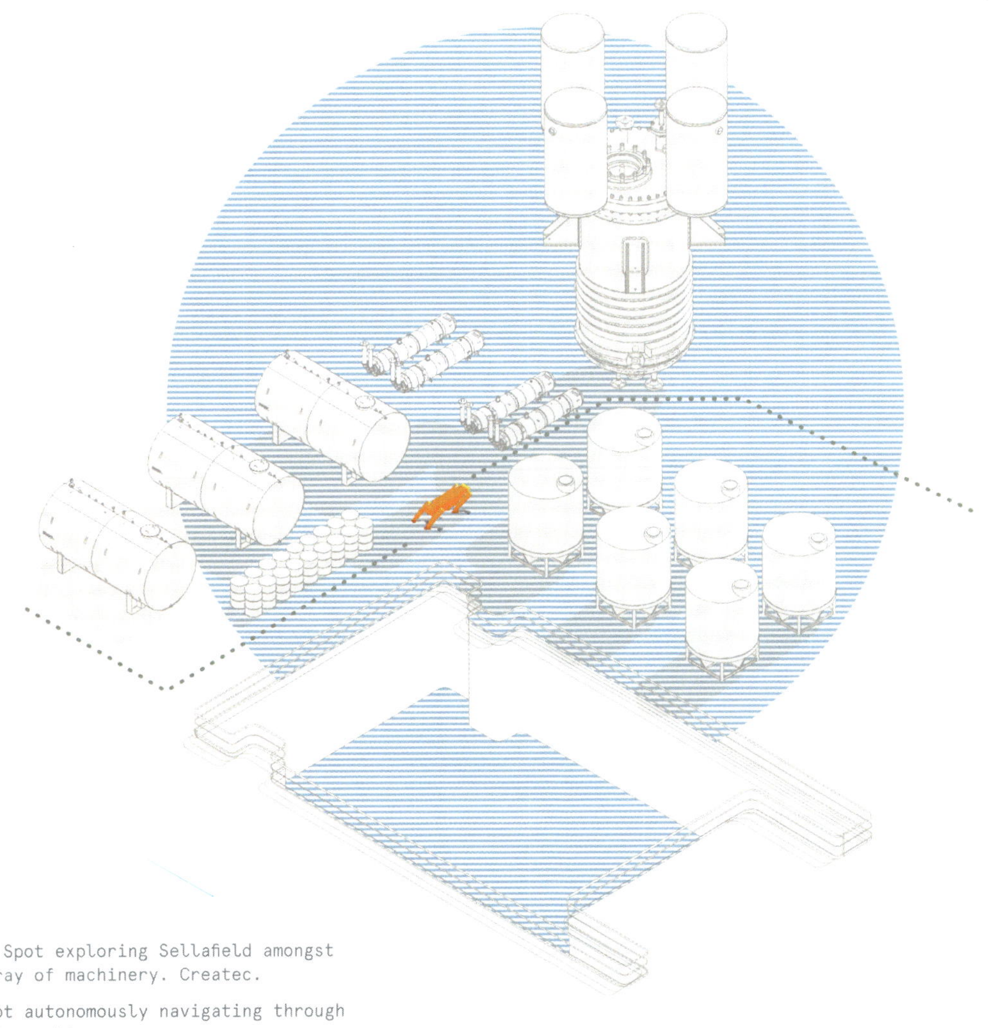

Opposite: Spot exploring Sellafield amongst a vast array of machinery. Createc.

Above: Spot autonomously navigating through Sellafield's machinery.

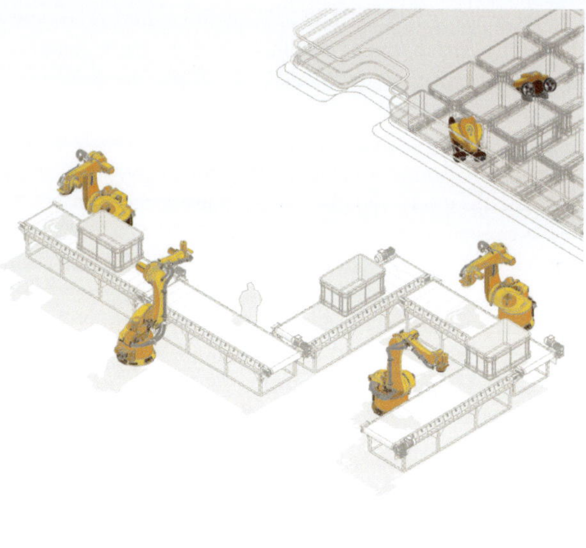

Automated dismantling machines and Raptor robot arms break up waste.

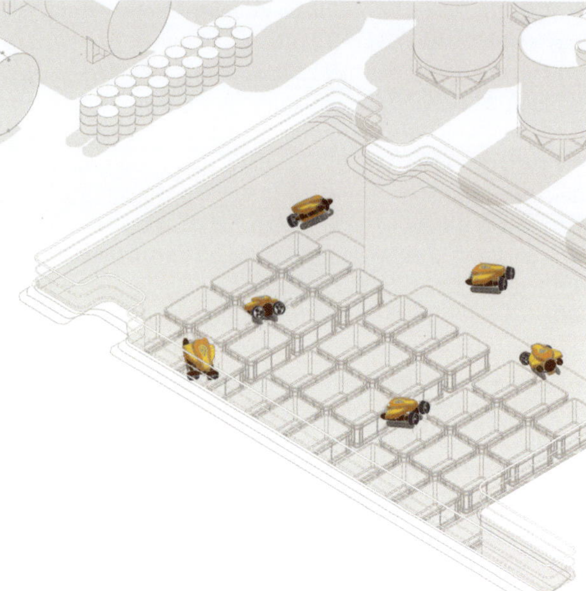

Amphibious robots chop up waste in pool.

to accommodate robotic repair, but designers must first understand what makes robotic repair unique.

Atomic types of Robo-Repair

In the 1940s, Sellafield was acquired by the British Government to research and produce nuclear weapons. Less than two decades later, a fire burned in the Windscale Pile reactor releasing radioactive fallout into the atmosphere that covered the UK and caused widespread sickness. The Windscale Fire was the worst nuclear accident in the United Kingdom's history.[3] To prevent future crises, Sellafield is undertaking a major robot-led decommissioning process to dismantle the plant's architecture piece by piece and treat the radioactive waste for longer-term storage. At the centre of the decommissioning process is a giant pool filled with water that constantly cools nuclear waste to a sufficient temperature. Once the waste is cool enough to be handled, it is chopped up, dropped into a basket and dissolved in chemicals.[4] All operations at the pool are undertaken by remote-controlled robotics. An automated dismantling machine and Raptor robot arm break up and move waste out of the pool, along conveyor belts and into storage. In other Sellafield buildings, endoscopes peek through holes in walls before robotic demolishers and slave arms take apart structures piece by piece. Once rooms are cleared and declared safe, humans can enter with protective clothing and continue cleaning tiny particles of radioactive dust from surfaces. These giant, heavy robots currently use outdated technology to perform tasks slowly and inefficiently. The addition of an agile and capable robot such as *Spot* to the family of robots at Sellafield will make the detection process more efficient and safer for people.[5]

Another robotics company named Createc has collaborated with Boston Dynamics to develop an attachment for the top of *Spot*'s body with the ability to laser-scan and detect gamma radiation.[6] Technicians simply direct *Spot* to move towards a set point, and the robot autonomously navigates around the map, scanning as it goes, adjusting course where the route might be obstructed by unpredictable terrain. The cameras and sensors attached to *Spot*'s body constantly detect and capture new data, which is downloaded at the end of each mission. The data is converted into colourised dots with specific tones signalling where radiation is located, linking the collected data to physical locations within Sellafield. Technical staff can then continue the decommissioning and waste planning processes without fear of contamination by avoiding areas identified as dangerous on the map. Sending *Spot* into hazardous locations with cameras and sensors means technicians do not need to go themselves, keeping the hazards for personnel as low as possible. However, there are some risks sending in a robot, including the effect of radiation on intricate and expensive electronics.

Safely getting the robot in and out of Sellafield and cleaned away are two very different stories. To ensure *Spot*'s

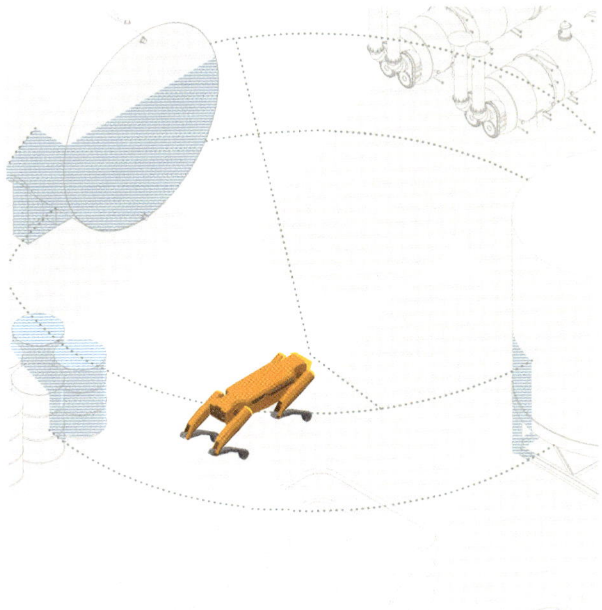
Spot scanning for radiation.

Family of robots at Sellafield.

longevity, the UK Atomic Energy Authority (UKAEA) has also collaborated with Boston Dynamics to develop a method of robo-repair designed to keep *Spot* operating.[7] Together they have fashioned a radiation-proof suit to clothe the robot and prevent *Spot*'s mechanisms from contamination. The transparent plastic suit shields *Spot*'s internal machinery from dangerous ionising radiation that works to destroy transistor electronics. With *Spot* clothed in the suit, tests were undertaken to understand just how much radiation the robot could withstand. *Spot*'s suit worked to absorb most of the radiation without failure, even with excessive exposure. Though the total amount the robot can absorb is still unknown, the knowledge that *Spot* can absorb levels present at Sellafield is instrumental to the decommissioning effort. Once a mission is over, the suit is removed and *Spot*'s body is monitored for radiation. If cleared, the robot can interact with technicians without risk. Due to the success of *Spot*'s new suit, the robot can leave Sellafield safely and be reused on other sites.[8] Finally, there is potential to move from nuclear sites to building sites and help architects out with construction.

Architectural Robo-Repair

Foster and Partners have adopted *Spot* to help them construct new homes at the Battersea Power Station residential development.[9] First designed in the 1930s, the Power Station produced enough electricity to meet the energy demands of Post-War Londoners. The energy plant is currently being renovated into 1300 apartments, including 103 affordable housing units.[10] The architects have designed homes to sit behind an undulating façade that allows light and fresh air to enter each room. *Spot* is placed on-site to monitor environmental conditions and ensure the unsafe air associated with the historic Power Station has been removed. Using its sensors, the robot tests the air to ensure the apartment is clean and well ventilated. As the architects work through design development, *Spot*'s detectors gather temporal and spatial information providing feedback on Battersea's interior environment. These intricate data collections show how people, furnishings and their surroundings interact in real-time. The ability to anticipate how apartments will feel assures designers they are delivering on their promise for liveable spaces.

Spot now attends places where ordinary people live and work using technology applied initially to detect radiation at Sellafield. Another method architects can use to track conditions on-site is to deploy *Spot* onto Battersea as a virtual avatar. *Spot* embodies the characteristics of designers by linking their screens to the robot's video camera, allowing them to experience Battersea virtually.[11] Technicians at Foster's login to *Spot* remotely from their London Campus and tap into the robot's controls. The design team can then move *Spot* around using *Spot*'s Autowalk functionality to comment on what they see virtually, intending to prevent design faults before they happen. By embodying the avatar of the architect at Battersea, *Spot* has become an additional team member,

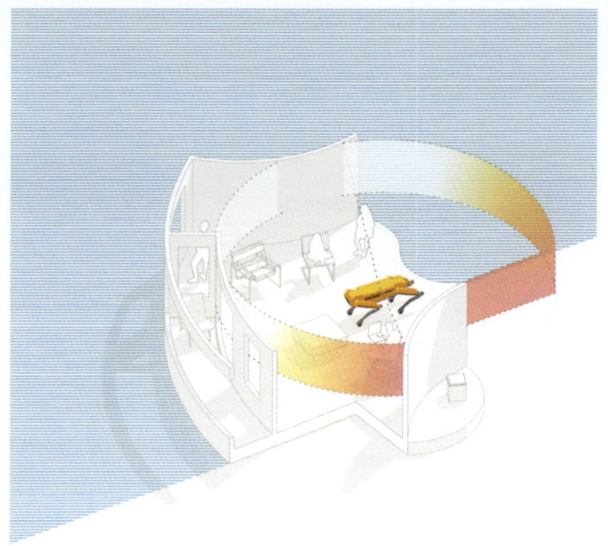

Spot monitoring Battersea construction.

Spot detecting temperature of an apartment.

collaborating with humans in the repair process. In this way, the Battersea Roof Garden is a collaboration between humans and machines, where robots become architects monitoring design defects. Foster and Partners are using *Spot* for more than just a tool for fabrication, turning the robot into a virtual being with the ability to assist designers in their roles.

At the Battersea Roof Garden stage of Battersea's development, *Spot* has replaced the architect as a site supervisor. With several contractors working on the Roof Garden at any one time, there is a need for a process that allows for rapid checking. Like Sellafield, Foster's team has designed a map for *Spot* to follow while scanning certain roof garden areas to capture measured data. As *Spot* repeatedly returns to site, the robot reruns the same missions with the same scanning routine. This yields a sequence of manageable data sets that helps to reduce post-processing times.[12] Designers can then check the real-world structure against their own design drawings, identifying where deviations have occurred. Sequential scanning completed by *Spot* means that designers do not need to supervise site progress and time and money is saved by the company. *Spot*'s successes on Battersea, combined with new opportunities in the construction industry, mean skilled and autonomous robots are participating in the built environment.

Spot's intelligence has been enhanced by Sellafield, becoming anthropomorphised with a heightened sense of smell, sight and walking ability. *Spot* has evolved from a hinged slave arm, a swivelling dismantling robot and a small snake-like detection endoscope into an intelligent and autonomous robot, with each evolution driven by a new problem to solve. Now highly evolved robots are arriving onto building sites, applying what they have learned from Sellafield to new issues. Architects are designing to accommodate these new recruits, making new buildings with the assistance of contemporary forms of repair. Foster + Partners adoption of *Spot*, has brought automation of the construction site into the realm of possibility. Soon cloned, copies of *Spot* will spread, multiplying in number and adding to maintenance teams eventually becoming as familiar as a bulldozer or a forklift.[13]

Spot will freely roam building sites with the capacity for self-repair while scanning. The limited battery life that powers *Spot* and impedes the robot from long missions will no longer be an issue. Having the ability to self-detect its own energy levels, the robot will decide on the time for recharging and walk towards a charging station.[14] Imparted with the cognitive faculty for self-charging, *Spot* can now undertake longer missions and operate amongst humans for extended periods of time. With constant improvements and updates, *Spot* will be tasked with more complex routes and given more autonomy. Ultimately, *Spot* will evolve from animoid to humanoid, with a consciousness to rival ours. On that day, a question will need to be asked either to restrict robots to the task of repair or let them transcend their original purpose and let the robots go free.[15]

01 Sellafield is home to 80% of the UK's nuclear waste. The sites buildings must not collapse as their destruction would cause widespread devastation. James Temperton, *"Inside Sellafield: How the UK's Most Dangerous Nuclear Site Is Cleaning up Its Act,"* Wired UK, September 17, 2016, https://www.wired.co.uk/article/inside-sellafield-nuclear-waste-decommissioning.

02 Boston Dynamics have created a new robot called Spot. This four-legged robot can navigate terrain with innovative mobility. *"SPOT® - Boston Dynamics."* Boston Dynamics, https://shop.bostondynamics.com/spot.

03 The plume from the Windscale Fire is thought to have covered most parts of England and Wales, brushing the east coast of Ireland. Public distaste about Nuclear accidents ignited protests around the world. Ireland was determined to stop the production of nuclear energy by their English neighbours. Veronica McDermott, *Going Nuclear: Ireland, Britain and the Campaign to Close Sellafield* (Dublin: Irish Academic Press, 2008).

04 The revolution in nuclear energy needs an evolution in robotics for the clean-up. David Hambling, *"Only Cthulhu Can Solve Sellafield's Sludgy Nuclear Waste Problem,"* WIRED UK, June 14, 2018, https://www.wired.co.uk/article/sellafield-nuclear-robots-cleanup-waste.

05 Spot is amongst a family of robots cleaning up Sellafield. Theo Leggett, *"The Robots Helping Clean up Sellafield's Nuclear Waste,"* BBC News, https://www.bbc.com/news/av/business-33847598.

06 Createc are integrating custom sensors into Spots hardware. *"Spot and Boston Dynamics."* Createc, July 23, 2021. https://createc.co.uk/spot.

07 The UK government is using robots to speed up the decommissioning process of Sellafield. Sellafield Ltd. *"Robotics in the Spot-Light."* GOV.UK, December 10, 2021. https://www.gov.uk/government/news/robotics-in-the-spot-light.

All images by author unless stated otherwise.

Below: Spot traversing in highly radiactive zone at Sellafield. Createc.

08 The robot completed its work wearing a suit specially designed and manufactured at the UK Atomic Energy Authority (UKAEA) which protected it from any radioactive contamination. This was provided via the National Nuclear User Facility for Hot Robotics. *"Spots Walkabout at Sellafield."* Hot Robotics: A National Nuclear User Facility, April 1, 2022. https://hotrobotics.co.uk/project/spot-deployment-at-sellafield/.

09 Robotic assistance is no longer a fantasy with Foster and Partners being the first architectural firm to adopt Spot. Andreea Cutieru, *"Automating the Construction Site,"* ArchDaily, June 14, 2021, https://www.archdaily.com/963301/automating-the-construction-site?ad_source=search&ad_medium=search_result_all.

10 Battersea is London's newest neighbourhood located on the river Thames. Foster and Partners. *"Battersea Power Station."* Foster + Partners, n.d. https://www.fosterandpartners.com/projects/battersea-power-station/.

11 Foster + Partners are pioneering the use of Spot as part of Boston Dynamics's Early Adopter Program. Foster + Partners. *"Foster + Partners Collaborates with Boston Dynamics to Monitor Construction Progress with Spot."* Foster + Partners, November 11, 2020. https://www.fosterandpartners.com/news/archive/2020/11/foster-partners-collaborates-with-boston-dynamics-to-monitor-construction-progress-with-spot/.

12 Ibid

13 *"Automating the Construction Site."*

14 Tsigkari, Martha, Anders Rod, Sherif Tarabishy, Khaled El-Ashry, and Adam Davis. *"On-Site with Spot: Robotic Refinement of Workflow Procedures."* Foster + Partners, December 20, 2021. https://www.fosterandpartners.com/plus/on-site-with-spot/.

15 Time will tell whether the presence of Spot is simply a by-product of the fashion of robots on construction sites or an integral moment to architectural history. Antoine Picon, *"Free the Robots!"* Log 36, Winter (2016): pp. 146-151.

TEMPORALITY

SHIPYARD 1862

Kengo Kuma & Yutaka Terasaki

Project location: Shanghai, China
Completion year of renovation: 2017

We have transformed a shipyard built in 1972 into a mixed-use complex comprised of a theatre, a multi-purpose hall and commercial spaces. The project's name '1862' is a direct reference to the date of establishment of the company who used to run the shipyard. Back in those times, plenty of factories were lined up along the streets in this area. However, when we visited the site in 2011, most of the factories had been demolished and were waiting for redevelopment.

Previously a place manufacturing large-scale ships, the Shipyard's architecture operates at industrial dimensions, thus giving it a subliminal sense of scale. The building is 200m in length and 45m in width with a height of 30m. There are not any walls in between, it is a one-room space with a void measuring 26m tall. Due to the lack of maintenance, the building was suffering from leaking problems at various locations. Rusted pipes that were presumably used during production times were lying around on the ground. The concrete columns supporting the building were weathered and marked by time. Yet when we witnessed the state of the columns, we did not look at it from a negative point of view. We were fond of this brutal space that carried its own history. During the revival of the building, we paid close attention, trying to explore ways to create a building for the future while maintaining the existing scale and texture of the architecture.

We responded by creating two atriums along the north-south direction which are then linked by another east-west facing, five-storey tall atrium. This compressed void evokes an ascending verticality which exacerbates the encounter between the human scale and that of the Shipyard's monumental structures. Here, the void not only exhibits the original columns and girders as an impressive spectacle, but also redefines them as the building's core where all events gravitate towards each other.

'Void' and 'Structure' tend to be antithetic concepts. The norm is for the structure to recede into the background in order to frame the emptiness of atriums. Instead, we deliberately inverted the relationship of the two by using the void to frame the raw, load-bearing structure built in the 1970s at the forefront. These aged concrete columns were kept in their original condition as much as possible. For instance, we kept the rusted steel staircase, the painted slogan and numbers which would be otherwise described as dirty and untidy. To preserve such rich textures, the supplementary structures were designed to be the least visible.

These days, commercial spaces tend to conceal the unsightliness of building structures with shiny surfaces, thereby redefining the visual identity of buildings. No matter what structure the architecture uses, the glamorous interiors that ultimately construct our spatial experience bear no relationship with it. As such, the world's commercial spaces have certainly become magnificent and glamorous, but also normalised and insipid.

Shipyard 1862 is a unique structure that is intended to create a 'barebones' commercial space by showcasing the unique structure in the most prominent location. Another critical consideration in the adaptive re-use of architecture is the rediscovery of a building's materiality and maintenance. Every architecture bears a unique texture that identifies it. Materiality imprints a deeper impression than form. If asked to describe the form of a building, the memory of it would be vague most of the time. However, the texture of the building leaves a clear impression behind. Materiality transcends beyond the visual experience, as it requires all five senses of the human body to engage it, to remember it. When the construction was completed, an elderly person who used to work in this exact factory came to visit. He put his hands on the preserved steel staircase and nostalgically began to share his personal memories of the place. He climbed onto the stair, saying that he used to invite a girl here on a date. We strongly believe this building is able to remind people of their own experience while connecting to the future.

Apart from the central commercial area, we planned an 800-seat theatre at the east side of the building. Here, we also worked hard to create the sense of scale and materiality. The ceiling of the theater exposes the existing concrete beams. In general, acoustics are the highest priority in theatre design and the structure is often invisible due to the acoustic clouds ceiling, but here we only met the minimum

Opposite & Middle: Image courtesy of Erieta Attali.
Above & Bottom: Image courtesy of Eiichi Kano.

requirements for the sound. Our focus was on creating an industrial atmosphere that is unique to the space. On both sides of the seating area, giant rusted pipes were recycled and deployed as HVAC ducts. After noticing these enormous pipes during our first site visit we have considered different ways to reutilise them. Eventually, we decided to conceal the HVAC ducts inside these pipes. This ensured that to this day, the pipe infrastructure remains one of the most distinctive characteristics of the theatre.

The materiality of this old shipyard bears a particularly colourful and tactile character. The design challenge for this project was to capture the material essence of the original brick walls. Due to the physical strength of the material and other legal aspects, traditional bricks were not selected. The shades and texture of bricks manufactured today tend to be very homogeneous, which makes it hard to emulate the rough and uneven textures of the shipyard's weathered brick walls. Our design proposal, a permeable brick wall, suspends a randomly arranged pattern using four types of coloured bricks along 8mm stainless steel wire fixtures (Fig.1). The gap between the bricks allows light and wind to pass through which is impossible if deployed on a traditional brick wall. The porosity of the design recalls the rough, weathered and particle-like qualities of the original wall.

On the one hand, the process of handmade bricks in the past has inadvertently generated flaws and defects. However, these 'flaws' and 'defects' create unintended randomness and noise, storing the memory of the building and the elderly man. Although there is no way to recreate those qualities with standard modern building techniques, it is important to reconsider the meaning of imperfection and how we can rediscover its essence in the contemporary world.

Left: Image courtesy of Shipyard 1862.
Right: Image by Author.
Middle (Fig. 1), bottom and opposite: Image by Eiichi Kano.

MASTERPLANNING ECOLOGIES OF REPAIR

Io Carydi

Introduction

The overarching intention of this article is to reveal how the notion of repair represents a multifaceted tool for architecture and urban design gaining multiple meanings within a masterplanning context. The aim is to show how the definitions of repair emerge in relation to the local requirements and spatio-geographical processes operating within the broader site context. By bringing this discourse into a design-based perspective and more specifically to the case-study of the award-winning Masterplan for the Regeneration of the Port-Industrial Waterfront of Lipasmata in Piraeus, Greece — a competition project won by the architectural team of Io Carydi — the article unfolds an amalgam of 'matters of repair' that become visualised as active aspects of redevelopment and regeneration. In what follows, repair is conceptualised architecturally as an interplay of repurposed buildings and infrastructures alongside the recovery of natural assets. Throughout the design process, the winning team felt that the context of repair could instrumentalise various aspects of the area's historical and cultural context, making the most out of the area's hidden social and spatio-geographical potentials. Repair is not only to be involved in the production of a new natural landscape, but rather, it informs a framework of knowledge for the experience of the place itself.

The team's work largely involved designs for the reconciliation of past contamination with future uses and the rehabilitation and conversion of existing buildings and infrastructures. The proposed masterplan sought to devise in-situ remediation processes alongside the retrofitting of existing infrastructure. Reconstruction involving decontamination through physical dynamics was particularly challenging. The complex design process had to be planned around staged recovery cycles and to make a large park in creating an integral part of the visitor's experience. Likewise, the team determined the new uses and scales of remedial operations by reference to other socioeconomic priorities. Combining new human activities with environmental processes and thinking about the site's *therapeia* ('cure' in Greek) helped to make the repair process more comprehensible to the wider public.

History & Context

The site is placed within a historically deprived region of North-West Piraeus. It occupies the coastal stretch and expands along the coast, between the container and the passenger port. The area has experienced cycles of growth and decay and its past industrial and maritime activities were closely associated to the immigrants and refugees that settled in the region affecting the flourishing of the industrial sector. The surrounding areas of Drapetsona and Keratsini, mostly known for the settlement of interior immigrants in the end of the 19th century and later the refugees from Minor Asia in the 1920s, became inseparable from the industrial sector as they increased the pool of low-skilled blue-collar workers. Socially and culturally, both areas have acted as melting pots over the last century giving an emerging working proletariat a distinctive identity.[1] Although these neighbourhoods are widely recognised for their cultural impact and the enrichment of the Greek culture, they have remained peripheral to planned urbanisation policies receiving limited access to social amenities and infrastructure. Even today, they are systematically associated with urban marginalisation, household racialisation, social outcasts and low-skilled working-class community.[2]

The region's deprivation is associated with environmental hazards. Its industrial networks have caused the past extensive depletion of the coastlines' natural and ecological assets. The two main bays of the area bear significant degradation of the marine system due to the combined action of untreated sewage deposited in the past — before Psyttalia island, opposite Drapetsona, was transformed to a wastewater treatment plant — and harmful heavy metals discharged to the sea by local industries.[3] Over the last century, the site quickly transformed to an organised hub for noxious and pollutant industries. It hosted several large industrial and harbour establishments that formulated a characteristic monolithic industrial block of activities segregating residential areas from the waterfront. Amongst the industrial complexes of the area, the most prominent was the Chemicals and Fertilisers industry, a phosphoric acid plant (in operation from 1909 till 1999) from which the area Lipasmata, meaning fertilisers in Greek, gains its name today. The plant formed a densely built complex of processing units and troughed belt conveyors. The plant produced decorative glass, glass panels, acid, chemical fertilisers and pesticides. Nearby industries comprised a gypsum production unit, a cement plant and an extensive array of petroleum and oil tank depots. The shutdown of most of these industries in early 2000 due to imposed de-industrialisation policies led to the site's gradual inertia and to its current condition of disrepair and obsolescence notwithstanding an implied loss of jobs in the manufacturing sector. The decommissioning of the Phosphoric acid production plant that began shortly after its closure revealed large concentrations of radioisotopes due to the produced phosphogypsum, a waste product from manufacturing fertiliser, which contains radioactive elements. Since this condition strongly impacted redevelopment perspectives and land value, the dismantling process turned to a disassembly and decontamination process from radioactive materials. This was the first one to be ever executed in Greece. The radiological decontamination process left no surface residual contaminants besides some small concentrations that where localised and buried deeply into the soil.[4] This process changed the image of the site from a densely built mass to a vast landfill from which only the glassworks plant, the silo, the chimney, the ammonia plant, the Chemistry & Agriculture Institute, the water tower and the electric power station remain as relics since they became listed as newer monuments of industrial heritage.[5]

Redevelopment Context

The hardened port-industrial zone of Keratsini and Drapetsona forms a vast brownfield, a barren land with decommissioned industrial plants, a dense network of road and port infrastructures and a high-density urban area with a marginal ratio of 1.5 m^2 of green spaces per inhabitant. The total area of 158 acres is distributed between public and private owners. The public share on the land is approximately 33%. The remaining percentage belongs to the Protypos Ktimatiki Company, a subsidiary of the National Bank of Greece that is the owner of Lipasmata and private landlords in the cement industry, port logistics and oil refineries. Lipasmata holds the largest share, owning one third of the port-industrial site and half of the coastal front. The Lipasmata zone forms the last remaining undeveloped space area on the waterfront. This is particularly significant for both western Piraeus and the Municipality of Keratsini-Drapetsona, as this zone constitutes a strategic intervention area for the qualitative upgrading of both western Piraeus and the surrounding neighbourhoods, capitalising on its proximity to the sea, its extensive waterfront and its significant historical and cultural background.[6]

Bird's eye view of the winning proposal of the architectural team of Io Carydi in the Architectural Competition for the Regeneration of 158 acres of port-industrial zone of Keratsini -Drapetsona.

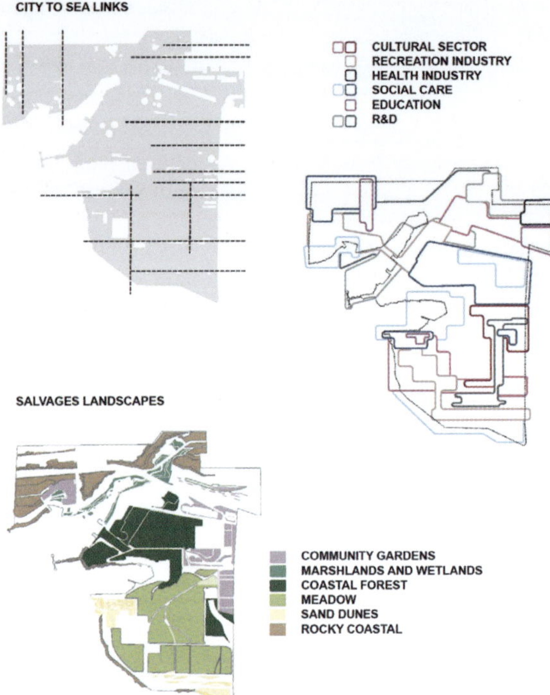

Green spatial planning initiatives and local communities' pleas for reclamation of the site as coastal park always remained overshadowed by aggressive land speculation perspectives that prioritised the site for densely built-up land under a high rise trend that echoed examples from Dubai and London's Docklands. One such major private investment project included 'a start from scratch' dense development that ignored all listed buildings. With increased building density at a factor 0.6–1.35%, the proposal aimed for new residential areas, a business shipping centre as well as areas for recreation and tourism.[7,8] Budgeted at €430 million for newly constructed buildings and €137 million for the infrastructure and public spaces, this project was quickly superseded by the economic recession that followed.[9] The resulting stagnant development and limited economic resources rendered the above plans non-bankable, while the remnants of sub-surface contamination restricted the possibility of large excavations required for creating a densely built urban fabric. This problem created an opportunity to think softer, prioritising the added value of the park alongside the repurpose of listed buildings. Under Law 4277 /2014 and its later reformations, the area was characterised as "Area for Metropolitan Interventions" and gained a new legislative land-use regime that restricted housing and industry. It called instead for soft-port activities, crafts and manufacturing, services, culture, education, sports, tourism and leisure. Within the scopes of the competition, the new building factor of the area was reduced to 0.15% and the development was oriented towards the regeneration of the area as a large park, supported by uses of culture, education, health, sports, green and recreation, securing open public spaces and restoring the lost continuity between city and sea. The competition's brief further demanded the protection and promotion of industrial heritage sites.

Repair as Urban Metabolism

Within this changed context, the winning proposal metabolises an inherited lag in progressive action by capitalising on the comparative advantages linked to the repair and refurbishment of the site's infrastructural assets. The design proposal aims to develop an exemplary developmental framework that fights back the effects of crisis on a local as well as metropolitan level. Repairing the site's past avoids taking the route of nostalgia. It avoids re-constructing an industrial scenery in the form of a passive icon with a dash of green in the background. Instead, the proposed park is conceived as a repair mechanism, hosting enmeshed and overlapping programs of history, culture, recreation, healthcare and sustainability. Urban reactivation and place-making also combined new infrastructures, urban artefacts and natural resources with new opportunities for turning tracts of contaminated ground into living laboratories for research. This aimed to facilitate the creation of self-sustained resources for the park's future needs. The delivered scheme provides form, identity and meaning to the site, but is resilient enough to adapt to changing ecologies, demands and uses over time.

The park offers an exceptional moment in an extensive and densely built urban landscape and accommodates a range of programmatic functions through a strategy of tactical and subtle insertions of small grain urban fabric in the landscape. The purpose of this park is not limited to the satisfaction of contemporary programmatic consumption; it aspires to become a productive landscape of metropolitan radiance through absorption of private and public investments for research and development, education, healthcare, community engagement, sustainability and culture. In doing so, the project draws from the regional and local specificities, as well as from the cultural and industrial heritage assets that weave together the physiognomy of local community.

Above: Intervention Diagrams. A) Urban Stitches as connections of city to sea. B) Mosaic ofoverlapping activities, as we forget zoning. C) Salvages landscapes.

Opposite: Masterplan of the winning proposal for the Competition for the Regeneration of Keratsini - Drapetsona.

Repurposed "nature"

The reclamation process for the landscape employs innovative and cutting-edge methods for the restoration of natural habitats and major natural ecosystems that are gradually re-established on site: the sandy-coastal, the rocky-coastal, the meadows and the maritime forests. The park's reclamation process is based on soil and water decontamination processes that are shaped through in-situ remediation, a more appropriate alternative to conventional expensive treatments that involve transporting and excavating materials abroad. The staged development introduced suggests familiarisation of the visitors with new types of green infrastructures that operate on site and under the public eye to provide securely accessible and low maintenance areas. Hazardous metals and toxic residues in topsoil surfacing are treated in-situ in phytoremediation farms that pair with research and development labs. Gridded armatures of bioremediation wells interweave with public paths in the oil tank districts to clean up petroleum hydrocarbons from the aquifer. Soil washing infrastructures are introduced on site to separate contaminated fine soil (silt and clay) from coarse soil (sand and gravel), the latter being reused in the surfacing of paths and piazzas. Soft swales subordinate parking and paved areas to recycle and purify run off before harvesting it for irrigation. An outdoor mussel farm is introduced in proximity to a bridged repurposed oil refinery infrastructure now designated to host a Museum of Benthic Communities of the Saronic Gulf and a research hub for the Hellenic Centre for Marine Research. The mussel farm acts as a bio-indicator of the quality of the sea water, as mussels absorb considerable amounts of heavy metals. At the same time, crushed shells are re-used as soil composting for the park. Biomass energy from tree cuttings and pruning activities, as well as an offshore wave energy production farm include infrastructures that complement the parks energy consumption and especially requirements for outdoor lighting.

Repurposed buildings

Rather than maximising new built-up spaces, the design proposal maximises the potential for refurbishing and converting existing infrastructure and listed buildings. This heritage-led approach was based on the survey and indexing of listed buildings and redundant infrastructures of the port's industrial waterfront. The rehabilitation of these buildings considered new programmatic possibilities, community engagement and job creation. These helped to understand how the regeneration of the site might be put into practice and identify the optimal architectural intervention for each type of asset.

Combining the rehabilitation and preservation of existing building stock and new building insertions — 55% and 45% of total built surface respectively — the proposal identifies three layers of networked activities and programs where listed landmark buildings and new embedded infrastructures become enmeshed into a wider socio-technological network. The pairing of old, listed buildings with new infrastructures orchestrates repair as change with a particular value-laden sense of use of the past, not as a narrative within a building's conservation, but as a path of interlinked activities in the park. As landmark buildings get enmeshed with new ones in contemporary themes, it is the new paths and interlinked networks of the park that evoke collective memories of the industrial site's heritage and immigration history. Responsive building envelops encourage synergies on multiple performative levels to satisfy cultural, recreational and educational needs as well as to provide space for much-needed healthcare services for the area. The rationale for repairing the existing building stock is that its refurbishment can generate new added value compared to sweeping dismantlement. Total demolition is often associated with large amounts of rubble that never returns to the material loop or fails to be properly upcycled. Past experience has shown that the environmental impact of re-use is significantly lower than that of new materials. In addition, rehabilitation of the port-industrial zone is an invaluable source of information and a constant learning process for the applied technologies.[10] Existing residual structures are not only a resource input for further production but a key element of the area's identity. Saving and maintaining these buildings is key to providing a strongly differentiated environment that celebrates the contrast between old envelopes and new components added to them. Thus, the main hall of the glassworks building turns what used to serve as a chamber of kilns and furnaces to a thalassotherapy — a form of therapy utilising seawater and other sea products — centre paired to a school of physiotherapy in the levels below and

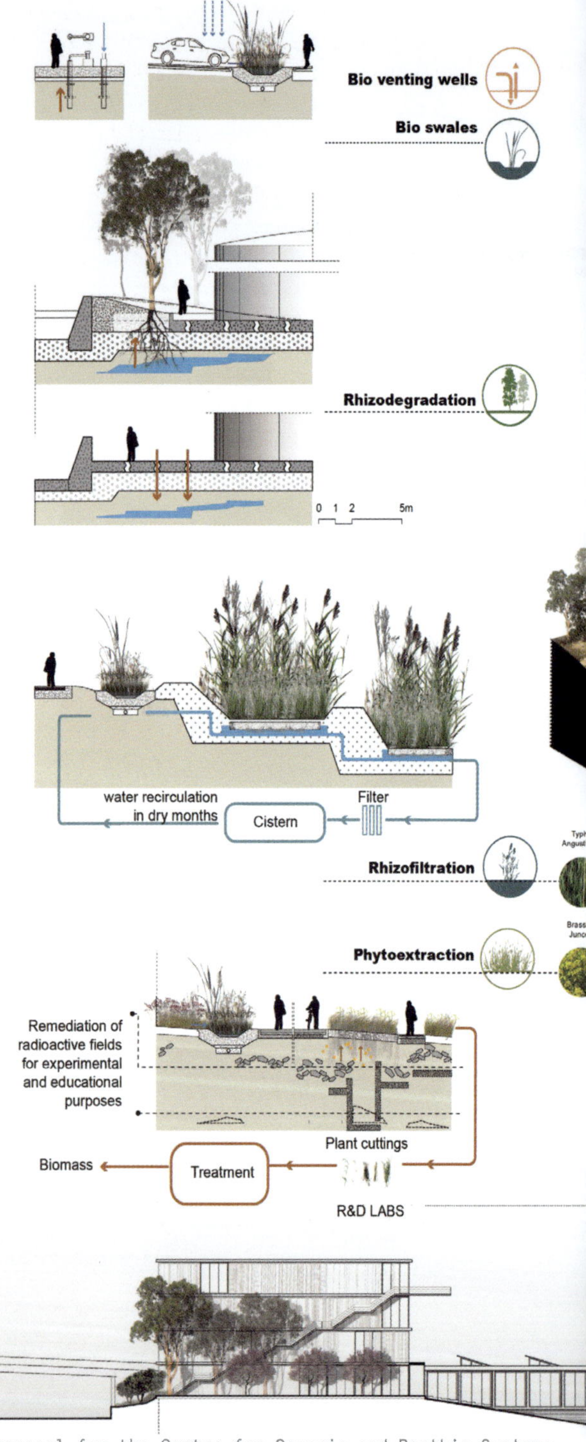

Proposal for the Centre for Oceanic and Benthic Systems Research, with Museum & Visitor Areas - Remediation processes of the rocky coast around Sfageion bay.

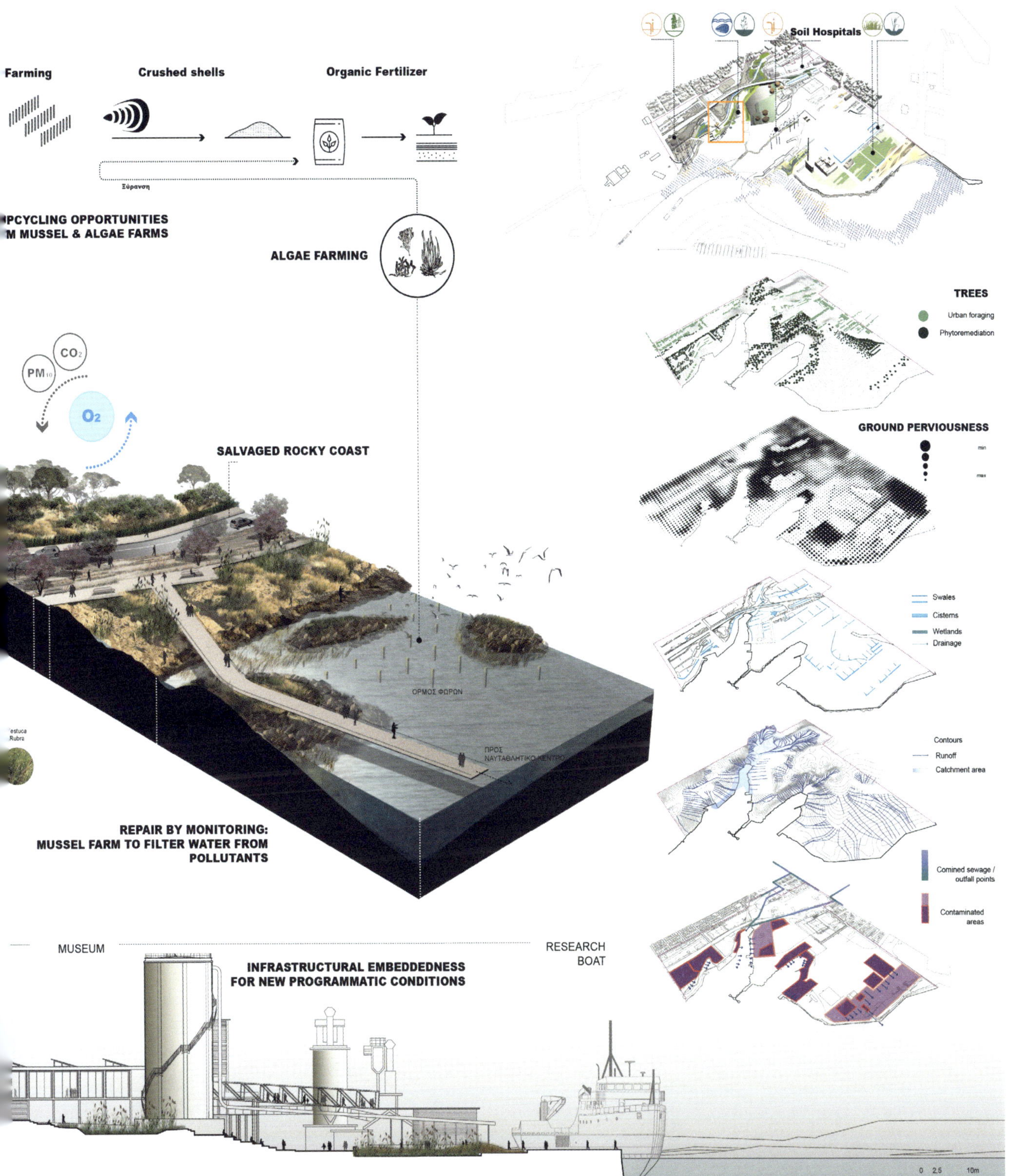
Farming
Crushed shells
Organic Fertilizer
Ξύρανση
PCYCLING OPPORTUNITIES
M MUSSEL & ALGAE FARMS
ALGAE FARMING
CO2
PM10
O2
SALVAGED ROCKY COAST
ΟΡΜΟΣ ΦΩΡΩΝ
ΠΡΟΣ
ΝΑΥΤΑΘΛΗΤΙΚΟ ΚΕΝΤΡΟ
REPAIR BY MONITORING:
MUSSEL FARM TO FILTER WATER FROM
POLLUTANTS
MUSEUM
INFRASTRUCTURAL EMBEDDEDNESS
FOR NEW PROGRAMMATIC CONDITIONS
RESEARCH
BOAT
0 2,5 10m
Soil Hospitals
TREES
Urban foraging
Phytoremediation
GROUND PERVIOUSNESS
min
max
Swales
Cisterns
Wetlands
Drainage
Contours
Runoff
Catchment area
Comined sewage /
outfall points
Contaminated
areas

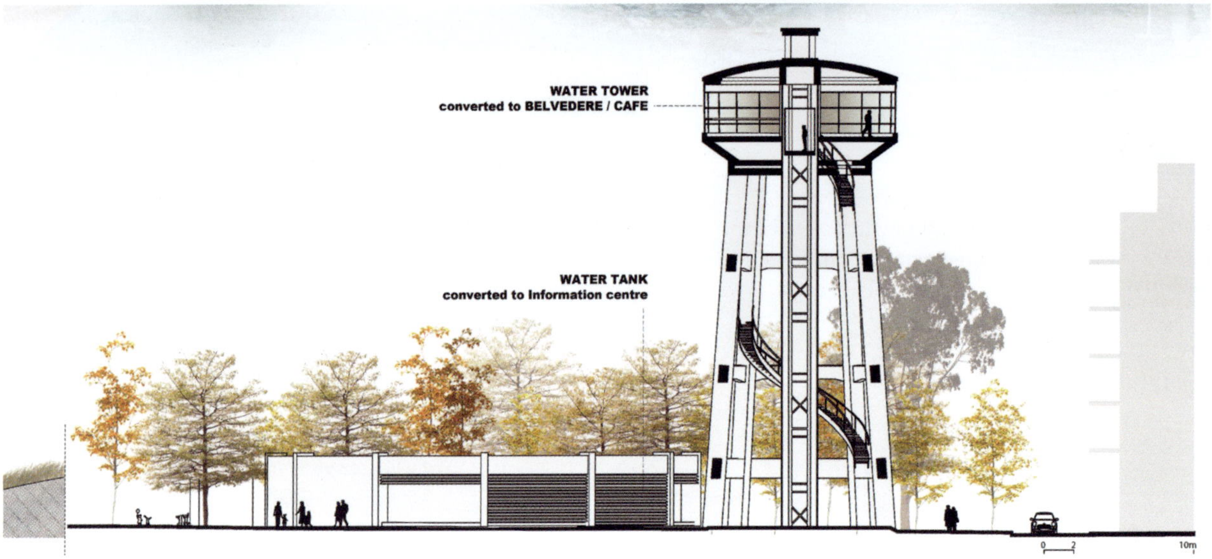

WATER TOWER
converted to BELVEDERE / CAFE

WATER TANK
converted to Information centre

0 2 10m

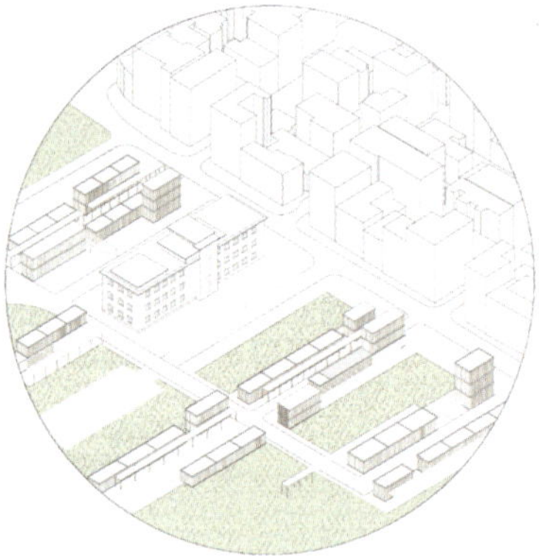

CIVIC & WELFARE GARDENS

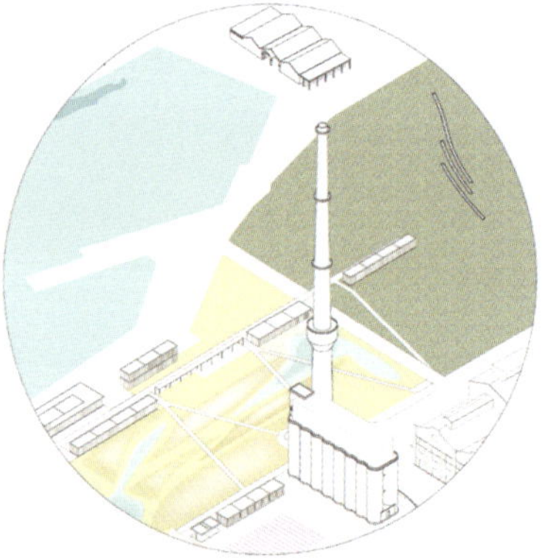

SANDY BERMS & SAILING CULTURE

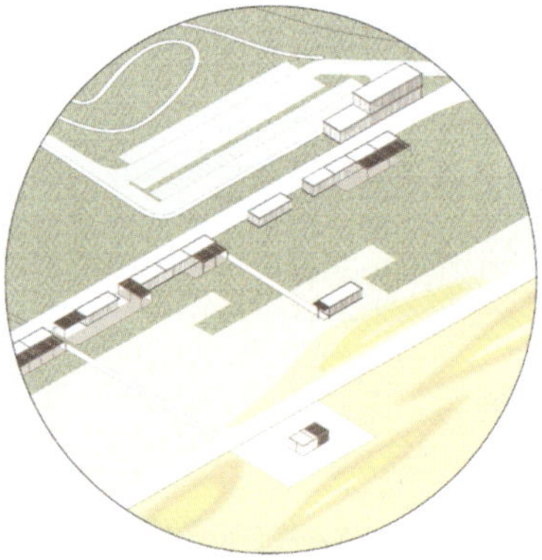

PHYTOREMEDIATION & LABORATORIES

a top floor viewing gallery with restaurants and museum spaces. As for the cylindrical oil tanks, each transformation overcame considerable design and construction obstacles by thoughtfully preserving and keeping historical characteristics where applicable. The repurposed oil tanks accommodate a wide variety of uses including a dance school, an auditorium, a 200-seated amphitheatre, art laboratories and several temporary exhibition spaces through minimal interventions. Inserted functions either deliberately maintain the existing vastness of the buildings allowing vaulted spaces to speak about their industrial past or dissect the existing structure, like in the case of the silo's refurbishment, to stress the comparison between new and old.

Design as repair economy

The metabolic process that characterises the recovery of the park is slow and gradual. It is presented through separate phases that introduce small changing steps that can be viable in the current economic context. The stages of repair inspire a process that gradually binds reclaimed green spaces with opportunities for employment and open programs for multiple users in previously 'no-go' areas together with environmentally aware and socially engaging citizens. Designing to repair generates social values through the provision and significance of recycling, amendment, care and maintenance of what is already there, what is already a tradition and a connection to the social, cultural and environmental history of the site.

Conclusion

The various constituent elements of the multifaceted proposal presented in this paper are directly associated with the following overarching premise: the use of repair as a means of situating nature within society and society within nature. Repair through design mobilises nature not as an external image but as a socio-technical construct. Avoiding the binary scheme of Nature–Culture, the repair strategy outlined above creates a necessity to closely interrelate architectural design with its surroundings and specific environmental issues.[11] The proposed re-programming and the listed possibilities for partnerships and employment opportunities it entails, brings design and the treatment of the ground, the buildings and infrastructures in new unexpected typological couplings.

Previous top: Conversion of the Water tower to belvedere/ café and of the Watertank to Information Centre.

Previous middle: The pairing of old listed buildings with new buildings and infrastructures.

Previous bottom: Conceptual image/collage of the repurposed waterfront.

All images pages 52-58 by Author.

Natural processes are harnessed within landscape repair processes and re-purposed buildings or infrastructures in dialogue with their immediate surroundings constitute new cultural artefacts.

01 The socially diverse climate of folk traditions brought from the immigrants' homelands blended with other cultures and everyday social practices giving place to new folk idioms such as the "rebetiko;" a genre of popular music that flourished in the streets and alleys of these districts. For a broader reading see: Lila Leontidou, "Slums of Hope", *Athens Social Atlas*, April 2017, https://www.athenssocialatlas.gr/en/article/slums-of-hope/

02 Alexandra Mourgou, "Rebetiko Neighbourhoods: Musical Encounters and Social Transformations in Drapetsona and Nea Kokkinia, Piraeus", *Balcanologie* 16, no. 1 (2021).

03 Vasilios Kapsimaliset, et al. "Pollution Assessment Of The Drapetsona Keratsini Coastal Seabed", *Bulletin of the Geological Society of Greece* 47, (2013).

04 V. Stamatis, et al. "Decommissioning a phosphoric acid production plant: a radiological protection case study", *Journal of Environmental Radioactivity* 101, no.12 (2010): 1013-1023.

05 "ΦΕΚ 1417/Β/7-11-2002," *Government Gazette* 2, 1417B, November 7, 2002. http://www.et.gr/idocs-nph/search/pdfViewerForm.html?args=5C7QrtC22wHghqNAYvmYB3dtvSoClrL89ciLegIW2m73U4LPcASlceJInJ48_97uHrMts-zFzeyCiBSQOpYnTy36MacmUFCx2ppFvBej56Mmc8Qdb8ZfRJqZnsIAdk8Lv_e6czmhEembNmZCMxLMtYnCIvYmiBXbrfOVOuwjA6cm1Q92ennVakyPPSe1uMhQ.

06 Municipality of Keratsini-Drapetsona, *Στρατηγικός Σχεδιασμός Δήμου Κερατσινίου-Δραπετσώνας 2020-2023* [Strategic Plan, Operational Program of the Municipality of Keratsini-Drapetsona 2020 - 2023], 2021.

07 Konstantinos Vergos, "Μετασχηματισμοί του αστικού τοπίου και κατευθύνσεις ενός χωρικού σχεδιασμού. Η περίπτωση των Λιπασμάτων Δραπετσώνας" [Transformations of the urban landscape and directions of a spatial design. The case of Drapetsona's-Lipasmata], (post-graduate research project, NTUA Athens, 2009), http://oldwww.arch.ntua.gr/sites/default/files/project/14925_/vergos_kostas_teyxos_a4.pdf

08 Dimitris Balabanides, "Αναπλάσεις σε παράκτιες λιμενοβιομηχανικές ζώνες. Το παράδειγμα των Λιπασμάτων Δραπετσώνας" [Reconstruction in coastal harbour-industrial zones. The Lipasmata factory case in Drapetsona], (post-graduate research project, NTUA Athens, 2009) courses.arch.ntua.gr/fsr/131680/teyxos%20ergasias-4.pdf.

09 Giorgos Lialios, "A massive new investment to revive Drapetsona", *Kathimerini*, September 13, 2006.

10 Susanna Moreira, "Deconstruct, Do Not Demolish: The Practice of Reuse of Materials in Architecture", *Archdaily*, December 25, 2021, https://www.archdaily.com/974056/deconstruct-do-not-demolish-the-practice-of-reuse-of-materials-in-architecture

11 Bruno Latour, *We have never been modern*, trans. Catherine Porter (Cambridge: Harvard University Press, 1993).

RECYCLING A TOWER

Dan Cruddace on behalf of BVN Architecture

Described as a 'once-in-a-generation project', Quay Quarter Tower looks to push the scale of adaptive reuse. AMP Capital engaged Danish architects 3XN and BVN to design and redevelop the existing 1976 tower in the Sydney CBD. Their choice to execute this simple act, as opposed to the norm of large-scale demolition, provided a world first design challenge: how do we repair what exists when it is easier to create anew? As the local architectural counterpart, BVN delivered this aspirational social and technological vision. Bridget McNab interviewed BVN's Dan Cruddace to understand the importance of this project in relation to the current architectural discourse.

Why was it important for this project in particular to address the climate crisis and the construction industry's contribution towards this?

Every project, no matter how big or small should contribute to mitigating the climate crisis. For us, having exemplary projects that show what can be achieved is key to bringing others along as well as deepening our own knowledge.

The construction industry contributes around 40% of global carbon emissions so, incremental change is not enough. Radical transformation, visionary leadership and design innovation is required to tackle the climate crisis whilst still enabling progress and financial success. The transformation in this instance, has been the literal transformation of an aging office building into a contemporary tower without simply knocking it down and building anew. Instead, it's a massive work of recycling, from the ground up!

Given its prestige, scale and global positioning it was very important for this project to positively contribute to climate crisis issues. Considered by some as the 'front-door' to Australia, AMP Capital's vision to transform this part of Circular Quay could not be anything other than an exemplar in design excellence, high quality architecture and sustainability innovation.

This is one of the reasons BVN was appointed as Executive Architect (3XN won the design competition while BVN led the development of this concept). Our collective has a deep sense of purpose around sustainable design and regenerative practice. Quay Quarter Tower (QQT) has been described as a once-in-a-generation project. It's a bold undertaking to radically adapt and up-cycle the 1970s building into a future-proof tower. It integrates technological and systematic innovation in achieving this act of sustainability.

Multiplex, as the construction company, aligned with this bold vision and saw Quay Quarter Tower as a key project to push forward their own sustainable policy and construction capabilities. For all involved in this project, it's been an opportunity to push our innovation and capabilities, identify what can be done through partnership that couldn't have been achieved alone, and to set a new bar to inspire.

Opposite: Quay Quarter Tower redevelopment diagram. 2022. Image courtesy of BVN Architecture.

What are the major design inclusions that address this problem?

One of the major design decisions on Quay Quarter Tower that sets a new benchmark in thought-leadership and design innovation is a radical adaptive re-use of the existing structure. In a world-first, approximately 65% of the original building structure frame and core was retained. AMP Capital's assessment of this key design move shows that there was an embodied carbon saving of c7,700,000kgs, compared to a conventional construction approach for a project of this scale.

This feat has been given significance when it was identified that the carbon saving is equivalent to over two years of operational emissions from essential building systems such as air conditioning, elevators etc.

This tower now stands as a physical representation and reminder of technological and systematic innovation in sustainability. How do you think the design and development industries can integrate this to be a norm?

The re-use of existing buildings, especially the structure, where the highest proportion of embodied carbon comes from, should be investigated at the conception of a project. It may not always be possible (for example — condition, configuration or future use), but the retention and integration of the structure alone can be a significant contribution to achieving sustainability goals and address the climate crisis issues.

Market forces push the availability and price of steel work up and up. This means that the retention of structure cannot only be a huge sustainability win but also benefit the project programme and cost plan. The continual review of material innovation will enable technical specifications to evolve in a truly sustainable way such that design and development industries will see advancements as the norm. This will extend to the point that previously conventional approaches will become obsolete, prohibited, or at least carry an industry stigma that suggest they won't likely to be used. Whether it be only procuring 'green' steel from suppliers who use renewable energy in production, or ensuring contractors progress new-build structure using lower carbon concrete solutions, the advancements in material sustainability credentials ought to become the norm.

Time within the design programmes to thoroughly investigate such concepts should be provided. QQT has been an exemplar project that proves that it can be done on a significant scale without compromising leasing flexibility, commercial viability or the quality required to meet market demands. Time was provided in the QQT design stages to investigate all options to optimise project outcomes with the support of cost and sustainability consultants. Sustainability-driven design also aligns well with tenant expectations. It isn't just a tick-box exercise to achieve a particular star rating or sustainable credit.

Why should they? Why shouldn't they?

We have no time to lose. The construction industry has a key role in the climate emergency that is upon us. We need to reduce embodied carbon now to reach climate targets that will allow us to avoid catastrophic climate change, as once these emissions are gone, there is no going back. Keeping as much existing building stock as possible is the first step.

Why shouldn't they? Excuses for not designing and developing sustainably is an archaic construct.

Above: Aerial view of Quay Quarter Tower. 2022. Image courtesy of BVN Architecture.

Repairing what already exists on such a large scale is evidently complicated and involves stepping outside the existing architectural and development norms. How did this process come about? What were some of the unexpected costs of repairing such a large-scale building? How did it become successful within the limitations of traditional norms and regulations?

The original 1970's AMP Centre was fully occupied by tenants as well as AMP themselves. The construction feasibility had to investigate all options including:

1. Refurbishment of existing building,
2. 100% demolition, re-build and new tower or
3. Substantial adaptive re-use and new-build hybrid.

The area uplift potential of options two and three were obviously attractive financial propositions if the existing building was going to be vacated. Numerous concept studies were undertaken at this time for all three options. AMP Capital's aspirations to create a showcase of sustainable design were at the centre of these early discussions. So too was analysis that revealed the time saved and waste avoided with a radical adaptive re-use scheme far outweighed the duration and material use of a full demolition-and-rebuild option.

As is always the case on large-scale complex projects, strict and continuous cost budgeting was undertaken throughout the process to ensure the bold sustainable vision could be realised. As part of this exercise there was input (and peer reviews) on the condition of the existing building and how it would perform during the partial demolition and when the proposed floorplate extensions were added. The original 1970's as-built structural drawings were retrieved from archive and proved to be valuable intel on what was reconstructed.

Cost plan contingencies were established to account for any unforeseen matters that are always likely in large complex projects. As the existing AMP Centre was gradually vacated, the condition and performance of the existing structure was surveyed and information incrementally added into the design documentation. This included areas where the retained existing structure was strengthened (eg. using carbon fibre strips). This also enabled the design life of the 50-year structure to be extended.

COVID-19 delays were an unexpected cost implication that impacted the entire construction industry. However, AMP Capital worked closely with Multiplex on the safe re-opening of the site to allow works to continue roughly on time.

The original building, built in 1976, holds 46 years of Sydney's city history. In what ways has this development chosen to conceal or showcase the original building's historical significance, function and architectural language? Why has this been important? In addition, what elements of the existing 1976 building required updating to fit in with the current function and context of the city? And on the contrary, what elements were still architecturally successful?

A full heritage review was undertaken by Urbis and the City of Sydney to determine the historical significance or otherwise of the original building. Much of the actual materials and historic documents have been kept, restored and put on display around the broader Quay Quarter Sydney precinct, for which we completed the initial masterplan. Showcasing the history of this site was very much a live discussion throughout the project.

Within the tower itself there are many examples of how historical design decisions have been celebrated. There was a strong vertical expression to the original building that remains with the retained perimeter columns on the western, southern and eastern parts of the floor plates. These vast 45-storey columns come to ground with the same dynamic expression as the original tower. The retained column shape on plan (with tapered nosings) has been maintained so the profile of the existing expression is legible, and to ensure the daylight onto the floor plate is maximised. All retained columns have a rectilinear expression, and all new columns are circular which has a certain honesty and subtly tells the story of the site and the existing building. The workplace strategies have been developed for the areas between the retained structure. These have proven to be very successful, providing a variety of office settings and privacy or shading opportunities.

The geometric plan module and building grid of the existing building (an imperial measurement construction grid) has been maintained for the new northern part of the tower to ensure the new façade system wraps harmoniously around the old and new components. Using the original building grid for the new-build portions also ensures building components could be standardised therefore minimising waste and maintenance logistics.

The interface with the adjacent 1950s AMP Tower at 33 Alfred Street (the first skyscraper in Australia) was considered to be of greater heritage merit than the 1970s AMP Centre. A new laneway called Goldsborough Lane was created to provide space for 33 Alfred Street to touch the ground with the same legibility as the original 1950s proposal, with activation on its previously hidden southern elevation now possible.

In the design process, what was identified as functional, contextual or social problems within the city that this project could address?

AMP Capital's vision for their asset – the Quay Quarter Sydney precinct — is a catalyst for the transformation of Circular Quay, to align with Sydney's vision as a global, sustainable city. In additon to that it will deliver a legacy of immense economic, social, community and cultural value for the people of Sydney. In the aftermath of the pandemic, the need for "neighbourhood making" became ever more potent and the project ever more relevant.

As the CBD transforms to become a place that is not just for working, but also for living and playing, Quay Quarter will help show the way to new kinds of city experiences. It is a global role model for future city neighbourhoods as a place that brings together workers, residents and visitors. The building will provide over one acre of green space in its terraces and podium gardens. The retail precinct and Market Hall in the podium will be zero waste environment, with a 100 percent diversion of landfill and a 100 percent recycling rate.

Quay Quarter is a destination where people will have exceptional public art, heritage interpretation, place activation and customer service strategies that support the vision for Quay Quarter Sydney to become a new neighbourhood and cultural destination in Sydney. Wellbeing for people working in the building will be enhanced through multiple measures, from daylight-filled workplaces, harbour views and high-rise terrace gardens through to soft-health training facilities and healthy food options in the podium retail.

Despite popular belief, a high rise can be extremely contextual. QQT is designed for both the tower user and the urban fabric by enhancing the daily experience through a socially dynamic workspace, while also increasing street activation and green space around its podium. QQT takes the ideas of urban public space and introduces that dynamism into a series of vertical, green villages up the tower.

Opposite: Quay Quarter Tower. 2022.
Image courtesy of BVN Architecture.

AMP
PARAGON HOTEL

Continuous architectural newness has created a mirage of material abundance, when in reality, resources are finite. Does this saving of embodied energy begin to alter the perception of infinite construction, and as a result what conversations does this stir within architectural practices, development businesses and regulatory bodies?

Operational carbon has been the focus in sustainability for many years and it is only recently that the focus has turned to embodied carbon, as the industry begins to understand the urgency to reduce emissions from construction materials. This project certainly provides an example of what can be achieved — the project is believed to be the biggest exercise in adaptive re-use in the world.

We hope that QQT will be a good example to follow. Existing buildings should be seen as a material bank, not as waste.

Design for disassembly is a major proponent within this building. How is this achieved and why is it an important part of sustainability and continuous repair? What does a sustainable building look like in this sense, in that its future is as important as its present?

All aspects of the construction of QQT have been developed to ensure safe maintenance and deconstruction or replacement if necessary. This includes all façade and plant components, which utilises a series of maintenance systems concealed in the roof structure.

Furthermore, the sustainable disassembly design of the atrium will future-proof the leasing flexibility and therefore safeguard the financial success of the building. A concept of 'de-constructable' floor plates was developed for the northern atriums to enable workspaces to be sculpted to suit changing tenant needs. Not building too much, and creating voids for additional daylight as well as visual and actual permeability, was a conscious decision. The purpose was to limit waste and therefore, limit the requirement of unnecessary changes or maintenance. Forward thinking on how the building can be continuously flexible, therefore minimising waste and maintaining the sustainable credentials of incoming tenants, was another major design consideration. Even the feature spiral stairs have been designed in smaller sections so they can be transported within the goods lifts.

The approach was to leave a legacy of long-term sustainability even as the individual spaces within the building may need to evolve over time. With flexibility built in, this evolution can take place without compromising its sustainability. The material sustainability and embedded energy conservation is a large component of the sustainability of this development.

As well as designing for disassembly, what other measures have been designed in to address the complexities of sustainable development?

The tower has a robust integrated technology system and smart-assisted digital technology to enable people to connect with the precinct's buildings, to each other and the neighbourhood. High levels of amenity and wellbeing for tenants and visitors have been achieved through a human-centric approach to Quay Quarter's digital infrastructure design. Seamless digital systems integration and innovative connectivity helps people to make the most of their day at Quay Quarter Tower. QQT utilises a passive sustainable approach to reducing thermal loads internally through the use of external sunshade hoods projecting from the high-performance, vision glass panels. The external sunshade hoods not only help reduce solar radiance, but through its staggered and repetitive frame, it creates a pattern that perceptually reduces the tower's scale.

A key leasing feature of QQT has been the demountable floor concept within the multi-level atria. This has enabled the client team to position QQT as one of the world's great flexible workplaces. The detailed design and coordination of this innovative technical strategy has been realised through the development of real innovation in construction. As well as providing the client with leasing flexibility, the tectonics of this future proofing system enables tenants to sculpt their space and develop the strategies for growth and business success.

In addition to the demountable floor concept, BVN led the design development and technical coordination of the visually stunning atrium spiral stairs that are a dynamic component of the workplace. These too have been engineered to be fabricated in smaller components so additional spiral stairs can be added in the future.

The Tower has a number of sustainability pillars. The building has achieved the following sustainability ratings:

- 6 Star Green Star Design rating V3
- 5.5 Star NABERS Office Energy Rating Base Building
- 4 Star NABERS Office Water Rating Base Building
- WELL Shell & Core

Facing the global realm of architectural spectacle phenomenon and the profit-oriented market, cities often compete for marketability, where money is often spent on creating architectural attractions that sometimes don't accurately address a city's needs. While recognising that raising capital is necessary in realising buildings such as Quay Quarter Tower, how do you see as the balance between sustainable innovation and financial success? How do you consider the role of architectural attractiveness in this?

If you consider financial success in the long-term, sustainable innovation is key. There is no future if the present is not sustainable. We depend on a healthy environment and society to have a healthy economy.

The role of 'architectural attractiveness" remains important. Not to be frivolous or for the sake of it, but to be responsive to the client brief, the context, behaviour, social requirements, and of course the environment. Being sustainable does not mean that architectural expression should be mediocre or banal. The more architecturally pleasing sustainable buildings there are, the more clients, city authorities and occupiers will no longer see sustainability as an add-on cost that compromises design quality. Fully integrated system and architectural propositions will surely lead to a richer urban fabric which in turn will assist financial success.

It is good to see within the industry that there is increased awareness and investor pressure to design and develop sustainably without compromising on architectural excellence and innovation.

In this system of architectural spectacle, what or what does not need repairing?

Quite often what needs repair in architectural propositions is the essential ingredient of 'future-proofing' and considering circular economy. Looking beyond day one and provide the client with cost effective design concepts that ensure the longevity of a development.

In an office development such as QQT, reflected ceiling plans, partition design sub-divisibility, atrium flexibility, infrastructure, system redundancy, kit-of-part core designs are utilise to minimise unique components and to create ease in maintenance. Transforming our own design processes and educating clients are items that all practices should continually strive to do to focus on designing for a better future.

Jeremy Till suggests that an architect who engages with architecture beyond mere building, indeed to the full extent of its spatiality, engages with the genuine social, global, ecological, and economical networks in which people operate within.[1] In this regard, how does Quay Quarter Tower engage with the fullness of where architecture extends, to where people and systems operate?

Danish practice 3XNs design was developed in partnership with BVN. Starting a project with this in mind changes the approach to design by focusing on the user experience. Dividing the tower into five separate volumes and placing atria throughout each, transforms the typical monotony and stack of a high rise into more human scaled spaces, creating intimate social environments. This encourages people to connect and interact over multiple floors; a design that positively shapes behaviour and enhances the everyday experience.

At 50 floors above the podium, the harbour views from inside are unrivalled. Multi-storey atriums with connecting spiral staircases make it one of the world's most spectacular workplaces. It's also one of the most flexible. A de-constructable floor system was developed that enables many of the tenancy neighbourhoods to be double height or more, creating a sense of vast open space even at the very top of the building. And they can change, as the individual pieces can even fit into the lifts. This adaptability ensures the tower has great leasing flexibility and will keep pace with the changing needs of its business tenants.

Playing host to 10,000 people a day, the tower presented a big challenge for pedestrian flow. Collaborative research led to design decisions ranging from the location of lobby doors and escalators, to the complex staging of over 40 lifts in 22 shafts. Walk around Quay Quarter Tower and you'll be struck by the sight lines – of the harbour, of public art, of gardens, of people. Because despite the technical and environmental complexities this building presented, it's a place for people.

Finally, what is the next step in large-scale innovation that truly addresses repair?

Technological innovation, development of smart buildings and assessing existing building assets prior to demolition and truly understanding the circular economy are several of the first steps. The development of a transparent product database that focuses on the circularity of the materials including its technical data, condition and quality will be a significant step forward in innovation. The notion of integrating repurposed and salvaged materials can be a complex one. There may need to be an assessment of warranties, statutory compliance and design certification that all need to be worked through thoroughly, but these issues shouldn't be a complete roadblock.

Circular economy has been helpfully defined recently in a publication by the European Parliament as "a model.... reusing, repairing, refurbishing and recycling existing materials."[2] The vision to upcycle 48 levels of existing structure (including podium levels) at Quay Quarter Tower epitomises this ethos. Further to this, the ability for architecture to adapt over the life of the building adds another facet to what architects and developers can do to combat the climate emergency we face.

01 Nishat Awan, Tatjana Schneider, and Jeremy Till. *Spatial Agency : Other Ways of Doing Architecture.* (New York: Routledge, 2011), under "Other Ways of Doing Architecture," https://discovery.ebsco.com/linkprocessor/plink?id=7f09ca1a-fb58-3132-b8e7-f358a28bcf1b.

02 "Circular Economy: Definition, Importance and Benefits." News | European Parliament, published April 26, 2022, https://www.europarl.europa.eu/news/en/headlines/economy/20151201STO05603/circular-economy-definition-importance-and-benefits.

Above: Initial render of Quay Quarter Tower platform, showcasing connective social devices. 2022. Image courtesy of BVN Architects.

DISMANTLING SECULARITY

LUTYENS' DELHI, THE CENTRAL VISTA PROJECT AND THE OPTICS OF A NEW RELIGIOUS NATIONALISM

Adrian Fernandez

At the centre of New Delhi lies the seat of the Indian Parliament. Designed by Edwin Lutyens between 1911-1931, it is widely regarded as one of the greatest compositions of Mughal-Islamic architecture in the world and an enduring symbol of India's independence and multi-layered complexity. Unsurprisingly, given recent history, the Islamic origins of this complex of buildings have greatly offended India's current ruling party. Narendra Modi and the Bharatiya Janata Party (BJP) are currently enacting plans to demolish the near 500,000m^2 complex of buildings and remake it in a new visage, the $2.8 billion Central Vista project.

The Central Vista project is Modi's and the BJP's most notable move in their overall goal of dismantling India's secularity, a fundamental tenet of its independence, working to replace it with barely-disguised Hindu nationalism. This project to reshape India's constitutionally protected secular Republic into a Hindu state has resulted in a vast rise in hate speech and extremist actions against India's Muslim population. These actions are being enabled — and even normalised — by political leaders, who in turn are enacting their own plans against the Muslim population. By reshaping the heart of India's political system, the BJP intends to establish total dominion over the images and space that define modern India, eerily reminiscent of British colonial oppression over pre-independent India and other Fascist movements throughout history. The Central Vista project is central to this, and all that it encompasses represents Indian psyche take-over by an ultra-nationalist regime.

The beginning, the Partition

Discussing modern India's complex relationship with its many competing identities must begin in 1947. It was that year, on the 15th of August, that the British pushed the button on their final act of violence against India. The first was marked in 1857, with the creation of the divide and rule policy that sought to establish a separate Muslim consciousness in India and cut ties between Hindus and Muslims, dividing the once unified country into what is now India and Pakistan. This separation set into action one of the largest migration events in history, resulting in the loss of around 2 million lives. However, it also led to a critical juncture in India's history. For the first time since 1757, where the British effectively took control of India after the Battle of Plassey, the people of India regained the authority to shape their own future and identities.[1]

Through the immense violence and mass movements borne by the Partition, the vital issue of navigating the complexities of India's multivalent religious diversity emerged. Whilst the First War for Independence was fought on the plan of equality of all faith traditions and of their followers, this quickly changed after the war was won and the actual work of deciding what an independent India entailed. The perception of equality changed, and certain sections of the Hindu majority began projecting their religion as inseparable from any notion of India's future ideologies. In response, Jawaharlal Nehru, India's first Prime Minister, and the Indian National Congress advocated for and enacted a form of 'composite culture,' referred to in India as 'secularism.' Secularity defined the nation's ways of operating, in both its people and governance, comprised of those who inhabit sovereign Indian territory and as a place where all citizens are equals.[2] Nehru believed that this 'secularism' was vital to India's existence, as he had seen firsthand the effect that 'communalism,' or the ideological forces that wanted to divide India along religious lines, had had on the country. On the other hand, Nehru believed that communalism — particularly Hindu communalism — resulted in the Partition of India in 1947, and thus, considered it a key threat to India's newfound independence. Nehru's vision of secularity was made concrete on 26 January 1950, when the Constitution of India was realised, setting out three tenets of this new nation, most notably a "liberty of thought, expression, belief, faith and worship."

Fig.1 (opposite): Raj Path, from India Gate looking to Rashtrapati Bhavan (formerly Viceroy's House) designed by Sir Edwin Lutyens. Image by Sondeep Shankar

The deconstruction of secularity

For the thirty years post Independence, up until the 1980s, Nehru worked to fight against all forms of communalism and never intended to separate politics and religion, stating that when "We talk about a secular state in India. It is perhaps not very easy even to find a good word in Hindi for 'secular'... What it means is that it is a state which honours all faiths equally and gives them equal opportunities."[3]

It was during the 1980s that the grand project of secularity began to show signs of stress, as a post-Nehru Indian Congress Party began making a series of decisions showing increasing signs of bias toward different religious communities. Indira Gandhi, the third Prime Minister of India, inaugurated the Bharat Mata Mandir, a Hindu temple constructed by the World Hindu Council. Rajiv Gandhi, Indira's son and India's sixth Prime Minister, invoked sharia as the template for Muslim communal law to mollify Indian Muslims. These actions, amongst others, severely damaged the credibility of secularity within India and, ultimately, paved the way for Hindu Nationalism to gain widespread political salience, culminating most notably through the formation of the Bharatiya Janata Party (BJP).

BJP and hyper-nationalism

The BJP, founded in 1980, is the political arm of the Sangh Parivar, formed from the offshoots of the Rashtriya Swayamsevak Sangh (RSS) party. From its earliest days, a vital project of the Sangh Parivar was the return to a Hindu nationalist India, or 'Hindutva.' Hindutva gained relevance in India's domestic politics in the 1980s but has almost a century of history behind it. The term originates from the 1923 book *Hindutva: Who is a Hindu?* which argued that native 'Hinduness' stemmed from three core traits; geographical unity, racial features and a common culture combing to unite Hindus against all 'others.'[4]

The strong undertones of Fascism are no coincidence, as Vinayak Savarkar, the author of *Hindutva: Who is a Hindu?* expressed support and admiration for the Fascist regimes of Germany and Italy before and during World War II, including the German occupation of Czechoslovakia, revival of Aryan culture, and the crusade against Aryan enemies. Savarkar had an affinity to and saw strong parallels to these Fascist regimes — particularly their oppression and violence towards those who did not align with their ideals — within the teaching of Hindu ideology, especially his belief in "super-savage cruelty" or the code of conduct for violence he argued Hindus had.[5]

This ideology formed the basis of the Sangh Parivar and its offshoot, the BJP. It has also been central to the rise of the BJP and its current leader Narendra Modi. Their rise was tied to two key groups; a collective who believed that Modi's rise would lead to the emancipation of the low castes of India because Modi himself was of supposedly low caste, and a collective of hardline Hindu nationalists who believed that Modi would deliver their vision of a Hindu nation due to his alignment with the BJP and their ties to Hindutva. Modi and the BJP would lean into their relations, particularly with the latter collective. They latched onto a series of perceived 'historical wrongs' that had been committed by the 'Muslim invader' against Hindus. The most significant in their eyes was the perceived destruction of a Hindu temple in the 16th century by Emperor Babur, the founder of the modern Mughal empire in India. They intended to 'right this historical wrong.'

The First Act of Architectural Violence.

The Babri Masjid (Fig.2) was a mosque allegedly constructed atop a former Hindu temple, and constructed in 1527 in Ayodhya in Uttar Pradesh, the largest state in India. Following the 'later Tughlaq' architectural style predominant at the time, the Babri mosque was a large imposing structure with three domes, one central and two secondary structures. It was surrounded by two high walls parallel to each other, enclosing a large central courtyard with a deep well known for its cold and sweet water. Fixed on the high entrance of the domed structure, are two stone tablets that bear two inscriptions in Persian declaring that one Mir Baqi built this structure on the orders of Babur. The walls of the Babri Mosque are made of coarse-grained whitish sandstone blocks, rectangular in shape, while the domes were made of thin and small burnt bricks. The mosque was well known for its advanced acoustics; in his book *Historic Structures of Oudhe,* Lord William Bentinck states, "for a 16th century building, the deployment and projection of voice from the pulpit is considerably advanced, the unique deployment of sound in this structure will astonish the visitor."[6] Another notable feature of the mosque was its integration of passive environmental control systems, with air cooling systems designed into Islamic architectural elements like vaults, domes and arches, and the use of large grille windows to allow ventilation of the spaces.

The mosque is a crucial part of a more extensive, contentious, near 500-year history of the site. A contested history of the site places the birthplace of the Hindu god Ram in this exact location, although there are no verifiable historical records to substantiate this claim. However, this contested history became canon to hardline Hindus, who used it as evidence to back up their claim to the site and its reinstatement as a Hindu temple. This tension was only exacerbated post-independence.

In 1949, Hindu activists entered the mosque and placed idols of Ram and his consort, Sita, in the main prayer hall, with Hindu priests occupying the once Muslim space to offer daily worship. This continued until a successful lawsuit by Muslim clerics resulted in locking the gates to the mosque, notably with the idols still inside.

Over the next several decades, Hindu and Muslim groups made many attempts to claim ownership over the mosque, yet neither side found success. It was not until 1984 that the World Council of Hindus intervened and began a nationwide campaign to garner public support for Hindu access to the mosque. It was this move that galvanised Hindu right-wing groups into action. On 6 December 1992, under the guise of reinstating the site to its 'rightful' use as a Hindu temple, 15,000 Hindu nationalists stormed the site and began destroying the near 500-year-old mosque.[7] As they tore down the mosque with pickaxes and hammers, they set off a wave of anti-Muslim violence, culminating in months of attacks resulting in nearly 7000 people dying (Fig.3).

By claiming that they were 'restoring' the Babri Masjid to its 'rightful' place as a Hindu temple, the Sangh Parivar and BJP enacted the first significant step towards legitimising the Sangh Parivar and BJP grand goal of returning India to a Hindu Nationalist state. It was revealed by Maloy Krishna Dhar's book *Open Secret*, that Sangh Parivar and the BJP planned and coordinated the mosque's destruction. Significantly, this was done in collusion with the then Prime Minister of India and leader of the Congress Party, P.V. Narshima Rao, whose tacit approval of these plans signalled the final death knell to secularity in India, and completed the legitimisation of the BJP in mainstream Indian politics, allowing them to move from a fringe political organisation to a national political party and culminating in their national election victory in 2014, with Narendra Modi at its head.[8] With this victory, the BJP and Modi shifted their focus to a much grander project, one that had once been the symbol of the British Raj, now a symbol of an independent India and in their view, a prime candidate for their continual manipulation of India's space towards a decidedly Hindu nationalist stance—the Rajpath, or the central axis of New Delhi and the heart of India's political systems.

Fig.2 (opposite top): The Babri Masjid mosque in the late 19th century, before its destruction. Image: Samuel Bourne

Fig.3 (opposite bottom): The destruction of the Babri Masjid. Image: T. Narayan

The British Raj and the destruction of India

The era of the British Raj brought about a significant change in how spaces were designed for the Indian populace. A lot of these changes were vastly inferior to what came before and were done in the classical colonialist mindset — to flatten and homogenise the culture they had taken over and oppressed in an attempt to instil their western sensibilities on the populace. What resulted was a confusing mess of styles and references, all implemented to import 'British-ness' to this new foreign setting. As the travel writer Robert Byron put it:

> In a country full of good examples, the English have left the mark of the beast… absolutely awful: Indian, Swiss chalet, French Chateau, Giotto's tower, Siena cathedral & St Peter's are to be found altogether in almost every building… Bognor roofed in corrugated iron and reassembled in the form of an Italian hill town... the whole of [British] India is a gigantic conspiracy to make one imagine one is in Balham.[9]

These failed attempts at enforcing an architectural style in India were just one facet of the overall oppression of India by the British Raj. They decimated the Indian economy during their occupation. In 1700, India was the world's richest country, accounting for around 27% of the global GDP. But in 1947, the year of Independence, India was reduced to one of the world's poorest countries, accounting for only 3% of the global GDP. This destruction of the economy was, as the American historian Will Durant put it when he visited India in 1930, "The British conquest of India… the invasion and destruction of a high civilisation by a trading company utterly without scruple or principle, careless of art and greedy of gain, over-running with fire and sword a country temporarily disordered and helpless… a plunder which has now gone on ruthlessly for one hundred and seventy-three years."[10] A further consequence of this decimation was the massive suffering the British Raj inflicted on the Indian populace. It is estimated that some 35 million Indians died in a succession of famines caused by British policy. The most notable was the Bengal Famine of 1943/44, where some 4 million people died due to the total redistribution of grain from Bengal to Britain to aid wartime efforts. When told of this, Winston Churchill notably replied, "Why hasn't Gandhi died yet?"[11]

It was only in the waning days of the Raj that a project merging of the two ideologically opposed cultures of India and Britain was conceived. In the Rajpath and the collection of buildings lining the boulevard, India had a powerful image that, albeit one still borne out of ethnonationalist beliefs, would define its post-independence era.

The Rajpath and the image of a new India

The project of the Rajpath (fig.4), and the new government buildings that anchored it (the Rashtrapati Bhavan — the President's Residence, or the Viceroy's Residence as it was known in pre-independence India — and the Secretariat building) was borne out of two lines of reasoning. The official one was that India's capital at the time, Calcutta, was too chaotic to be the capital. Thus, a new capital was required to build a proper capital complex. However, the unofficial, and arguably truer reason, was that this was "a move undertaken in large parts to enable the government to escape the uncomfortable political atmosphere of Calcutta, marked by continued and often violent demonstrations of nationalist sentiment since Lord Curzon's 1905 partition of Bengal."[12] This line of reasoning continued the British policy of 'divide and rule' by shifting focus away from Calcutta, which had become a focal point for Indian dissent and pushback against British rule by that time.

Designing this new capital was primarily assigned to two architects, Edwin Lutyens and Herbert Baker. Both were initially very dismissive of traditional Indian architecture, with Lutyens stating "I do not believe there is any real Indian architecture or any great tradition. There are just spurts by various mushroom dynasties with as much intellect as there is in any other art nouveau."[13] Both Lutyens and Baker believed that the new capital buildings needed to speak of the imperial ideologies of the British Raj and that the 'superiority' of European classicism would be privileged, with the "peculiar genius of the Indian workman lying only in ornament and decoration."[14] These racist sentiments were typical of the views of the British Raj on India's architectural heritage. The input of Swinton Jacob, Lutyens' and Baker's architectural advisor, and the then Viceroy Lord Hardinge induced Lutyens and Baker to take a closer look at the ancient site of northern and central India for ways to incorporate Indic elements into their proposals. Through this, features like the chhatri (elevated dome-shaped pavilions), chhajja (overhanging eaves or roofs with large ornate support brackets), jaali (pierced stone lattice screen), and the four-centred Mughal arch were incorporated into the Rajpath. Whilst there was a closer reading and incorporation of Indic elements into the project, it was clear that the architecture still privileged the ideals of the British empire, with Indian features only incorporated at a subordinate level.

Despite the grandeur of the project and its clear attempts to impose British ideologies onto the most prominent architectural project in India's colonial history, the completion of the project in 1931 is widely seen as the beginning of the end of the British Raj. Metcalf notes, "Lutyens' use of Indic features too, while innovative, reflected the loss of imperial self-confidence."[15] In the 20 years it took for the Rajpath to be completed, from 1911-1931, the British Raj had dramatically weakened as the anti-colonialist movement that began in Bengal had spread nationwide. This, coupled with the outset of World War II, led to the end of the near 200-year oppression of the Indian continent by the British, and, at the stroke of the midnight hour, as Jawaharlal Nehru gave his famous 'A Tryst With Destiny' speech, thousands of Indians converged on the Rajpath, liberating it from a key image of the British Raj into arguably the most prominent symbol of India's independence, the largest public space in the city, and the stage upon which modern India was born.[16]

The Central Vista project and the second act of architectural violence

Whilst campaigning for re-election, Narendra Modi, the current Indian Prime Minister and leader of the BJP, made repeated references to his inability to win over the 'Lutyens world,' whilst in the same breath reminding voters he was a man of the people, from humble beginnings as the son of a tea-seller rather than a member of the elite. Through this sentiment, Modi was directly targeting those who had held the balance of power in Indian politics since it became an independent nation and who had made the Rajpath their main base of operations, revealing his and the BJP's innermost desires to dismantle the Rajpath — or Lutyens' Delhi as it is known — to strengthen their hold on the country and continue pushing their goal of pursuing Hindu nationalism.

Their proposal to do this, the Central Vista project, involves the construction of a new parliament, converting much of the existing Ministry buildings into a national museum. All these ministries will be relocated into a series of new secretariat buildings along the 3km Central Vista, or Rajpath. Furthermore, several significant cultural buildings will be demolished, including the National Archives, the Indira Gandhi National Centre for the Arts and the existing National Museum (Fig.4). Modi's justification for this project is ostensibly an effort at modernisation and repair. The buildings, infrastructure and public spaces that make up the Rajpath are, he says, in need of restoration and India's growing population, it is argued, requires more parliamentary representatives that the current buildings supposedly can not accommodate.

In a presentation by the lead architect, Bimal Patel of the firm HCP Design, Planning and Management, asserted that the incremental changes to the Rajpath over the years have 'violated' the symmetry of Lutyens' design, rendering it 'disorderly and incoherent.' Comparing his proposal to the Apple Headquarters, he stated that the intent is to make "government function more efficient and productive…where you can sit in one place and run the business of government."[17] Patel describes this project as 'efficient,' 'productive,' 'the business of government' a language reflective of the projects goal to prioritise efficient space over public space. The new Central Vista project disregards the historical significance of the space, and is little more than a tool of the BJP, historical revisionism, with a grand goal of rewriting Indian history to privilege Hindu ideology above all else. This move towards rewriting history takes its most insidious form in destroying the National Archives, National Performing Arts Centre and National Museum. Whilst there have been reassurances that they will be relocated and their content safely stored during this process, no proper plans for any of this have been forthcoming. The vague proposals around the preservation of more than 25,000 manuscripts, 100,000 maps, 130,000 Mughal documents, 200,000 artworks and 4,500,000 other files creates a vacuum where the BJP could edit and rewrite these historical documents. This has happened before, with Modi's government accused of modifying school textbooks to reflect their ideological leanings in the past. If the same fate befalls these essential collections which tell India's true histories, it will only serve to expedite India's journey towards a Hindu majoritarian country.[18]

This project aims to neutralise the secular, democratic nature of the Rajpath and replace it with an architecture evocative of the insidious relationship between governance and Hinduism that Modi and the BJP are working towards. In its current form, the Rajpath is known as "the lungs of the city," providing over 80 acres of green space in a city with very little green space. This green space is also regarded as the democratic heart of the city, providing a space for festivals, protests and demonstrations to take place, a vital part of the checks and balances of democratic processes. The new version of the Rajpath cuts that green space to only nine acres, cutting out this key democratic and environmental asset, replacing it with a faceless colonnade of office buildings locked behind a highly securitised gated compound that will only increase congestion and pollution in an already congested and polluted city.[19]

Lutyens' original design for the Rajpath envisaged a series of axes connecting significant landmarks — the Jaipur column in the forecourt of the presidential palace to the India Gate, the Parliament building connecting to Connaught Place, and beyond that connecting the Rajpath to Old Delhi, the Jama Masjid, the Red Fort and St James's Church. These axes form a non-hierarchical interface between the city's major governmental, religious and cultural centres, allowing these different demographics and users to interact and move in a democratic setting. The plans put forward intend to destroy this non-hierarchical interface, replacing this network of axes with a single axis connecting the two ends of the new Rajpath, from India Gate to the Akshardham Hindu temple. In this new connection between the Parliament, India Gate and the Hindu temple, there is a clear symbolic alignment between political power, the military establishment and the Hindu religious establishment — the underpinning of Modi's new India.

The new structures and space will not only destroy the legacy of the reclamation of British oppression into a symbol of India's secular, democratic legacy, but it will also destroy the legacies of the many empires that have held New Delhi as its capital: from the Rajputs to the Delhi Sultanate to the Mughals. Each has left behind a layer of architecture, a palimpsest of the various societies and complexions of the city. The new structures and spaces will not add to this palimpsest; they will not bear any history of embodying the collective memories of the battles lost by the colonial power and won by the struggles for independence, citizen demonstrations, and protests against government policies and celebrations. They will instead symbolise only the overwhelming desire for the personal glory of a ruling class that wants to forget and rewrite the democratic past of India, however flawed its history might have been.[20]

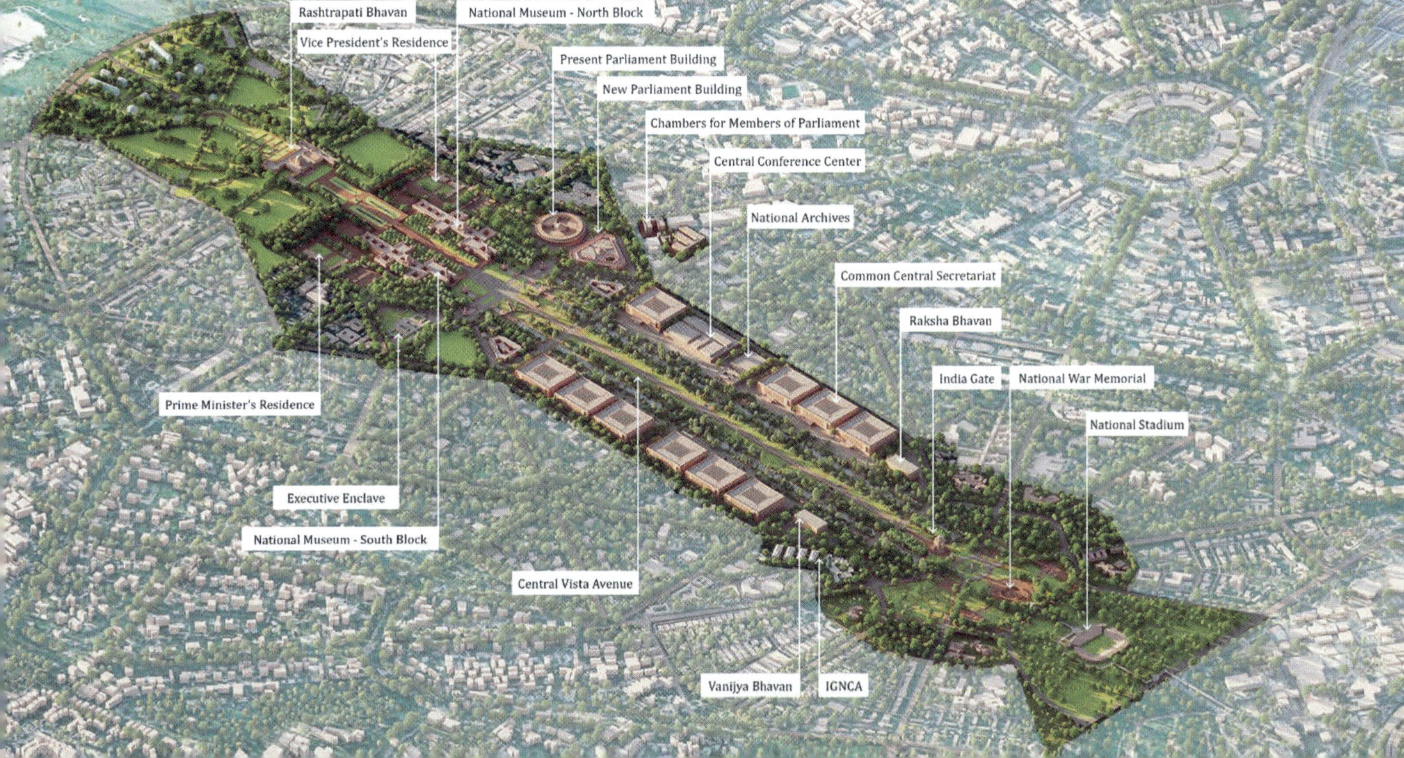

Fig 4: Aerial view of the proposed Central Vista redevelopment. Image: *HCP Design Planning and Management Private Limited.*

Conclusion

This is the behaviour of conquerors, not democratically elected leaders, and that is how the BJP wants to be seen. The Central Vista project is the latest and grandest move in a long line of oppression against those who do not fit into the narrow ideals they espouse, from migrant workers, to farmers, to the Muslim populace. Conquerors, throughout history, have shown no obligation to the laws, customs, values or norms of the society they conquer. This psychology of conquest explains the contempt the BJP has for the law, press, honest elections, the Constitution and any form of dissent.

Apart from a desire for expansion, power and glory, the ultimate vision behind this conquest is a re-conquest. A reclamation, restoration and reformation all at once, and Delhi and the Rajpath are its most precious prizes. This re-conquest requires humiliation, destruction, ethnocide and pillaging. The conquerors are permitted to destroy spaces, rewrite histories and terrorise members of the public deemed to violate their oppressive ideologies.

The Hindu nationalist re-conquest of India requires the Rajpath to be destroyed and to organise this destruction in public view. After all, is any conqueror ashamed to display their newfound power? And the total subversion of every law, regulation and norm which governs urban design, architecture, construction or environmental change in Delhi is not a hidden means of slipping through the cracks of India's legal provisions. Still, it is a naked assertion of the death of India's Constitution, the Rajpath and India as a nation in one reciprocal act.

01 Sarah Ansari, "How the Partition of India happened - and why its effects are still felt today," *The Conversation*, August 10, 2017, https://theconversation.com/how-the-partition-of-india-happened-and-why-its-effects-are-still-felt-today-81766.

02 Christophe Jafferlot,"The Fate of Secularism in India," *Carnegie Endowment*, April 04, 2019, https://carnegieendowment.org/2019/04/04/fate-of-secularism-in-india-pub-78689.

03 Ibid.

04 "What is Hindutva?" *Medium*, October 17, 2018, https://medium.com/@stophindutva/hindu-fascism-101-what-is-hindutva-75105e71f5e1.

05 James Robertson, "Modi's Philosopher," *Jacobin*, April 10, 2019, https://jacobin.com/2019/10/vinayak-damodar-savarkar-chaturvedi-hindutva-bjp-modi-hindu-nationalism.

06 "Babri Mosque Uttar Pradesh," Winentrance, accessed March 22, 2022, https://www.winentrance.com/general_knowledge/mosques_india/babri-mosque-uttar-pradesh.html.

07 Amalendu Misra, "Ayodhya: the history of a 500-year-old land dispute between Hindus and Muslims in India," *The Conversation*, April 16, 2019, https://theconversation.com/ayodhya-the-history-of-a-500-year-old-land-dispute-between-hind us-and-muslims-in-india-114471.

08 Harold A. Gould, "The Babri Masjid and the Secular Contract," *Contributions to Indian Sociology* 32, no. 2 (November 1998): 507-26.

09 William Dalrymple, "The Rubble of the Raj," *The Guardian*, November 13, 2004, https://www.theguardian.com/artanddesign/2004/nov/13/architecture.india.

10 "Britain's Shameful Colonisation of India," Asian Century Institute, published December 9, 2019, https://asiancenturyinstitute.com/development/1568-britain-s-shameful-colonisation-of-india.

11 Sandhya Ramesh, "Proved by science: Winston Churchill, not nature, caused 1943 Bengal famine," *The Print*, March 31, 2019, https://theprint.in/science/proved-by-science-winston-churchill-not-nature-caused-1943-bengal-famine/214942/.

12 Thomas Metcalf, *An Imperial Vision: Indian Architecture and Britain's Raj* (London: Oxford University Press, 1989).

13 Pavan K Varma, "Remaking Delhi's beloved heritage," *The Times of India*, November 8, 2019, https://timesofindia.indiatimes.com/blogs/toi-edit-page/remaking-delhis-beloved-heritage-why-are-open-design-competitions-not-held-for-drastic-changes-to-national-capitals-heart/.

14 Ibid.

15 Metcalf, *An Imperial Vision*, 85.

16 Adrija Roychowdhury, "New Delhi architecture was meant to soften nationalism, Parliament House was always meant only for Indians," *Indian Express*, December 12, 2020, https://indianexpress.com/article/research/new-delhi-central-vista-capital-parliament-house-rashtrapati-bhawan-architecture-7101680/.

17 Kai Friese, "Modifying Lutyens," *India Today*, June 1, 2020, https://www.indiatoday.in/magazine/interview/story/20200601-modifying-lutyens-1680798-2020-05-23.

18 Kensiya Kennedy and Abhinav Padmanabhan,"India's Central Vista Project," *South Asian Voices*, June 16, 2021, https://southasianvoices.org/indias-central-vista-project-and-the-optics-of-a-new-nationalism/.

19 Ibid.

20 Debika Ray, "Is Modi out to destroy New Delhi?" *Apollo Magazine*, May 4, 2021, https://www.apollo-magazine.com/new-delhi-architecture-narendra-modi/.

RHIZOMATIC REJUVENATION

ARCHITECTURE & NATIVE GRASSES IN THE LATROBE VALLEY

Andrew MacKinnon

The Latrobe Valley has been the centre of extraction in Victoria for over a century. Under unprecedented climate change, we are seeing a reluctant phasing out of coal for alternative energy sources. The township of Morwell and its neighbouring communities, of low to middle socio-economic status, were dependent on mining work and will now require alternative industries of employment.[1] Current plans to flood the Morwell Open Cut Mine threaten the Latrobe River, Morwell River, ground water and downstream Ramsar wetlands with industrial contamination, increased salinity and water exhaustion.[2] The region requires ecological repair in the face of increasing temperature, fires and floods. It does not need another tabula rasa project poised for lucrative short-term gains. The need for resilient agriculture, protected environments and public access to regional land and water is essential for our future.

Rhizomatic Rejuvenation is a speculative project that investigates the implementation of a decentralised architecture and native grass ecosystem to rejuvenate the post-extractivist landscape of the Morwell Mine for walking, camping, farming, baking and brewing.[3] Gilles Deleuze and Félix Guattari's concept of the rhizome, a way of understanding the relationship of things through the principles of connection, heterogeneity, multiplicity, rupture, cartography and decalcomania, conceptually frames the project's research and design, emphasising the complex organisation of the site, its history, its ecology and its human and non-human inhabitants.[4] The project's architecture within a grassland is dependent on its relationality, what, Édouard Glissant can be called a 'poetics of relation', that forms an adaptive assemblage of programmes that increase habitat for endangered species and allows communities to participate in native grain agriculture.[5] Expanding on Guattari, Glissant and Gregory Bateson's ecological and decolonial thinking, a carefully considered network of architecture support systems establish an economic, social, psychological, cultural and environmentally extended ecology.[6]

Situated in the Latrobe Valley

The Morwell Mine is situated in the Latrobe Valley between the Baw Baw and Strzelecki Ranges at the confluence of the Latrobe and Morwell Rivers. The valley was once a rich system of native grasslands, riparian zones and woodlands, and home to many animals. For over 60,000 years, the Braiakaulung people of the Gunaikurnai Nation coexisted with the land, having a deep understanding of its cycles. They were aware of the British arrival, having witnessed ships off the east coast, but did not encounter colonial settlers until 1836 when squatters began to travel through what would become regional Victoria. In 1840, squatting became legal, and parts of the Latrobe Valley were settled for livestock farming. Tensions between settlers and the First Nations people arose after the massacre of 30 Gunaikurnai people in an opportunistic land grab.[7] The invaders brought cows, horses, pigs, goats and sheep that ate their way through native grassland, while dogs, cats and rats turned feral and ravaged small marsupial and bird populations.[8] The region's agricultural industry continued to expand while the feral species thrived.[9]

The agricultural centre of the Morwell River flats was transformed into the site of the Morwell Mine in 1964. Lignite or brown coal, the lesser cousin to anthracite, sub-bituminous and bituminous coal, was once plant material and peat, until transformed under immense pressure and heat. It rested in the ground, with clay, sand, humus and basalt, a benign soil enhancer, before becoming a necessary component for global industrialisation. Over time, the extraction of brown coal would see the mine grow to engulf more land. The agrarian territory was reterritorialised through a network of excavations, roads and railway lines. Nature learned to inhabit the liminal spaces between the active mines, as it had done with the farms and the towns. But soon it was also humans that had to contend with the growing mines. On the periphery of perceived civilisation, on the 'frontier,' the mine and the newly established urban domain engaged in a tussle for land.[10] In 1968, the State Electricity Commission announced the closure of the township of Yallourn, with the town being completely engulfed by the expanding mine by 1983. The small town of Hazelwood, now Churchill, was established in 1964 for workers at the new Hazelwood Power Station.

While temperate and dry during the summer and autumn, the area experiences large amounts of rainfall during winter and spring. The landscape's fluvial geology comprises alluvium, sand, gravel and silt, and was once riparian habitat well adapted to flooding. To prevent the mines flooding, the Morwell River was redirected around the Morwell Mine and a causeway was constructed to carry it through the Yallourn Mine to reach the Latrobe confluence. In 2012, after intense rainfall, the Yallourn Mine wall collapsed, and flood waters rushed into the mines. This was not the first flood (2007) to break the wall and it would not be the last (2021).

Like much of Australia, the Latrobe Valley is prone to bushfires. In 2014, a nearby bushfire ignited a 45-day fire in the mine that covered the township of Morwell and much of the Latrobe Valley in smoke and coal ash.[11] The toxic smoke caused nausea, vomiting and coughing amongst residents, and the long-term effects of cancers and respiratory problems are only now beginning to reveal themselves.[12] A Royal Commission into the fire led to a $2 million fine for ENGIE, the French multinational energy company in charge of this Australian mine, and a State Inquiry announced new security bonds totalling $591 million for the government to use if mine operators fail to meet their rehabilitation targets.[13]

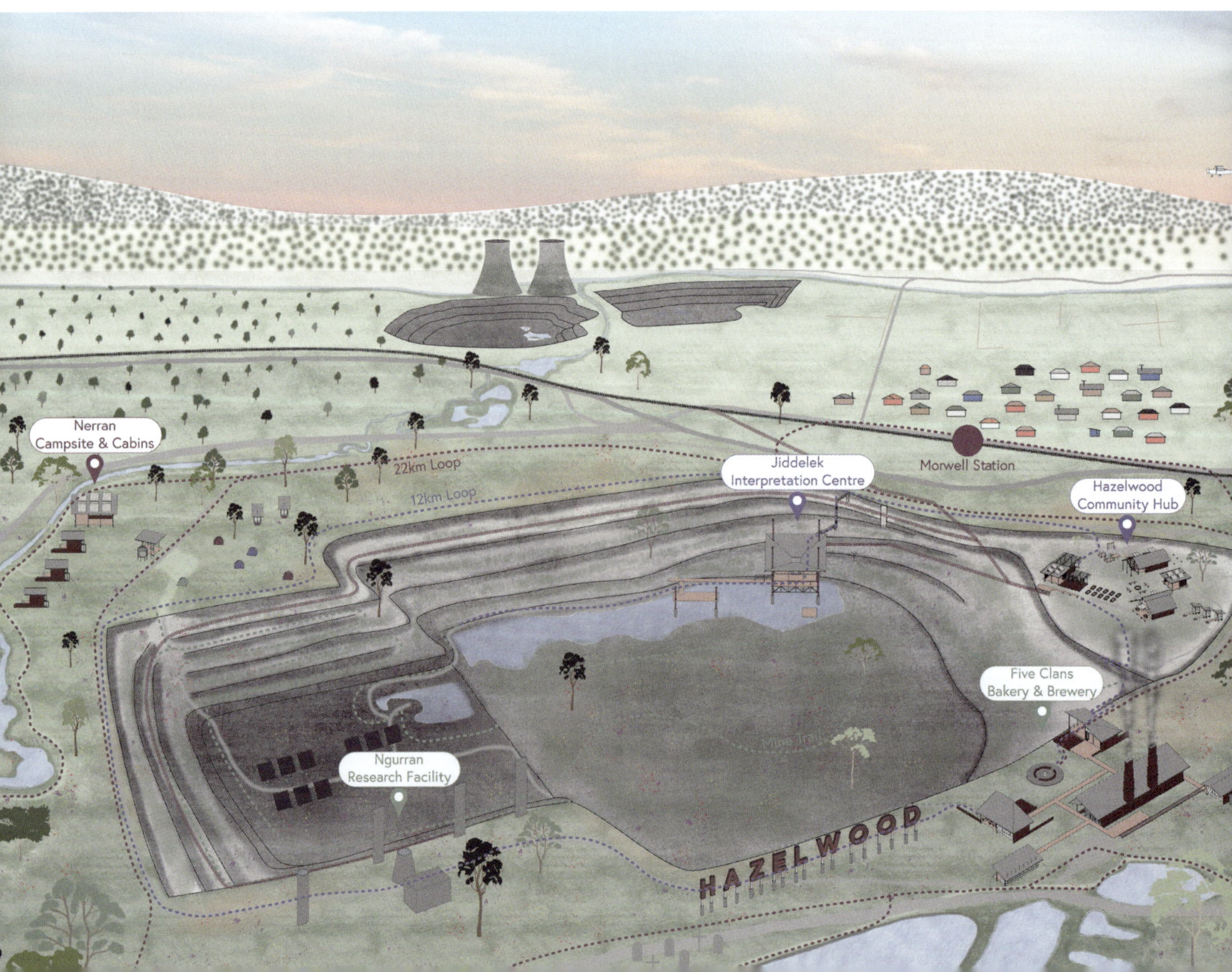

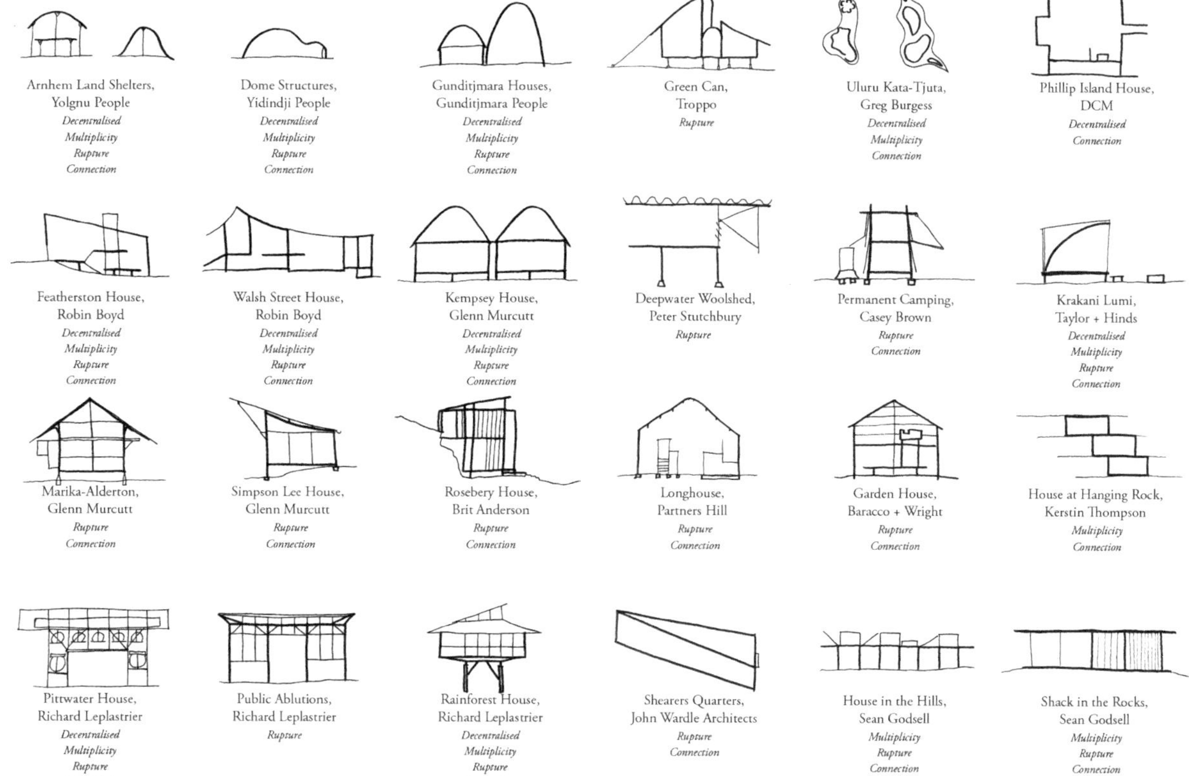

Following these series of catastrophic events, and the continuing pressures to phase out coal, the Hazelwood Power Plant was decommissioned. In 2020, the plant was demolished with explosives. The very equipment that destroyed the landscape was made redundant in an equally destructive fashion. Of all eight chimneys, four boiler houses and many dredgers, only the iconic neon Hazelwood sign was preserved.[14] After 53 years of service, there was no attempt to retain, restore, repair, or leave parts of the mine as a form of industrial cultural heritage. In 2021, the adjacent Morwell Power Station was also demolished. A total of 40,500m^3 of asbestos was removed from the site and 18,000 tonnes of steel was recycled.[15] The Briquette Works is the only building that remains on the site due to tenuous heritage protection.[16]

In 2019, ENGIE and Arup released a Concept Master Plan for the mine's afterlife.[17] They proposed transforming the 4000 hectare site into a lake and mixed-use hub for tourism and agriculture. Environmental groups have criticised the plans due to the tremendous volume of water needed and potential leaching of contaminants.[18] The mine void is approximately 0.74 billion cubic metres and would need 740 gigalitres of water to fill, the equivalent of 296,000 Olympic swimming pools. With Yallourn Mine and Loy Yang A and B to be closed in 2028 and 2048, respectively, these plans are short-sighted and do not consider the whole valley's future potential.[19] ENGIE predict their legally required rehabilitation work to be complete by 2023, leaving a 1281 hectare, 100 metre deep hole in the ground.

Post-Extractivist Landscapes

Post-industrial and post-extractivist landscapes proliferate much of our planet following a century of immense mineral exploitation and production. Late 19th century industrialisation, intense capitalism and our current consumption of technologies have now become synonymous with the degradation of natural ecosystems and the global climate crisis. Our survival in the uncertainty of the ending Holocene (Anthropocene, Capitalocene, Chthulucene, Plantationocene, Wasteocene or Rhizomocene) depends on our environment-world, our milieu and how we make sense of it, remaining habitable.[20] Feral Atlas (2020), an online

Fig.1 (opposite): Project Panorama. 2021. Image supplied by the author.

Fig.2 (above): Rhizome in Precedents. 2021. Image supplied by the author.

platform featuring a collection of ethnographic stories of diverse hybrid nature-culture milieus, invites us to embrace the complexity of these damaged sites in order to survive during an age of unparalleled geological, ecological and climate change. Similarly, the projects featured in *Geostories* (2018) examine speculative futures of an earth designed in the event of climate crisis to render visible the problems and possibilities of design and engineering. Such contemporary projects follow a lineage of written and designed provocations that critique the present and aspire for a better future, such as Rachel Carson's *Silent Spring* (1962), Stewart Brand's *Whole Earth Catalog* (1968), Superstudio's *Supersurface* (1972) and Donna Haraway's *Cyborg Manifesto* (1985).

Post-industrial or brownfield sites need to undergo a process of remediation to prevent contaminants from harming people and the environment. These sites have always been alluring to architects due to their scale and location, such as Freshkills Park on Staten Island. The forms and rarity of the existing infrastructure can also inspire refurbishments, such as OMA's Zollverein Kohlenwasche, or additions to buildings that complement the site's heritage, such as New Architekten's Coking Plant Monument Path. The scale of post-extractivist sites demand multidisciplinary designs that encompass landscape and built form. Peter Zumthor's Old Allmannajuvet Zinc Mines in Norway curates a visitor experience through three buildings: a museum, a café and a facilities block.[21] The project's minimal architectural moves emphasise the journey through the site's landmarks. The Brick Pit Ring by Durbach Block Jaggers erected a circular gantry for visitor circumambulation around the old pit that was transformed into a wetland habitat for the endangered Green and Golden Bell Frog (Litoria aurea). While grand projects like the Eden Project are well-known, it is the more subtle projects that resonate with the Australian context.

Australia's slow transition to renewable energy and its inability to meet global emission reduction targets (due to our dependence on coal exports and energy production) is cause for national embarrassment. The current climate data from the 2021 IPCC Report demands new approaches to agriculture that can withstand extreme weather events and demand less water and land.[22] There are also calls for a return to ecological farming practices that respect natural cycles, indigenous practices, biodiversity and seasonal harvests.[23] Native grasslands once covered much of Victoria but are now critically endangered with only 1% remaining following widespread agriculture, mining, plantations and urbanisation since colonisation.[24] Unlike introduced grains, native grasses are naturally adapted to fires, drought and extreme temperatures, grow quickly, and require less pesticides and irrigation.[25] Their root and rhizome structures penetrate deeper into the soil than invasive species, reducing water loss and runoff into river systems. Native grasses such as kangaroo, weeping, windmill and wallaby grass are all native to the Gippsland area, as are their companion species, quolls, bandicoots, wallabies, insects, birds and reptiles. These fields of grass are not monocultures, but rather a biodiverse array of grasses, flowers, and tubers, including murnong, bulbine lily, matted flax-lily, prickly lettuce, water ribbons and samphires.[26] For the Morwell Mine, these grasses could help remediate the contaminated ground, stabilise the soil and create habitat.[27] The Bell County Mountain Top Removal project by David Ledford and the accidental rehabilitation of the Ravensworth Mine exemplify the phytoremediation potentials of native grasses and their capacity to design the land.[28] The use of plants for creating awareness of biodiversity, climate change, Indigenous cultures and endangered ecosystems has been exemplified by Agnes Denes' *Wheatfield* installation at the Battery Park Landfill in Manhattan and Baracco, Wright & Tegg's Australian Pavilion at the Venice Biennale.[29] Gilles Clément's Jardins du Tiers-Paysage utilised plants to curate a walking experience through an old submarine factory. Clément's concepts of the Third Landscape and the Planetary Garden value plants as the designers and humans as the caretakers and gardeners.

Designing for an Extended Ecology

The history of architecture is presented from a Western perspective as an arborescent lineage of progress. The European notion of an architect or master builder, contrasts to most vernaculars where people built for themselves with traditional techniques and local materials. It has been traditionally understood that architecture has evolved from the primitive, Laugier's Primitive Hut, to Modernism. Sir Bannister Fletchers *Tree of Architecture* (1896) exemplifies this growth from 'primitive' cultures through Enlightenment towards a projected modern architecture. This linear progression suggests that later periods of architecture are more complex and superior to earlier architecture. Charles Jencks' *The Century is Over, Evolutionary Tree of 20th-Century Architecture* (2000) diagram proposes a greater complexity and interconnection between the 20th-century's architecture movements while still implying progress. The Morwell Mine site is a palimpsest of historical events from the geological deposits of rock to the eventual extraction of coal, all moments in time that affected the site's future are present on the site today. A contemporary proposal for the future of the site must make visible all these past complexities, to create a nuanced relationship between the past, present and future.

In a state of decolonisation, Australia is in search of a contemporary identity that is inclusive of Aboriginal Australians, migrants and other minorities. Like other post-colonial nations searching for an identity, there will always be a conflict between the vernacular and modern. Navigating the repercussions of designing with traditional approaches, international influences, colonial hierarchies and cultural differences is a dilemma. Many Australian architects have grappled with the tensions of what Australian architecture is. Aboriginal Australian architecture was temporary, built with natural materials and responding to environmental and cultural requirements. Invasion saw the introduction of formal Colonial European styles and the colonial-settler agrarian shed. Australia transitioned through the various periods of colonial-settler architecture until reaching today's eclectic mix of architecture, famously critiqued by Robin Boyd as 'featurism' in *The Australian Ugliness* (1960). Today, there appears to be a continuum between two strains of architecture. One that celebrates eclecticism and the building as an autonomous object and one that returns to an essentialism and functionalism.

In searching for an appropriate architecture for the context of decolonisation, climate change and repair, can themes of simplicity, compassion and austerity drive design? Through avoiding categorisation and hierarchy, can an architect begin to design without the burden of lineage or rules imposed by the western canon? Can the contemporary Australian architect become a rhizomatic designer, a bricoleur, an assembler of relationships? As a tool the concept of the rhizome does not demand anything. It simply allows for an assemblage of things. Those things do not necessarily need to be aesthetically related, as their relationality is enough. This rhizomatic architecture is not static, nor is it centralised or hierarchical.[30] The rhizome does not call for an architecture that mimics organic growth but is abstracted into design tools based on the principles of decentralisation, multiplicity, rupture and connection. Architecture might become like the lines of flight, or ruptures, from the leakage of the site's past. A rhizomatic architecture offers a design approach open to a greater network of influences and connections to an extended ecology. It considers how we put together an array of architectures that not only follow aesthetics, but also material flows, energy, waste and labour.

Rhizomatic Rejuvenation

In critical distinction from precedents of amphitheatres, hotels, flooded lakes and geodesic domes, *Rhizomatic Rejuvenation* proposes a composition of architectural objects to support a native grassland. The decentralised rhizomatic architecture forms a framework for human coexistence within an ecosystem of slow repair. After situating myself in the Latrobe Valley, the site was deterritorialised through mapping the entanglements of water courses, roads, homes, agriculture and historical events. Although the Morwell Mine site is expansive and seemingly disconnected from the township of Morwell, its relationality and imbrication with ecological and social fields informs various design decisions. The architecture becomes the lines of flight from the flat surface where intersections occur, reterritorialising, resettling, but with complexity. Rather than erecting autonomous monuments in a vacuum, the architecture is critical of its presence. It provides shelter from the sun, wind, rain and fire and allows for the various programmes to coexist. Two temporalities emerged from the design process. The first indicates a sense of impermanence, the ability to perish in fire, decay over time or become overrun by vegetation. The second demands a sense of permanence to protect against fire and flood.

Rhizomatic Rejuvenation proposes five buildings. Each consists of small pavilions, sitting on support structures, and are activated by their connection to each other. The buildings connect to the landscape, express refuge, are elevated above the ground, and maintain a humble scale. The buildings are located adjacent to landmarks and industrial remnants. Influenced by Donna Haraway's *Staying with the Trouble*, the mine and any remaining equipment is left as it was when extraction ceased.[31] The past is not forgotten but becomes a reminder of past material realities. The architecture, as ruptures from the horizontal organisation of grasses, look to materials that are either reused from the existing power station, locally sourced, dirty and earthen, impermanent or strategically enduring. The overburden, dried grass and fly ash are all harvested and transformed into air-dried mud bricks at the old Briquette Works. This process embeds the site's past and present, while demanding a connection between material, labour and product. Over time, the decomposition of the bricks will return the site's soil to the ground from where it came. The demolished power stations provide recycled steel framing and steel sheeting for fireproof cladding. Corrugated iron roof sheeting references the vernacular of the historical cottages and nearby agrarian sheds. The timber, initially sourced from the neighbouring Jeeralang Plantation, will eventually be harvested from onsite trees. Permanent footings will be made from concrete that utilises aggregates from the overburden, sands from the redirected Morwell River and fly ash from the Yallourn Power Station.[32] As a staged project, the construction of the architecture coincides with the rehabilitation of the mine.

The project establishes three stages:

1. the remediation of the site through native grasses;
2. public access for recreation;
3. and the production of grains.

The phytoremediation of the mine is the first stage of rejuvenation. Current remediation practices, involving capping the contaminated soils with a geomembrane and fresh soil, are expensive and require the relocation of additional soil. Phytoremediation, the repair of soil via natural plant processes, can offer an affordable and more effective alternative.[33] The process involves the backburning of invasive species, the broadcasting of native grass seeds, and the repetition of regular cultural burning to destroy contaminated plants and activate the soil. The plants are the designers, and the humans are the caretakers. The reintroduction of native grasses and trees will bring animals back to the mine. The foraging and burrowing habits of marsupials such as the bandicoot are vital for ongoing soil health, overturning large amounts of soil, reducing hydrophobia and fire risk. The combined faeces from marsupial and bird species will fertilise the soil and spread the grass seeds across the site.[34] The initial architecture on the site is small in scale and has an impermanence. Indigenous precedents suggest temporary forms of habitation on the site. *Krakani Lumi* exemplifies a site sensitive design that recognises its Indigenous past. The *Rolling Huts* and *Freycinet Lodge* offer examples of cabins that are small and respectful of the landscape, while *Dômes Charlevoix* mimic that aesthetic of the tent, producing comfortable accommodation for glamping. The Nerran (moon) Cabins are an example of the simple architectural structures that will be scattered around the 22km Yarram (river) walking trail. Timber based community-built rest areas, cabins and toilets, as well as campsites, will allow visitors to stay overnight for free.

The second stage of welcoming visitors into the mine can begin after the remediation of the upper portion of the mine. The Hazelwood Community Hub, closest to the town of Morwell, becomes the community gateway to the project. Rather than one large building with internal divisions, the Hub is composed of a series of buildings that are activated by their proximity to each other and the grasslands. The programme of a shared event space, meeting room, community garden, book swap, seed and plant nursery and creative space encourage a range of uses, and a connection to Country through storytelling and gardening. A simple post and beam structure supports operable steel facades that allow for seasonal change in sun and wind. The Hub uses peg and key joint timber construction, allowing community members to assemble and disassemble the structures. The same tectonic language is used to create woven dried grass sliding screens that provide shade and wind breaks. The buildings accept the temporality of architecture in the face of destructive bushfires. The sacrificial timber structures allow the architecture to remain an ongoing material process that

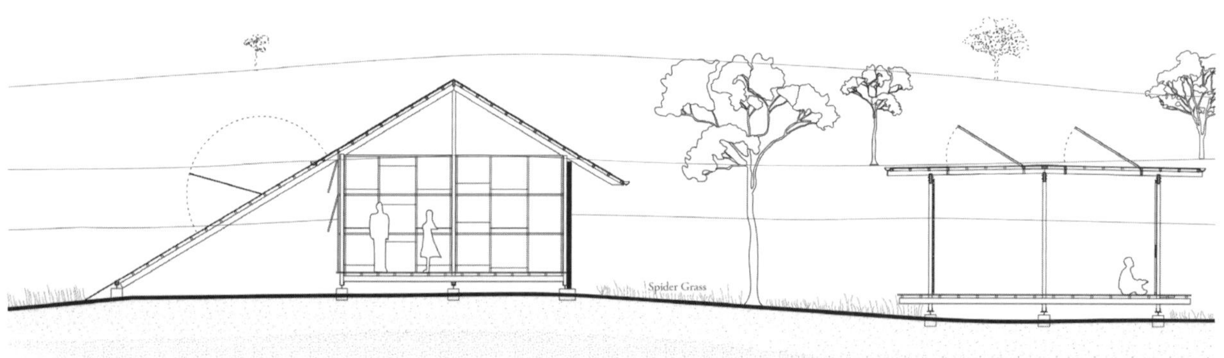

Above: Hazelwood Community Hub Section. 2021. Image supplied by the author.

Opposite: Jiddelek Interpretation Centre Section. 2021. Image supplied by the author.

can be adjusted, changed, expanded or contracted as the community sees fit. The concrete footings and steel stirrups remain as a mnemonic device for perished buildings and as an invitation to rebuild when required.

At the bottom of the mine, the Jiddelek (frog) Interpretation Centre is established amongst an emergent wetland. The Centre orients visitors on the site and juxtaposes the raw coal with the rupturing architecture, newly sprouting natives and settling sediments. It orients visitors on the site, with information boards and a smartphone audio tour, explaining the application of grasses, the rejuvenation process, the companion animals and the entangled history of the site. The building is supported on hydraulic piers that allow the building to move up and down with the seasonal water level of the wetlands. Raising the building allows marsupials and the growling grass frog to easily access the water of the wetland. The open structure is made from the powerplant steel and floats on recycled oil drums. The Centre is a place for humans and animals to coexist and observe one another, and a place where cultural practices such as making stringy bark canoes and boomerangs can continue.

By stage three, the mine is deemed safe for harvesting native grains to produce beer and bread. In the spirit of Bruce Pascoe, Vandana Shiva and Masanobu Fukuoka, a biodiverse, chemical free agriculture is established with weeping, kangaroo and common wheat grass, and native millet.[35] While there are many spaces across the site for hand milling grains and baking on open fires, the Five Clans Bakery & Brewery serve as a more practical and accessible way to interact with the native grains. Located on the foundations of the Hazelwood Power Station, the series of small buildings have views across the mine, and towards the refurbished neon Hazelwood Sign. A stone mill, a bakery, a café and a microbrewery are housed in four connected buildings that join onto a space for eating and drinking by a fire that rests on the foundations of one of the original chimneys. The architecture is expressed through the thick and the thin, the permanent and impermanent. Thick masonry walls provide a backbone for programmed activities that open onto outdoor spaces through thin timber and glass facades. The shifting of spaces through pavilions removes any true focus, allowing for a decentralised plan. Further affected by the connection to necessary agrarian support structures, shed and silos, that proliferate the site. While the site runs entirely on solar power, there is also a traditional oven and boiler that uses coal or wood to preserve knowledge of past practices. The Power Station's existing carpark is retained for visitors and will be used for future growth when grains, beer and bread are to be transported and sold offsite. The existing mine railway that once connected the V-Line tracks, Morwell Power Station and Yallourn Power Station will be reinstated, easing movement of grains, equipment, materials and people between the site's main buildings.

The Ngurran (Emu, Southern Cross) Research Facility supports research into the potentials of native grasses for biomedicine, bioplastics and biofuels.[36] It is a protected underground complex that houses an office, laboratory, archive, seed bank and fire shelter. It is one of the few buildings on the site that is built with permanence in mind. It is the inverse of the surface ruptures, delving into the mine wall and interacting with the remaining coal. It protects endangered seeds, expensive equipment, archived research and human life in the event of an uncontrolled fire or severe climate change induced weather. The facility, although underground, is oriented to take in the vistas of the mine. Changes in ceiling

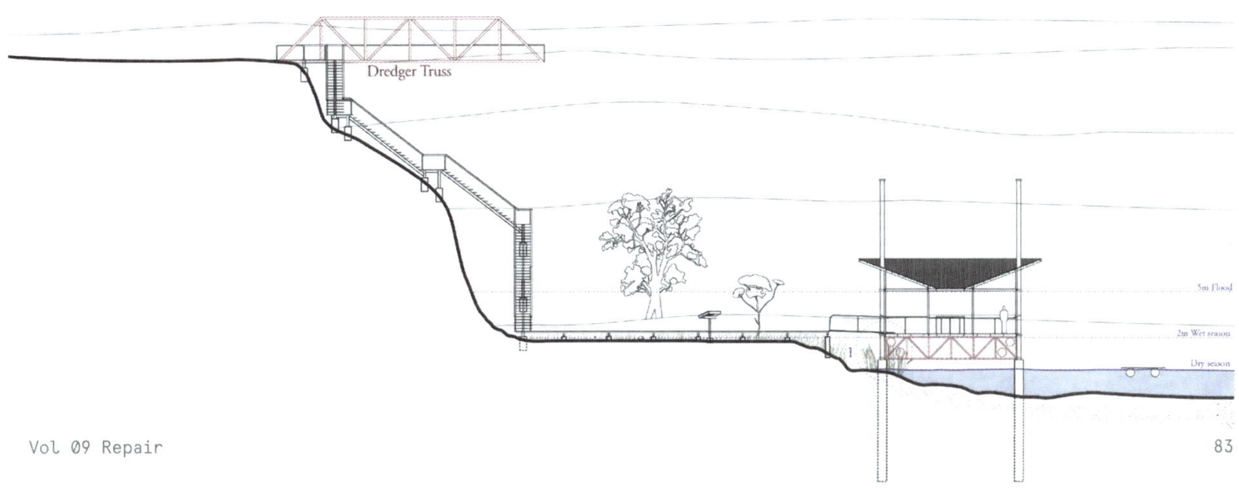

level and the tactility of the sprayed fly ash concrete create a dynamic interior space and vertical light wells allow for comfortable spaces and internal courtyards.

Rhizomatic Rejuvenation's speculative programme advocates for Aboriginal Australian led consultation and collaboration to champion food sovereignty and continue traditional epistemologies.[37] The Gunaikurnai people gained Native Title in 2010 and in line with the *Victorian Traditional Owner Native Foods and Botanicals Strategy,* can begin to regain agency over land use.[38] Through an ethic of care and maintenance, governance of the site could be shared by a collective of Gunaikurnai people, local residents, Latrobe City Council and Parks Victoria.[39] While mining has made the site unrecognisable from its previous state, the reintroduction of native plants and land practices such as cultural burning aim to reconnect to Country.[40] Income for the scheme will come from the wholesale of grains, the bakery and brewery, and education, looking to shift from a capital-based income model to a custodial one. The demand from brewers, bakers and chefs for the unique flavours and gluten free nature of native grains will only increase over time.[41] The site's connection to the M1, trains, nature walks, growing urban centres and the proposed Great Victorian Bathing Trail all support this proposal.[42]

As our climate crisis intensifies, the urgency for action must be reflected in the projects we embark on. Complacency, standardised solutions and techno-fixes will not suffice. Privatisation, social and economic hierarchies, and the bifurcation of scientific and indigenous knowledges are failing our environment.[43] We must rethink architecture and its ability to become an armature for repair.[44] *Rhizomatic Rejuvenation*'s humble architecture simply supports a grassland ecosystem and activates the landscape.[45] The conceptual lens of the rhizome attempts to synthesise the entanglements of the site's ecologies into a holistic proposal for a sustainable future.[46] Allowing for complexity of use, mixing human and non-human, recreation and agriculture, landscape and architecture, has revealed an assemblage of onsite activities that renew the Morwell Mine. The project sets a precedent for both the Yallourn and Loy Yang mines, possibly connecting the Latrobe Valley through walking trails, community activities, employment, nature corridors and native grasses. Rather than neglect, this project explores the potentials of 'staying with the trouble,' transforming the Latrobe Valley from a mining region to a resilient, biodiverse ecology.[47] With the uncertainty of our future there is hope that returning to native ecosystems, traditional land care practices, and localised natural agriculture can reduce our impact on the planet, and even begin to repair our damage.

01 "Socio-Economic Advantage and Disadvantage," *Australian Bureau of Statistics*, 2016, https://bit.ly/3ABAc2S.

02 Jarrod Whittaker, "Water shortages, pollution mean Latrobe Valley mine lakes plan not viable, environment groups say," *ABC,* December 11, 2020, https://ab.co/3mep8oF.

03 *Rhizomatic Rejuvenation* is my Master of Architecture independent thesis project supervised by Professor Hélène Frichot, undertaken at the Melbourne School of Design. María Puig de la Bellacasa, Matters of Care: *Speculative Ethics in More than Human Worlds* (University of Minnesota Press, 2017).

04 Gilles Deleuze and Felix Guattari. *A Thousand Plateaus*, translated by Brian Massumi. London: The Athlone Press, 1988.

05 Édouard Glissant, "Errantry, Exile," in *Poetics of Relation,* translated by Betsy Wing (Ann Arbor: University of Michigan Press, 1997), 11.

06 Doina Petrescu and Katherine Gibson, "Diverse economies, ecologies and practices of urban communing," in *Architecture and Feminisms,* edited by Hélène Frichot, Catharina Gabrielsson, and Helen Runting (Routledge, 2017); and Céline Condorelli, Support Structures (Sternberg Press, 2009), 29.

07 "The Killing Times," The Guardian, accessed August, 2021, https://bit.ly/3jwcdvf.

08 Department of Agriculture, Water and the Environment. EPBC *Act Protected Matters Report.* (Department of Agriculture, Water and the Environment, 2021).

09 Anna Tsing, Heather Swanston, Elaine Gan, Nils Bubandt, eds, *Arts of Living on a Damaged Planet* (Minneapolis: University of Minnesota Press, 2017).

10 Laura Junka-Aikio and Catalina Cortes-Severino., "Cultural studies of extraction," *Cultural Studies* 31, no. 2-3 (2017): 178, doi: 10.1080/09502386.2017.1303397.

11 Tom Doig, *The Coal Face* (Australia: Penguin, 2015).

12 Nicole Asher and Jarrod Whittaker, "Hazelwood Power Station operators fined nearly $2 million," ABC, published May 19, 2020, https://ab.co/3iu2lTe.

13 "Hazelwood Mine fire inquiry," State Government of Victoria, accessed August, 2021, https://www.vic.gov.au/hazelwood-mine-fire-inquiry-victorian-government-response-and-actions.

14 "The ENGIE Hazelwood Rehabilitation Project," Engie, accessed August 2021, https://www.hazelwoodrehabilitation.com.au/

15 "Media Release," Energy Brix Australia, April 2021, https://ebacdemolition.com.au/demolition-stages/.

16 "Morwell Power Station and Briquette Factory," Heritage Council Victoria, 2021, https://vhd.heritagecouncil.vic.gov.au/places/200429.

17 Arup, Hazelwood Concept Master Plan, (Arup and ENGIE, June, 2019), https://bit.ly/3k1OTFW.

18 Whittaker, "Water shortages, pollution mean Latrobe Valley mine lakes plan not viable, environment groups say."

19 Jarrod Whittaker and Mim Cook, "Victorian coal plants likely to close early," A45 BC Gippsland, published May 3, 2021, https://ab.co/3xu4ClS.
20 Hélène Frichot, *Creative Ecologies: Theorizing the Practice of Architecture*. London (Bloomsbury Publishing USA, 2018), 26-27, accessed August 7, 2021. ProQuest Ebook Central.
21 Amy Frearson, *Peter Zumthor creates buildings on stilts,* Dezeen, published June 2016, https://www.dezeen.com/2016/06/10/peter-zumthor-architecture-wooden-buildings-on-stilts-tourist-trail-norway-allamannajuvet-mine/.
22 Bruce Pascoe, *Dark Emu* (Broome, Western Australia: Magabala Books, 2014); and IPCC, "AR6 Climate Change 2021: The Physical Science Basis," 2021, https://www.ipcc.ch/report/ar6/wg1/#FullReport.
23 Pascoe, *Dark Emu,* 229; and Masanobu Fukuoka, The One-Straw Revolution, translated by Chris Pearce, Tsune Kurosawa and Larry Korn (Emmaus: Rodale Press, 1978).
24 Bill Gammage, *The Biggest Estate on Earth: How Aborigines Made Australia* (Sydney: Allen & Unwin, 2011); and Foreground. "'Wild' grasses are in vogue as priceless native grasslands disappear." Foreground, May 9, 2019. https://www.foreground.com.au/agriculture-environment/wild-grasses-are-in-vogue-as-priceless-native-grasslands-disappear/.
25 Louise Wright, and Mauro Baracco, "Designing For Repair," *Landscape Architecture Australia,* 159 (2018): 59.
26 Gammage, *The Biggest Estate on Earth,* 23.
27 Anna Tsing, Jennifer Deger, Alder Saxena Keleman, and Feifei Zhou, eds, *Feral Atlas: The More-Than-Human Anthropocene* (Stanford University Press, 2020), https://feralatlas.supdigital.org/?cd=true&bdtext=what-is-the-anthropocene.
28 Charles Huxtable, Rehabilitation of Open Cut Coal Mines Using Native Grasses, (Department of Sustainable Natural Resources, 2003); and Leslie Nemo, "From Defiled to Wild," *Scientific American,* published July 2018, https://www.scientificamerican.com/article/from-defiled-to-wild-can-a-spent-coal-mine-be-reborn-as-a-nature-conservation-center/.
29 Linda Tegg, "Grasslands," accessed August 2021, http://www.lindategg.com/grasslands.html.
30 Ian Buchanan, "Assemblage Theory and Its Discontents," *Deleuze Studies* 9, 3 (2015): 382-392, doi: 10.3366/dls.2015.0193.
31 Donna Haraway, *Staying with the Trouble: Making Kin in the Chthulucene* (North Carolina: Duke University Press, 2016), accessed August 11, 2021. ProQuest Ebook Central.
32 Kate Stephens, "Hopes a new eco-friendly concrete can rise from the ashes of coal power," *ABC News,* September 21, 2021, https://www.abc.net.au/news/2021-09-18/geopolymer-concrete-coal-mining-town/100464518.
33 "Phytoremediation Potential of Abandoned Mines," Power Plants Phytoremediation, accessed August 14, 2021 https://bit.ly/3lZkvi5.
34 Adrian Marshall, Nicholas S.G. Williams and John W. Morgan, eds., *Land of Sweeping Plains: Managing and Restoring the Native Grasslands of South-Eastern Australia* (Victoria: CSIRO Publishing, 2015), 94, accessed June 13, 2021, ProQuest Ebook Central.
35 Vandana Shiva, *The Vandana Shiva Reader*. University Press of Kentucky, 2014. http://www.jstor.org/stable/j.ctt12880j6.
36 Institute of Agriculture, "Native grains from paddock to plate," (Sydney: University of Sydney, 2020).
37 Gunaikurnai Land and Waters Aboriginal Corporation, *Gunaikurnai: Whole Country Plan* (Gunaikurnai Land and Waters Aboriginal Corporation, July 2015); and Russell Kennedy et al., Australian Indigenous Design Charter (Burwood, Vic, Australia: Deakin University, 2016).
38 "Gunaikurnai Native Title Agreement," Victorian Government, 2010, https://bit.ly/3CPacTN; and Federation of Victorian Traditional Owner Corporations, *Traditional Owner Native Foods and Botanicals Strategy* (Federation of Victorian Traditional Owner Corporations).
39 Mauro Baracco, Louise Wright and Linda Tegg, "Seeing and Acting," in *Critical Care: Architecture and Urbanism for a Broken Planet,* edited by Angelika Fitz and Elke Krasny and Wien, Architekturzentrum (Cambridge: MIT Press, 2019). 65.
40 Danièle Hromek, "Reading Country: Seeing deep into the bush," Architecture AU, May 27, 2021, https://architectureau.com/articles/reading-country-seeing-deep-into-the-bush/#.
41 Bruce Pascoe and Jack Pascoe, "Bruce Pascoe and his son on farming Indigenous foods," May 27, 2021, in *Life Matters,* interview by Hilary Harper, Podcast, 54:35, https://ab.co/3ANeut0.
42 Matt Sykes, *The Great Victorian Bathing Trail* (Regeneration Projects, 2019), https://www.peninsulahotsprings.com/wp-content/uploads/2021/03/The-Great-VIC-Bathing-Trail.pdf.
43 Frichot, *Creative Ecologies,* 24.
44 Rania Ghosn and El Hadi Jazairy, *Geostories: Another Architecture for the Environment* (Barcelona and New York: ACTAR, 2019).
45 Renata Tyszczuk, and Stephen Walker, eds. *field: Ecology* 4, 1 (December 2010), http://field-journal.org/wp-content/uploads/2016/07/field-journal_Ecology.pdf.
46 Felix Guattari, *The Three Ecologies,* trans. by Ian Pindar and Paul Sutton (London: The Athlone Press, 2000 (1989)).
47 Haraway, *Staying with the Trouble.*

Rhizomatic Rejuvenation is MacKinnon's Master of Architecture independent thesis project supervised by Professor Hélène Frichot, undertaken at the Melbourne School of Design.

REPOSITIONING ARCHITECTURE

Kirsten Day and Daniel Huppatz

Introduction

Architecture holds a place of respect and admiration in a deadening global culture. Its outcomes define spirit, place and people. It is an art and a functional tool; its history is writ large, it embodies public memories. Or such was the view of architecture before architects ceded control of their professional role and allowed others to intercede in overseeing construction administration, project management and building realisation. Their traditional role as ethical, creative and quality controller was sold off by processes such as novation, so they no longer acted as agents for their clients but became minions in the industry with a reduced impact on the built environment. The system needs repair.

Others have noticed, architecture is a constructed morality, and an architect requires passionate integrity and steely determination to deliver on that task. Today, many professionals call themselves 'architects.' Engineers, project managers, drafting services and developers, could employ one architect and attach the title to their business charter. Architecture became a commodity. In the process, the built city became less inventive and more banal. Financial operations ruled decisions and architecture became the business of procuring commodities to enable profits, the city a spreadsheet of returns on financial investment, not a place designed for the betterment of people.

Value? And Work

Our contemporary use of the word 'value' — like many — is used interchangeably and, in the process, loses its central meaning. Shifting between noun, verb, and context — misinterpretation is easy and frequent. It is worth interrogating the definitions of 'value' and use within the context of the architectural design, construction and use of the built environment. A word or sign is determined by context; even within the confines of a single discipline (such as architecture) our interpretation of a single word can be multifaceted. For example, designing a building using the 'value' of equity and human rights ensures universal access.[1] However, during the 'value' management of the project, steps are included because the levels were 'not quite right,' the wheelchair lift was not installed or underspecified, or 'disabled access' is via the delivery bay at the rear of the building near the rubbish bin storage. Design values are different to procurement values.

Through a semiotic lens, 'value' is the place or function of a sign within a system of signs from which we derive meaning; a shape or symbol that can be used out of context, exaggerated, inverted, coloured, distorted — the playground of image-based architects who imagine themselves provocative.

From a sociological perspective, 'value' describes principles or standards of behaviour — a judgement of what is important in life. General guides to conduct the principles or moral standards, held by a person or social group; the generally accepted or personally held judgement of what is valuable and important in life. In 2021 we saw changes to the Architect's Act in Victoria and their value/definition of a natural person — or, who is permitted to use the legal title 'architect.'

Finally, we cannot ignore value as the material or monetary worth of something — the amount at which something may be estimated in terms of a medium of exchange, as money or goods, or some other similar standard, which is equivalent to a fair or satisfactory equivalent or return. This is the reality of architectural practice in a global developer-driven neoliberal economy.

Architecture Commodified

In Australia, as with many other global locations, we have a fixation with housing prices. The home being the single most expensive investment a person might make in their lifetime. Matthew Soules identifies how this changes or limits how we might design:

Opposite: Nightgale Housing Project. Image by Author.

THE COMMONS
Nº 9
SPRINKLER
BOOSTER
OPEN

> As architecture has become finance and finance has become architecture, key aspects of both have changed, these changes involve how buildings are conceptualised, used, and managed and at the same time how they are designed, entailing everything from their proportions to their programmatic composition.[2]

There are 'workarounds;' such as the Nightingale and Assemble housing projects in Melbourne which explore financial options as alternatives to developer led models.[3, 4] However, these approaches remain embedded in home ownership.

The dark side to this is the procurement models, and how many of our apartments are built. The 'poster child' of the Shergold Weird Report — Icon Apartments in Sydney and Lacrosse in Melbourne exemplify this problem with 'value.'[5] Material substitution and pushing down design decisions to subcontractors to save money and time have resulted in severe building failures across Australia. These have had significant repercussions across the industry, with architectural registration in NSW and recent changes to the Architects Act and the Heritage Act in Victoria.

The impact of global systems on architecture is fundamental to understanding why we do and what we do. Jeremy Till writes "Architecture at every stage of its existence — from design through construction to occupation — is buffeted by external forces ... Architecture is defined by its very contingency, by its very uncertainty in the face of these outside forces."[6] While there have been several studies on global systems in general, their impact on architecture (as professional practice or in the education of architects) has gone mostly undocumented.[7] While Peter Raisbeck describes the global system that applies specifically to the practice of architecture — the broader ecosystem of people and materials — the financial system that pays for architectural production has much greater sway on the operations and education of architects than we care to acknowledge.

The implication of these financial mechanisms has ultimately been influential in redefining architecture in terms of valuing architecture as a 'product.' Matthew Soules writes:

> Finance capitalism has an especially pronounced effect on architecture. This is not merely because it is the dominant contemporary economic mode that, by necessity, impacts all sociocultural conditions, but rather because real-estate in one of the primary mediums through which finance capitalism operates.[8]

The commodification of architectural output means that home is an 'asset' and part of a larger financial system.[9] A 'residence,' for example, is no longer assessed as a place where we dwell but a physical asset that we buy and sell. It is part of a global asset class.[10] This view of asset architecture is foreign to the pedagogical landscape of architecture schools–aside from formal explorations of the pentominium, the gigamansion, zombie and ghost urbanism.[11, 12, 13, 14]

The reality of architecture as a real estate asset is the subjugation of the architectural ideal in a developer-led environment. While universities comply with competencies to train architects to address issues such as carbon footprints, sustainability, ecological responsibility and design with Country, the role for which non-traditional contracts within the construction industry employs architects can be viewed as little more than window dressing. Contractually, architects may have little influence on any strategy to improve the environment — unless it is mandated by law and can stand up to the 'value management' processes in Design & Construct and novated contracts.

In the Australian construction industry, developers are responsible for funding buildings — reinforced via a banking system that is reluctant to operate outside of this established model.[15] Beyond the façade of buildings is a robust financial system with specific locations in which these projects can be built due to the ability to justify the development to mortgage lenders.[16] The architect's role within this system is defined primarily as the designer of a product, the building as an asset.

Procurement and Novation

Procurement methods and contractual agreements have been at the front and centre of numerous reports concerning failures in the building industry and the lack of confidence in investment. The Shergold Weir Report was commissioned to investigate issues concerning catastrophic building failures exemplified by the case studies of the Lacrosse Tower in Victoria and Icon Apartments in NSW.[17] In the case of Lacrosse, materials substitution was determined to cause the fire that engulfed the façade of the building in 2017.[18] For the Australian construction industry, this was the equivalent of the UK's 2017 Grenfell Disaster (thankfully, without loss of life) which led to serious questions about risk, responsibility, and accountability within the construction industry.

In the Lacrosse Tower case, the building was signed off under a novated contract which places all responsibility for the completion of the project (and the budget) in the hands of the builder. In this case, the builder successfully implicated the building surveyor, the architect and the fire engineer to be liable.[19]

The prevalence of design & construct and novated contracts restrict the management on site by the design consultant team. This 'ensures' that budgets are met. While there is little evidence of these benefits, there is evidence that the quality of projects is diminished in this 'value management' of the project.[20] While this suits the developer and builder, the investors, or future occupants, are often left with substandard builds or high ongoing maintenance costs. Once the keys have been handed over, there is no current liability for the developer.

The novated contract is redefining the architect's role, particularly for large, commercial projects. Architectural generations are not only facing a loss of tacit knowledge, but are also experiencing the push of contract administration firmly toward project management. Surprisingly, project managers do not carry any indemnity for decisions made, which is mandatory for architects and other design consultants. For architects, the idea of serving the public good as a long-term goal, or addressing issues of climate change mitigation, or of Country, becomes secondary in such a context.

The Professional Architect

The idea of the professional architect — a person whose specialised knowledge and skills engage "human problems amenable to expert service" — has changed over the past century.[21] In the 20th century, professional associations in law, medicine and architecture set standards for fitness, practice and conduct through frameworks for education, accreditation, registration, and on-going evaluation. Beyond knowledge and skills, the professional was also governed by an ethical code, a responsibility for collective life and prestige associated with their social contribution.[22] The professional was a trusted public figure whose judgement was based on their expertise in a specific field and their independent advice was given fearlessly and honestly.

The regulation of professional expertise via standards and accreditation resulted in a monopoly of services, one long-standing critique of professionalism.[23, 24] More recently, the status of professions as a category of special occupations further lost prestige.[25] Access to online information (and misinformation) has resulted in public scepticism surrounding expertise (from climate change denial to alternative medicines), attacks on 'elitism' in the political sphere, and increased competition, specialisation, and automation increased pressure on contemporary professions.

Researchers have completed studies examining the standard skills and knowledge (competency requirements) of professions such as medicine and engineering.[26, 27] Aside from architectural engineering, scholars have neglected issues surrounding the implementation, assessment, or regulation of competencies in architecture.[28] This is a significant omission, given their importance in defining and regulating the architectural profession.

The misalignments between competencies, education, and professional practice outlined above raise several issues for the architectural profession. Perhaps the most pressing is that of identity and purpose. While insecurity has been part of the profession from its beginnings, the ongoing popular association between architecture and aesthetics, combined with the marginalisation noted above, has created a situation where architects seem more dispensable than ever.[29] However, while the body of specialised knowledge remains contested, scholars such as Flora Samuels have mounted an argument for the value of architects as "socio-spatial problem-solvers, integrators of complex bodies of information and masters in space-craft."[30]

But exactly how such masters of space-craft emerge from the competing interests of educational institutions, professional accreditation boards, and practice is unclear. Andrew Leach notes "a mismatch between the influence that national associations exert on architectural education, and the influence that they exert on the general marketplace," a mismatch that certainly coincided with the contemporary Australian context.[31] Part of the problem is the changing construction industry — more global, more competitive, but above all, dedicated to lowering costs and increasing speed in constructing a finished asset.

Part of the problem is a loss of connection between building and the public good or any ideals about the social or ongoing purpose of the built environment:

> Over the past 30 years the construction industry has become ever more strongly biased towards easy project delivery rather than questioning what should or should not be delivered, or what its long-term value to society ought (or ought not) to be. Rather than studying requirements, exploring options and measuring potential benefits in terms of public good or added value, what has come to matter most to many, if not quite all, architects

> and other building professionals is very close to the interests, often very short-term, of the construction industry itself.[32]

The role of the professional architect, once central as a mediator between clients (and society), trustee of the built environment, and of various suppliers and those employed in the construction industry, has become increasingly marginalised. The short-term nature of so much building today means there is a failure to consider how buildings are used over time.

While the Architects Accreditation Council of Australia (AACA) assume the architect as a leader within such contexts, their role is typically only at the front–design–end of projects which are commercial services provided at the beginning of a building project, with the final product as an end goal. There is little interest in Post-Occupancy Evaluation, especially the ongoing building management or future adaptability or reuse.[33] The means to participate in a longer-term process are generally not available within the contemporary context of the construction industry. There is, then, little value in long-term environmental impacts or the social issues associated with building on Country.

Immediate financial cost rather than trust, judgement, or expertise — those attributes associated with the professional — is typically the determining factor and initial price, not long-term use, benefits, or longer-term value. Yet there is still a role for professionals and standards: "Now it is clients, even that mega-client, the state (now, in some countries, fully deskilled in design and construction matters) that need protection from the huge, powerful and rapidly globalising delivery machines that parts of the construction industry have become."[34]

Changing Roles?

Two routes have emerged recently with regards to the future role of architects. The first is a move towards de-professionalisation. As Leach argued, for example: "there seems to be little sense in using accreditation to protect the name of the architect in a professional context where the position of the architect seems to have become increasingly marginal within the building industry."[35] In a sense, this amounts to a kind of resignation that the system is too difficult to change and architects should find alternative means. Alternatives take various directions, including alternative practice models.[36] At one extreme, Peggy Deamer, for example, recently advocated 'deprofessionalisation,' making a case for getting rid of registration and licensing of architects altogether. Her alternative, referencing the Swedish model whereby there is no licencing and registration of architects, relies instead on education:

> And because the government has a vested interest in the competency — both because their economy is based on innovation technology and because they will be the clients of most architects — it gives large sums of money to the universities for forward-looking approaches to architecture and to architectural offices for research grants.[37]

However, this is far from the situation for Australian governments or universities, both seldom invested in competencies within the built environment.

Another model consists of embracing the construction and development industry to regain control for architects — that is, to become developers.[38] Recent projects in Melbourne in this vein include the Nightingale projects, beginning in 2014 with The Commons and Assemble Communities. Nightingale is a successful and ongoing non-profit organisation that combines architecture, development and construction with financing to design environmental, social and financially sustainable apartments — in short, more than simply assets (see Nightingale Housing). [39]

Education Accreditation and Registration

The state's role within Australian higher education is a significant driver of change, with the federal government providing the primary funding for universities. Originally designed to educate students for the public good, universities have shifted since the 1960s "from a liberal, openly accessible, lesser time pressured and broadly based education to more vocational forms of Higher Education that focus on the commercialisation and marketisation of teaching and research for industry and business."[40] The impact of these changes, accelerated in the last two decades, has had several effects. Universities have looked to alternative revenue streams, primarily through international student fees and research partnerships with industry. Universities have increased their emphasis on institutional branding (including new buildings, logos, and promotional material), increased centralised managerialism, precarious short-term casual and contract staff, and a focus on competitive individualism rather than collective futures. Educators have had to adapt to a new culture, driven by top-down 'managerialism' that:

> … has undermined academic democracy (power of central managers and deans rising, departmental

> decision-making declining, students redefined simply as customers). Management's search for a cheap and flexible labour force has had a dramatic educational effect: though universities do not advertise this fact, around half of the undergraduate teaching in Australia is now done by casual labour.[41]

Centralisation within universities means decisions regarding pedagogical structures, class sizes, contact hours and delivery modes come from above, resulting in less autonomy for architecture schools and academics. Finally, with an ever-greater emphasis on fees, students are encouraged to perceive education as a commodity and universities as service-providing industries that provide a ticket to a job.

In addition to the commercial pressures, universities have faced government pressure to align pedagogy and research with technology-driven solutions and new ideals of professional work. For architecture students, this means that the individual and creative practitioner are emphasised to be working in a hyper-competitive and hyper-productive studio. The model student is understood as an individual entrepreneur rather than a professional with a network of collaborative or consultative relationships more common in practice. Other challenges include increasing staff-to-student ratios, pressure on academics to complete research outputs and administration, and the distance between academics and practising architects, with many academics not involved in practice or only practising a long time ago. Jack Self makes the critical observation that:

> The key ambiguity at the core of neoliberal education is whether the student is the product of a system (in which the ambition of the institution is the homogenisation of subjectivity through pedagogic discipline and vocational training), or the consumer of a service (with all the rights and responsibilities that this entails, such as value for money, quality control and other diverse guarantees). In other words, is the student receiving an education, or merely purchasing an educational experience? [42]

In 2010, the Bologna process was implemented in Australia around the idea of developing a 'global knowledge society' and providing greater options for students and graduates, specifically to facilitate the international student market. Herman Neukermans (KU Leuven) was critical of the implementation of the Bologna Model in architectural education in Europe.[43] In particular, he raised the concern that the Architect's Directive in the EU stipulates that training for an architect should be a minimum of four years. This conflicts with the three plus two model, with the two years being the accredited course of study. The Architect's Council of Europe, the International Union of Architects (UIA) and UNESCO advocate for a minimum of five years of training on the basis that architecture schools train students to be self-employed architects and liable for the projects designed.

The Bologna Model is also the basis for the AACA to assess providers' architectural education and the expectation of knowledge and experience. However, this creates tension between generality (the expectations by accreditation and examination bodies) and specialisation (preparing students for a variety of professional settings). Specialisation then provides a new set of problems — who can and cannot practise as an architect. However, when Australian architectural schools adopted the Bologna model, it meant an alignment with European institutions and accreditation standards.

As architects have moved away from professional and ethical responsibility, through commercial processes like novation, there has emerged a raft of concerns about the global environment: energy and sustainable issues, circular economies, cultural inequalities and indigenous values, heritage, ethics, gender imbalance, health and ageing, the human condition related to gender, political stupor, and more. Yet there is an opportunity to reposition architects in the creative and ethical practice of providing and delivering a better constructed world. If architects return to the values of an ethical, socially responsive constructed morality, they will regain respect and reposition themselves as the leaders of what a better built environment should be.

01 United Nations, "Convention on the Rights of Persons with Disabilities (CRPD)," (United Nations, December 2006).
02 Matthew Soules, *Icebergs,Zombies,and the Ultra Thin: Architecture and Capitalism in the Twenty-First Century,* First edition, (Princeton Architectural Press,2021), 33.
03 Assemble Communities build purpose built rental housing with supported pathways to home ownership. Assemble Communities, "Assemble Futures" (Assemble Communities,2022), https://assemblecommunities.com/.
04 Nightingale is a not-for-profit organisation where future owners ballot to be part of a deliberative development project. Nightingale Housing, "The Nightingale Model" (Nightingale, 2017), http://nightingalehousing.org/model.
05 Peter Shergold,and Bronwyn Weir,"Building Confidence: Improving the Effectiveness of Compliance and Enforcement Systems for the Building and Construction Industry across Australia," February 2018.
06 Jeremy Till, *Architecture Depends* (MIT Press, 2013), 1
07 Peter Raisbeck, *Architecture as a Global System: Scavengers, Tribes, Warlords and Megafirms* (S.l.:

EMERALD GROUP PUBL, 2019), 1
08 Soules, *Icebergs,Zombies,and the Ultra Thin*, 31.
09 Sassen, Architects Saskia, "Predatory Formations Dressed in Wall Street Suits and Algorithmic Math," *Science, Technology and Society* 22, no. 1 (March 2017): 6-20.
10 Soules, *Icebergs, Zombies, and the Ultra Thin*, 36.
11 Portmanteau of penthouse and condominium where each floor contains a single penthouse with all that entails.
12 A gigamansion is a home of at least 1,850 m2 and sells for more than USD $50 million.
13 Zombie urbanism is defined by a state of reduced occupancy in an area - thus impacting on the local community.
14 Ghost urbanism is distinguished from zombie urbanism by higher vacancy rates and the perception of failed community.
15 Steven Rowley, Greg Costello, David Higgins, and Peter Phibbs,"The Financing of Residential Development in Australia (Project Number: 81009)," Final, *AHURI Final Report*, No.219. Melbourne, Australia: Australian Housing and Urban Research Institute Limited,25 February 2014. https://www.ahuri.edu.au/research/final-reports/219, 75.
16 Andrea Sharam,"Nightingale's Sustainability Song Falls on Deaf Ears as Car-Centric Planning Rules Hold Sway," *The Conversation*, 25 November 2015, https://theconversation.com/nightingales-sustainability-song-falls-on-deaf-ears-as-car-centric-planning-rules-hold-sway-50187.
17 Shergold and Weir, "Building Confidence: Improving the Effectiveness of Compliance and Enforcement Systems for the Building and Construction Industry across Australia".
18 Hanmer, Geoff, "Lacrosse Fire Ruling Sends Shudders through Building Industry Consultants and Governments," *The Conversation*, 5 March 2019.
19 Victorian Civil and Administrative Tribunal, "VCAT Reference No BP350/2016," in *Civil division, Building and Porperty list* (Melbourne: Victorian Civila and Administrative Tribunal, August 2018).
20 Australian Institute of Architects, "The Benefits and Challenges of Novation for Architects - Victoria," (Melbourne, Australia: Australian Institute of Architects, August 2019), https://www.architecture.com.au/wp-content/uploads/Australian-Institute-of-Architects_Novation-Survey_Victoria-2019.pdf.
21 Abbott, Andrew Delano, *The System of Professions: An Essay on the Division of Expert Labor* (Chicago: University of Chicago Press, 1988).
22 Rudolf Stichweh,"Professions in Modern Society," in *International Review of Sociology* 7, no. 1 (March 1997): 95-102, https://doi.org/10.1080/03906701.1997.9971225.
23 Macdonald, Keith M, *The Sociology of the Professions*,(Calif: Sage, 1995).
24 Aboelela, Sally W, Elaine Larson, Suzanne Bakken, Olveen Carrasquillo, Allan Formicola, Sherry A. Glied, Janet Haas, and Kristine M. Gebbie, "Defining Interdisciplinary Research: Conclusions from a Critical Review of the Literature," *Health Services Research*, 42, no. 1p1 (February 2007): 329-46. https://doi.org/10.1111/j.1475-6773.2006.00621.x.
25 Thomas Kurtz,"The End of the Profession as a Sociological Category? Systems-Theoretical Remarks on the Relationship between Profession and Society," in *The American Sociologist* 53, no. 2 (June 2022): 265-82, https://doi.org/10.1007/s12108-021-09483-3.
26 Epstein, Ronald and Hundert, Edward "Defining and Assessing Professional Competence," in *Journal of American Medical Association*, 287, no. 2, 2002, pp.226-35.
27 Male, Sally A., Mark B. Bush, and Elaine S. Chapman. "Understanding Generic Engineering Competencies,"in *Australasian Journal of Engineering Education* 17, no. 3 (November 2011): 147.
28 Parasonis,Josifas, and Andrej Jodko. "Architectural Engineering as a Profession: Report on Research Leading to a Curriculum Revision," in *Journal of Civil Engineering and Management* 19, no. 5 (1 October 2013): 738-48, https://doi.org/10.3846/13923730.2013.812980.
29 Flora Samuel, *Why Architects Matter: Evidencing and Communicating the Value of (*New York: Routledge, 2018), 13.
30 Samuel, Why Architects Matter, 2.
31 Leach, Andrew. "The (Ac)Credit(Ation) Card," in *The Architect as Worker: Immaterial Labor, the Creative Class,and the Politics of Design*, edited by Peggy Deamer,(London; New York: Bloomsbury Academic, 2015), 228-40.
32 Francis Duffy and Andrew Rabeneck, "Professionalism and Architects in the 21st Century," in *Building Research & Information*, 41, no. 1 (February 2013),115-122,https://doi.org/10.1080/09613218.2013.724541.
33 Lance Hosey,"Going Beyond the Punchlist: Why Architects Should Embrace Post-Occupancy Evaluations," in *Metropolis*, 6 February 2019.
34 Duffy and Rabeneck, "Professionalism and Architects in the 21st Century".
35 Leach, "The (Ac)credit(ation) Card".
36 Harriss, Harriet, Rory Hyde, and Roberta Marcaccio,eds, *Architects after Architecture: Alternative Pathways for Practice* (NY: Routledge, 2020).
37 Peggy Deamer,"Deprofessionalisation,"in *Architects after Architecture: Alternative Pathways for Practice*, edited by Harriet Harriss, Rory Hyde, and Roberta Marcaccio, (NY: Routledge, 2020), 184-190.
38 Zogolovitch, Shouldn't We All Be Developers?
39 Nightingale Housing, "The Nightingale Model".
40 Troiani and Dutson, "The Neoliberal University as a Space to Learn/Think/Work in Higher Education".
41 Raewyn Connell,"The Neoliberal Cascade and Education: An Essay on the Market Agenda and Its Consequences," in *Critical Studies in Education* 54, no. 2 (June 2013): 99-112. https://doi.org/10.1080/17508487.2013.776990.
42 Self, "Factories or Malls?".
43 Herman Neuckermans, "Assessment in Architectural Education," in *Shaping the European Higher Architectural Education Area*, edited by Constantin Spiridonidis, Maria Voyatzaki, and European Association for Architectural Education, 171-79,(Thessaloniki, Greece: The Authors and the EAAE, 2003).

Opposite: Lacrosse building. Image by Author.

REPAIRING CHINESE CITIES

SPATIAL JUSTICE IN URBAN REGENERATION

Dr. Guanghui Ding

Abstract

Over the past four decades, China's urbanisation under a socialist market economy can be described as a process of 'creative destruction.' The continual expansion of the urban environment profoundly transformed society, economy and lives of its inhabitants.. This process of urbanisation was associated with the loss of balance between people, nature and the built environment. In an attempt to address these unbalanced circumstances, a state-led campaign of top-down interventions for urban repair and ecological restoration (*chengshi shuangxiu*) was promoted and implemented in 2017, aiming to create a better environment for better life. Aided by central governmental support, various local authorities, design institutes and construction companies were involved in the process, committed to restoring ecologically damaged landscapes, treating polluted water bodies, building pocket parks, constructing pleasant waterfront spaces and preserving historic built heritage, among other things. This article reviews the origin, strategies and implications of this urban repair movement, focusing specifically on the issue of spatial justice. It uses the Laoximen urban regeneration project in the city of Changde, Hunan Province as a case study, because it demonstrates a deep commitment to skilfully integrating new buildings, historic fabrics and material culture into dynamic urban complex with strong humane concern. The Laoximen project was not a spontaneous, grass-roots community construction in the conventional sense, but a remarkable state-invested urban regeneration with positive contributions from various stakeholders. This article contends that the emphasis on spatial justice in the Laoximen project, a project that facilitated ordinary people access to urban space, helped forge a sustainable community with social, cultural and environmental vitality.

Introduction

As China's economic development has entered a 'new normal' (shifting from a high to a medium-high rate of growth), by the mid-2010s its urban growth gradually transitioned from land-focused, incremental expansion (*zengliang kuozhang*) to people-centred improvement of the status quo (*cunliang tisheng*).[1] The former implies that large-scale urbanisation functioned as the developmental engines in pursuit of economic growth and social stability, while the latter refers to the process of urban regeneration that intends to fix various physical, spatial and social problems within the existing urban fabric. The shift mode of urban transformation implies that the previously debt-based urban expansion, closely bound up with economic growth momentum and profoundly limited by land resources, was unsustainable and likely to engender a potential financial crisis.

To some extent, the 2015 Central Urban Work Conference (*zhongyang chengshi gongzuo huiyi*) in Beijing marked a significant transitional moment in China's urban development model. Shortly after—and even before the conference, local governments in Beijing, Shanghai and Guangzhou began to underline and implement the policies around urban regeneration. The problems to be resolved by urban regeneration in China is more about the scarcity of well-designed public and urban space, the uneven distribution of public service facilities such as affordable housing, schools and hospitals and ecological degradation, rather than the increasing privatisation of urban public spaces. Local authorities played a directing and guiding role in encouraging architects, planners and landscape designers to use their professional knowledge to transform Chinese cities into liveable and sustainable places.

In Shanghai, for example, urban regeneration was carried out across two different scales. At the macro level, the isolated and fragmented landscapes on both sides of the Huangpu River and Suzhou River have been transformed into continuous, vibrant and pleasant public spaces along the waterfront (Fig. 1).[2] At the micro level, the Shanghai Urban Public Space Design Promotion Centre (*Shanghai chengshi gonggong kongjian sheji cujin zhongxin*) encouraged designers to participate in the transformation and enhancement of city streets, community centres and abandoned urban spaces.[3] In Nanjing, the urban regeneration practice represented by the Xiaoxihu project, demonstrates the multidisciplinary collaboration between local planning department, academics,

students and practitioners from architecture school, residents, public and private investors and construction companies, that could reshape decayed areas into liveable places with socially inclusive dynamics and hope.[4]

Despite the significance and relevance of many noticeable works emerging in the context of China's urban regeneration, this essay uses the Changde Laoximen project as a case study, examining how the project deliberately addressed existing problems in social, spatial and cultural urban dimensions. The reason for this selection is three-fold. Ideologically, the project challenges the political and economic logic of mainstream urban regeneration that either perfunctorily follows top-down bureaucratic process or pursues maximised profit. Physically, it combines new buildings with old cultural relics and weaves them into an inclusive, multicultural waterfront block. Socially, it achieves a subtle balance between the well-being of local residents, the expectation for an updated urban image by local government and developer and the creation of a vital commercial and cultural block.

The Laoximen project, designed by the Beijing-based Ideal Space Studio of Zhongxu Architectural Design Co.Ltd., is a large-scale, process-based urban redevelopment. This 600-metre long reconstruction consists of a wide range of commercial, cultural and residential buildings and public facilities such as plazas, waterfront streets, outdoor theatres, parks and bridges (Fig. 2). These new buildings forged a dense urban texture, respected the site's history and culture and provided inclusive urban public spaces that are accessible to the general public. As a critically acclaimed work widely published in both scholarly periodicals and social media in China, the project received professional recognition from public and private institutions and academic discussion.[5] These publications appreciate the project's contribution in exploring an alternative model of urban construction.

Fig.1: Waterfront Public Space on Shanghai's Huangpu River, 2017. Image courtesy of author.

As a complement to the existing literature, this essay focuses on the issue of spatial justice embedded in the urban repair process. Spatial justice, for geographer Edward W. Soja, involves the fair and equitable distribution in space of urban resources and opportunities that the city provides.[6] The inclusive result of Laoximen urban repair process was shaped through long-term collaboration by enlightened officials, socially progressive architects, committed landscape designers and skilled builders. The bold urban intervention reconstructed the city's physical, spatial and social environment and produced a sense of gain for local community and residents.

Urbanisation under Neoliberalism

Since the 1980s, Chinese central and local governments have been struggling to upgrade dilapidated inner city areas and create new districts, in order to improve the economic,

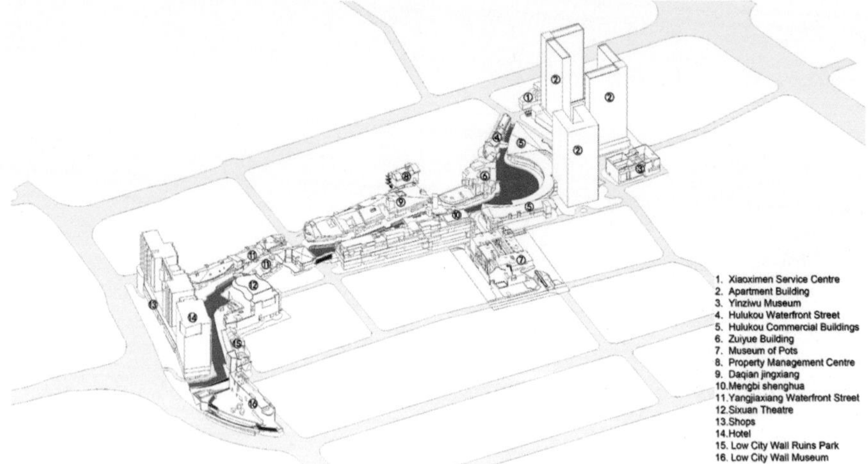

physical, social and environmental conditions of cities. This rapid urban process—urbanisation rate increases from 18 percent in 1978 to 64 percent in 2020—was entangled with domestic political and economic reforms and globalisation. At a macro-level, China's urbanisation was closely bound up with the global expansion of capitalism.[7] In order to solve the problem of excess, capital needs to seek accumulation and proliferation opportunities in the global market. The construction of cities, factories, transportation hubs, various infrastructures and other spatial production is the main form of global capital flow. This is what geographer David Harvey calls 'spatial fix.'[8]

During the early period of reform and opening-up policy in the 1980s, the transformation of urban areas in major cities relied on available Foreign Direct Investment (FDI) which was first and foremost embodied in the construction of high-end luxury hotels for accommodating international visitors. The White Swan Hotel in Guangzhou's inner city, jointly invested by Hong Kong Tycoon Henry Fok Ying Tung and local authorities, demonstrated the power and impact of global capital flow. This 28-story, 100-metre tall modernist building, erected on the shore of the Pearl River, next to the historic Shamian island, represented an explicit intention to modernise the city's image and upgrade its infrastructure and thus becoming an iconic project in south China's economic liberalisation and urban transformation (Fig. 3).

In the 1990s, urban transformation was driven by profit-seeking land speculation activities and primarily led by emerging public and private real estate developers. Their strategy was to bulldoze small-scale old buildings and replace them with high-rise apartments and high-end office complexes. The pursuit of maximised floor areas and plot ratio, ensuring the maximisation of investment returns through market sales, often led to the appearance of super-sized constructions. One can easily see the massive buildings that contradicted and conflicted with the scale and fabrics of the old city in Guangzhou (Shangxiajiu Distric), Shanghai (Jing'an Temple District) and Beijing (Wangfujing Street). As local governments faced a shortage of funds for urban development, the power of capital often took a dominant position in the struggle between cultural preservation and economic development, a trend that continues unabated in the early 21st century.

By the early 2000s, the pace of urbanisation accelerated, due in part to the fact that China has obtained more foreign currency through export trade after joining the World Trade Organisation (WTO) in 2001 and in part to the increasing flow of large amount of Foreign Direct Investment into the country. This urban expansion manifested in the fact that many local governments started to plan new Central Business Districts (CBD), such as Shanghai's Pudong New District, Guangzhou's Zhujiang New Town and Zhengzhou's Zhengdong New District. One of the main instruments to address funding scarcity was to rely on the so-called 'land finance model' (*tudi caizheng*)—local governments' heavy reliance on land-leasing revenues to compensate for an unbalanced tax system that provides them with insufficient revenue to meet their budgets.[9] Local authorities transformed arable land that belonged to farmers into newly proposed towns, selling large plots for real estate development in an attempt to promote economic (Gross Domestic Product or GDP) growth. This model often sacrifices the benefits of rural regions and farmers, without proper compensation for the

loss of their land and future livelihood. The intention to plan large plots and build super-block communities and wide roads was closely associated with profound economic factors, because local authorities could gain maximised revenue and eliminate financial pressure in constructing infrastructure. Hardly surprising, the task to build roads, schools and public utilities within the community became the developers' main responsibilities.

Another institutional way to raise money for urban construction is to issue quasi-municipal bonds by the state, provinces, cities and other governmental entities. The state's debt-financed investment in architecture and infrastructure quickly transformed many new districts. In these newly planned towns, government agencies tend to occupy the central location, surrounded by grand theatres, museums, art galleries, libraries, a youth palace and other cultural and institutional landmarks. These iconic buildings are projects that international architects strive to win in competitions. Consider, for instance, the once booming construction of the grand theatres in the coastal and inland cities, a typical manifestation of China's urbanisation and new district building in the first two decades of the 21st century (Fig. 4).[10]

Land lease and speculation have provided lucrative opportunities to local governments, officials and developers, in many cases at the expense of the interests of villagers and the less well-off. The brute scenario of displacement in many regions exposes the neo-liberal nature of China's urbanisation, characterised with the process of 'accumulation by dispossession.'[11] This liberalisation process was quite different from western experience, in the sense that the Chinese state plays a crucially important role in steering the process of economic development and urbanisation as what can be described as 'state entrepreneurialism'—the state uses the market approach as an instrument to developing economy while realising its monopoly on social control.[12] However, without efficient democratic management and adequate legal control, this urban process driven by 'finance, corporate capital and an increasingly entrepreneurially minded local state apparatus' inevitably engendered potential catastrophic consequences.[13] For example, due to the lack of mature institutional arrangements in land property acquisition, radical methods often adopted include: forcible demolition, cutting off water and electricity to isolate individual owners (*dingzihu or nail household*) and occasionally providing high compensation.[14]

What has happened during this unprecedented urban revolution, however, is the disappearance of the previously balanced relationship between man and nature, between rural and urban environment. For architects Wang Shu and Lu Wenyu, these dynamic and harmonious relationships existing in ancient China and suppressed for almost one century was quickly transformed into a predominant world system in recent decades.[15] Human construction activities in the built environment that demand resources and the disposal of

Fig.2 (opposite): Diagram illustrating the programme distribution of the Laoximen project. Image courtesy of Ideal Space Studio.

Fig.3 (left): The White Swan Hotel in Guangzhou's Shamian Island, 2017. Image courtesy of author.

Fig.4 (right): Henan Art Centre, Zhengdong New District, Zhengzhou, 2018. Image courtesy of author.

waste without restraint have created new social, spatial and ecological crisis. How do we address these urban problems? Or put it another way, what is the role of architectural interventions in repairing the physical, cultural and social ruptures and reconstructing a sense of continuity between the past and the present?

Urban Repair: A Political Will

Urban repair (*chengshi xiubu*), a recently promoted concept by the Chinese government, refers to the 'organic' process of urban regeneration that tries to avoid large-scale deconstruction and rapid reconstruction (*dachai dajian*). However, its meaning was often entangled with similar policies previously highlighted by the authorities, such as urban renewal (*jiucheng gaizao*), urban regeneration (*chengshi gengxin*), organic renewal (*youji gengxin*) and micro-regeneration (*wei gengxin*). Although these concepts put forward in different historic periods had differential focuses and strategies, the key challenge was to address the tension between the new and the old during urban development.

Urban regeneration becomes a global phenomenon, manifesting how governmental decision makers in many countries are willing to invest public funding and resources to address the previously mentioned urban problems. In the Chinese context, solving urban problems were emphasised by top political leaders, demonstrated in the holding of the Central Urban Work Conference in 2015 in Beijing. This is the fourth meeting since the founding of the People's Republic of China and it has been 37 years since the last meeting was held in 1978. During this period, Chinese cities have undergone tremendous changes. Despite profound progress, Chinese cities still face many thorny problems, including urban sprawl, traffic congestion, environmental pollution, ecological imbalance, housing shortage, social services scarcity, unreasonable industrial structure, poor urban liveability and weak sustainable development capabilities. It becomes increasingly imperative to 'cure' these omnipresent urban maladies (*chengshi bing*) through top-down political, institutional and professional interventions.

This high-profile political meeting can be described as both a forward thinking of future urbanisation and a revision and reflection of current mode of urban development. The conference proposed comprehensive solutions to address existing urban problems in planning, design, construction and management, highlighting the instrumental role of urban design, urban repair and ecological restoration in dealing with urban maladies. The conference statement largely reflected mainstream views of leading Chinese planning technocrats and design experts, whose professional knowledge was transformed into legally binding policies.

When addressing the urban issues that became the political will of the central government, it implies that ministries and local governments would quickly follow up and issue relevant policies. For example, on 10 December 2016, the Ministry of Housing and Urban-Rural Development convened a national 'urban repair, ecological restoration' meeting in the city of Sanya, Hainan Province, inviting about 150 people in charge of various local urban construction committees across the country to attend and inspect the city's on-going practice of urban repair. Before the 2015 Beijing conference, Sanya was selected by Chen Zhenggao, the then Minister of Housing and Urban-Rural Development, as a pilot site for urban repair experimentation. The city of Sanya was presumably selected for three reasons: 1) After three decade's of rapid development, the city faced a wide range of urban ills as many other cities encountered as well; 2) as a coastal, tropical city well-known for domestic tourism, the city had rich economic and financial conditions; 3) Sanya is a place frequently visited and inspected by top governmental leaders, with political significance and potential demonstration effect.

Commissioned by the Ministry, the China Academy of Urban Planning and Design, a state-owned flagship planning institute, together with Beijing Turen Landscape Design, were responsible for the design and coordination of urban repair in Sanya. A series of comprehensive projects have since 2015 been carried out, including urban repair endeavours such as upgrading infrastructure, improving urban transportation system, transforming urban villages, coordinating building colours and ecological restoration efforts like restoring ecological wetlands, increasing the number of urban parks and creating urban green space systems. In regard to Sanya's urban structure, the design team from the planning institute selected some representative nodes to provide suggestions of waterfront skyline control, architectural colours, outdoor advertisement, urban lighting, village renovation design and traffic upgrading, aiming to make the city more humane and liveable.[16]

If we say the urban repair practice embodied an attempt to re-forge the links between the quality of life and the built environment, then the ecological restoration intended to rebuild the damaged relationship between man and nature. In the Sanya Mangrove Park design, Turenscape designers strategically transformed a waste site vulnerable to flooding into an ecologically designed waterfront park, rehabilitating the mangrove ecosystem resistant to typhoon flooding and pollution (Fig. 5).[17] Turenscape's design approach, or what its director Yu Kongjian described as the 'big feet'

Fig.5: Sanya Mangrove Park, 2020. Image courtesy of Turenscape; photo taken by Li Liang.

aesthetics (*dajiao meixue*), emphasised the interaction between design and plants, water, climate, ecology and human recreational behaviours on the larger urban scale, subtly and controversially critiquing traditional Chinese garden design that tended to pursue formal delicacy and spatial sophistication within limited space.[18]

Parallel to Sanya's urban repair initiative was a series of government-led urban regeneration endeavours taking place in other major and second and third-tier cities, such as Shanghai, Beijing, Jinan and Jingdezhen, where local governments issued a large number of implementation methods and model projects. Among these cities, Shanghai has moved one step ahead, as local authorities initiated remarkable participatory and community-engaging projects and encouraged officials, designers, academics and local residents to work together to improve the city's urban public spaces.[19] Of particular interest were Shanghai's community garden design efforts, organised by the Clover Nature School (*siye caotang,* launched by landscape designer Liu Yuelai, architects Fan Haoyang and Wei Min), a non-profit organisation concerned with environmental practice and education based at Tongji University. The urban gardening initiative intended to build small-scale, accessible gardens as inclusive places of social interaction, transforming abandoned left-over urban spaces into landscaped public realms. From 2014 to 2022, the programme went through a transition from a few fragmented pilot projects to more than 200 networked community engaged activities, demonstrating its environmental concern, social cohesion and spatial impact (Fig. 6).[20]

Whereas Turenscape's Sanya Mangrove Park was a large-scale—100,000 square metres, designer-oriented project with one-off government investment prioritising ecological restoration, the Clover Nature School's initiative was small-scale—garden sizes usually span from 3 to 10 square meters, bridging the public and private sectors through active public participation. The former, determined by political and professional decision-makers, was centralised power described as 'urban landscaping;' a top-down effort to compensate for the loss of ecological sustainability. The latter, characterised by decentralisation of power, can be classified as 'urban gardening.' In this case, the designers as project coordinators collaborate with local residents, leading to a set of social actions directed towards design, organisation, realisation and cultivation of crops and ornamental plants in (semi-)public spaces.[21]

The Laoximen Project

To some extent, the Laoximen urban regeneration project was not a product that appeared to respond to the central government's urban repair movement. Instead, it originated in 2011 and was built in the four-tier city of Changde, Hunan Province, with a less developed economy but rich history of culture. However, compared with the many urban repair projects emerging in response to the governmental call, the Laoximen project demonstrated an ideological foresight and awareness that a great city should be built with humanity, patience, diversity and creativity; a principle that was promoted by Jane Jacobs in her 1961 book *The Death and Life of Great American Cities*.[22] The Laoximen project differentiated itself remarkably from the politics-driven, speed-prioritised and profit-focused development in the conventional sense, in that it paid careful attention to the cultivation of urban vitality and cultural renaissance.

At the beginning Laoximen, literally, the old west gate, was a dilapidated old town in Changde. Like many decayed inner-city areas, it faced the multiple challenges of material, spatial and environmental renewal, cultural revival and personnel resettlement. It is obvious that this would not be a profitable real estate development project that can be seen in many new districts under urban expansion. Compared with a *tabula rasa* construction site, Laoximen was built on the ruins of the Ming dynasty city wall, the hidden, polluted moat, the remains of blockhouse during the anti-Japanese war of the 1930s and 40s, the remains of local traditional *yinziwu* (a sub-cellar house typology), the local theatre base during socialist period and the demolished deep mansions, former residences of celebrities.

In their design, Qu Lei and He Qing, the principal architects of the Ideal Space Studio, carefully preserved, re-configured and reinterpreted the site's profound, multi-layered history, memory and culture. What they intended to do is to repair the site from three levels:

Socially, re-forging the links between people and place
In order to allow the local residents to continually and fully 'settle down in place' (*jiudi anzhi*) instead of being displaced and relocated in remote suburbs, the architects designed three high-density U- and L-shaped tower buildings consisting of small and medium-sized units and at the same time created abundant public spaces between floors and towers in the sky and on the ground. The coexistence of extremely compact living units and convenient and comfortable community public places not only meets the needs of dwelling number, but also provides spaces for social interaction under the condition of high density. The complementarity between compact living and dynamic public space is similar to the living model in Hong Kong.

Whereas the capital-led urban transformation often led to the loss of local residents and gentrification in the old city, the approach of settling down in place helped build a more humanistic urban life with spatial justice. In the context of the Laoximen project, the traditionally un-privileged urban population were able to easily access highly valued urban centre with education, health and transportation facilities, rather than being relocated to urban periphery without sufficient public services. Appreciation, celebration and articulation of ordinary people and everyday life helped generate an inclusive urban environment.[23] The attitude towards humane concern in urban design, partly influenced by the architects' transcultural experience (living, studying and working in Canada for several years), reflected their ideological identification on Jacobs' critique of 'orthodox' urban planning and rebuilding that destroyed diversity and vitality.

Spatially, integrating buildings within the city fabric
Architect Yung Ho Chang critiqued 'the city of objects,' a phenomena that the once uniform urban landscape now becomes a metropolitan field inundated with skyscrapers and individually expressive architecture in a disorganised or even non-existent urban fabric. The Laoximen project created a cluster of buildings with formal and spatial interactions, or 'a city within a city.'[24] In particular, the efforts to reshape urban vitality and improve the commercial value of the location are reflected in the creation of open spaces along the waterfront. The pleasant commercial streets dissolve the oppression of residential towers and facilities such as squares, covered bridges and stage theatres. They have become indispensable elements of urban living rooms. This heterogeneous nature of programme and space was embodied in the everyday life surrounding the place: visitors walking on the streets or siting on the waterfront benches drinking tea or coffee, residents sitting under the arcade or playing cards, children sketching the street-view and fans participating in music festivals or watching outdoor performances.

In many small cities in China, as Qu Lei remarked, local officials normally lacked critical imagination towards future development, but tended to simply follow the development model of large cities, particularly the omnipresent super-block, large-scale model, which, under the restriction of financial pressure, succumb to the interests of larger real estate developers.[25] What he promoted and explored is a thesis of 'small city story' – urban regeneration and development in small cities should be small-scale, process-oriented and encourage the participation of multiple stakeholders, rather than the domination of a single developer. While the Laoximen project was invested in by a

Fig.6: The urban gardening project, Shanghai, 2020. Image courtesy of Liu Yuelai.

local state-owned developer, the architects were fortunate to work with a client who supported their regeneration-driven design ideas.[26]

Historically, repairing the rupture between tradition and modernity

By weaving multiple pieces of historical ingredients into coherent narratives, the architects created a mixed condition of time. At completion, these grey-faced brick and black-tiled buildings did not appear to be particularly novel and after a few years, they were not dilapidated either. With a sense of history, the commercial blocks showcased the durability of materiality, the thickness of time and the consistency of experience.

Within the modest atmosphere of the block, two individual buildings stand out immediately. One is the Museum of Pots, a three-story red concrete building with idiosyncratic formal languages. This bold colour symbolises flame and passion while the rough concrete surface is reminiscent of the terracotta-made pots. As a direct expression of the architect's personality, it jumps out from the surrounding grey buildings. The building function seen through photographs does not seem to be thoughtfully considered and articulated. Instead, its public spaces, including inner courtyards, stairwells, conical light wells and roof gardens, are the focus of formal expression and bodily experience.

In comparison, the *yinziwu* museum that seems to be formally restrained adopted a mixture of old and new materials, traditional and contemporary craftsmanship and formal language. The pitched roofs used 200,000 pieces of recycled old tiles and the facades were built with recycled old bricks and small components such as wood and stone carvings. Skilled local craftsmen were invited to use traditional and modern construction methods to create a unique spatial effect for this building using internal patios. The hybrid design and construction, neither a restoration of historical prototype nor a nostalgic innovation, aimed to creatively restore the memory of the space and show the history of *yinziwu* house.[27]

As the whole block consisting of more than twenty individual buildings were designed by one studio, the architects employed mixed, changeable and sometimes flamboyant vocabularies. For some fastidious critics, the appropriation of many formal sources may give rise to a sense of familiarity and discontent. The boldness of eclectic approach to aesthetics, for the general public, generated diversity. The mixture of different volumes, forms, materials, colours, styles and spaces, from the point of view of Jacobs, may constitute a necessary condition of vibrant urbanity.

Conclusion: Towards Spatial Justice

Within the context of China's urban regeneration movement, the Laoximen project was an exception, not a rule. This exceptionality was demonstrated in two fundamental aspects: for one thing, the project expanded, spatially, the site's programmes and changed the skyline of the city centre. This expanded approach in height, volume and scale, particularly the building of three high-rise residential towers, provided enough affordable accommodation for local residents and respected their interests and living styles. However, this design strategy can hardly be replicated in traditional historic cities such as Beijing, which legitimately restrained large-scale redevelopment in the inner city.

For another, the project was a decade-long collaborative practice, thanks to the dedication and patience from architects and clients. This 'slow' process contrasts sharply with conventional urban development that tends to seek for short-term economic profit by real estate developers and immediate political performance by local officials. Nevertheless, the approach of spatial innovation, the strategy of slow development and the attention to social concern, as useful solutions to repair existing urban problems caused by the predominant neo-liberal policies, can be adapted to similar urban regeneration projects in different contexts.

It should be noted that appropriate architecture, urban design and landscape design maintains the potential to create public spaces that are accessible to everyone, should its creative autonomy and social commitment be respected by various decision-makers. Socially engaged projects may raise people's awareness of spatial justice and allow people to access public resources. The implication of spatial justice lies in the resistance to the domination of market logic in space making which tended to overlook social, environmental and cultural benefits. However, this mode of urban regeneration is indispensable from the close collaboration between committed architects, (usually state-owned) developers, local officials and residents.

Due to the developer's leadership change, the Laoximen project faces insufficient investment. In addition to the impact of the COVID-19 pandemic on the local economy, tenants often withdraw their leases and the vitality of the Laoximen commercial street was seriously challenged. This kind of follow-up management is also a problem faced by many urban regeneration projects. Although the project design is completed, the maintenance of vitality requires continuous investment and creative operation.

Acknowledgements:
I am grateful for the meticulous editorial support from editors Yutong Jin, Anna Mueller and Patrick Hayes. Thanks also go to Liu Yuelai, Qu Lei and Sun Zhe for providing images.

01 Shenzhen Municipal Planning and Land and Resources Commission, *Zhuanxing guihua yingling chengshi zhuanxing [Transition Planning Guiding Urban Transition]* (Beijing: China Architecture and Building Press, 2011).

02 Harry den Hartog, "Shanghai's Regenerated Industrial Waterfronts: Urban Lab for Sustainability Transitions?" *Urban Planning* 6, no. 3 (2021): 181-196.

03 Ma Hong, Ying Kongjin, "Micro-regeneration of Community Public Space: Exploring Approaches to Community Building in the Context of Organic Urban Regeneration in Shanghai,"in *Shidai jianzhu [Time + Architecture]*, no. 4 (2016): 10-17.

04 See, for instance, the special issue on the Xiaoxihu project, *Jianzhu xuebao [Architectural Journal]*, 2022(01). Wang Hui, "Interpreting 'Spatial Justice' of the Xiaoxihu Practice in Nanjing,"in *Jianzhu xuebao*, no. 01 (2022):47-49.

05 Zhu Jianfei, "Reflections on the Urban Renewal Project of the Laoximen in Changde, Hunan,"in *Jianzhu xuebao*, no. 09 (2016):1-3; Wang Hui, Changde Laoximen: An Alternative Space Production,"in *Jianzhu jiyi [Architecture Techniques]*, 27, no. 08 (2021):87-94.

06 Edward W. Soja, *Seeking Spatial Justice* (Minneapolis: University of Minnesota Press, 2009).

07 Yawei Chen, "Neoliberal-inspired Large-scale Urban Development Projects in Chinese Cities," in *The Routledge Companion to Urban Regeneration*, eds. Michael E. Leary and John McCarthy (London and New York: Routledge, 2013), 77-87.

08 David Harvey, "Globalization and the 'Spatial Fix'," in *Geographische Revue* 2, (2001), 23-30.

09 Heran Zheng, Xin Wang and Shixiong Cao, "The Land Finance Model Jeopardizes China's Sustainable Development,"in *Habitat International* 44, (October 2014): 130-136.

10 Charlie Xue (ed.), *Grand Theater Urbanism: Chinese Cities in the Twenty First Century* (Singapore: Springer, 2019).

11 David Harvey, "Neoliberalism as Creative Destruction,"in *The Annals of the American Academy of Political and Social Science* 610, (2007): 22-44.

12 Fulong Wu, "State entrepreneurialism in urban China: A critique of the neoliberal city," in Debating the Neoliberal City, eds. G. Pinson and C. M. Journel (Abingdon: Routledge, 2017): 153-173.

13 David Harvey, "The Right to the City,"in *New Left Review* 53, (2008), 23-40.

14 Tang Yan, Yang Dong and Zhu He, *Chengshi gengxin zhidu jianshe: guangzhou, shenzhen, shanghai de bijiao [The Innovation of Urban Regeneration Institutions in China: Experienc e from Guangzhou, Shenzhen and Shanghai]* (Beijing: Tsinghua University Press, 2019), 30.

15 Wang Shu and Lu Wenyu, "Poetics of Construction with Recycled Materials: A World Resembling the Nature," in *Shidai jianzhu* 2, (2012), 66-69.

16 Zhang Bing, ed., *Cuihua yu zhuanxing: chengshi xiubu, shengtai xiufu de lilun yu shijian [City Betterment and Ecological Restoration: Catalysts in Transitional Development of China]*, 2nd edition (Beijing: China Architecture and Building Press, 2019).

17 Yu Kongjian, "Sanya Mangrove Ecological Park," in *Jingguan sheji [Landscape Design]*, no. 04 (2020):4-8.

18 Yu Kongjian, Wang Xin, Lin Shuangying, "Urban Design Needs a 'Big Foot Revolution': The Practice of Sanya's Urban Double Repair,"in *Chengxiang jianshe [Urban and Rural Construction]*, no.9 (2016): 56-59.

19 Hua Xiahong and Zhuang Shen, "Promoting Everyday Public Space through Design: A Review of Urban Micro-Regeneration Practices in Shanghai,"in *Jianzhu xuebao*, no. 03 (2022):1-11.

20 Liu Yuelai, Yin Keluan, Sun Zhe, Yu Hai and Mao Jianyuan, "Cooperative Landscape: A Case Study of the Experiment of Integrating Public Space Renewal and Social Governance of Community Gardens in Shanghai," in *Jianzhu xuebao*, no. 03 (2022):12-19.

21 Chiara Certoma, Susan Noori and Martin Sondermann, eds., *Urban Gardening and the Struggle for Social and Spatial Justice* (Manchester: Manchester University Press, 2019), 7.

22 Jane Jacobs, *The Death and Life of Great American Cities* (New York: Vintage Books,1961)

23 Cui Kai, Qu Lei and He Qing, "A Symbiosis of the City and Urban Life: A Conversation of the Urban Renewal Project of the Laoximen Area in Changde,"in *Jianzhu xuebao*, no. 09 (2016): 4-9.

24 Yung Ho Chang, "City of Objects, a.k.a. City of Desire," in *Writes* (Beijing: SDX Joint Publishing Company, 2003), 218-31.

25 Qu Lei and He Qing, "Interview of the Renovation Design of Changde Laoximen," in *Jianzhu jiyi* 27, no.8 (2021): 84-86.

26 The author's interview with architect Qu Lei, Beijing, 16 April, 2021.

27 Qu Lei and He Qing, "Reconstruction of Laoximen Comprehensive Area,"in *Jianzhu xuebao*, no. 09 (2016):10-25.

THE RIGHT TO MESSINESS

Ayomi Olasoji

Mess

The co-existence and acceptance of differing sociocultural contexts has actively defined the contemporary urban experience of societies such as Australia, with the country accommodating over 270 unique ancestral identities and housing one of the oldest continuous cultures on earth.[1] Linked to this diversity is the potential for unique representations of economic and cultural environments that routinely adapt to its social reality. Consequently, the primary quality of a diverse environment is its aptitude for instability; conceptually, the built environment works to authentically reflect the lived experiences of its inhabitants through its vernacular. With even the smallest of changes in sociocultural makeups withholding the capacity to shift the characterisation of space altogether, the concept of clashes and intersections are the innate framework upon which the atmosphere contemporary urban spatial contexts are rooted in.

In establishing this premise, it is fair to conclude that cultural complexity should manifest 'messy' architectural languages, particularly in urban contexts where diversity is increasingly prominent. However, this miscellany is siloed across western regions, inaccurately representing the cultural fabrics which constitute public urban space. As represented in figure one, hegemonic architecture (as defined by western spatial ideals) has dominated global representations of the urban, contributing to an overwhelming sense of sameness across various international urbanities. These urban spaces typically present themselves as such out of a fear of 'messiness.' Abdin Kusno notes that the very concept of mess is encoded by colonial ideas of its equivalence to underdevelopment; moreover, aesthetic assimilation has long been regarded as having the ability to garner respect by proximity and association.[2,3]

By drawing on an observed western hyper-fixation with the organisation of the built environment as a means of purveying an urban ideal, we need to re-assess how diversity truly manifests in designed spaces through means of layered authorship as opposed to authoritative imaginations in a bid to create self-repairing urbanities. In questioning the contemporary claim of desiring a heterogeneous societal makeup despite these environments suggesting otherwise, it reinforces how urban expressions are innately skewed in favour of social capital. We can then, as a result, begin

to interrogate the intended user of the public space in urban contexts and institute practices that promote equity, particularly upon acknowledgement that the 'mess' derived from contemporary diversity is ingrained in transience.

Transience

To fully grasp what socioculturally complex architectural expressions may actualise as, defining 'mess' and understanding its fluidity is crucial. By leaning into Helene Frichot's understandings of complexity underpinning the virility of social space, 'mess' in this context is described as evidence of negotiation between differing social, economic and cultural participants.[4,5] In contrast, ordered space is the consequence of design or legislative actions which group like with like, typically through the imposition of social territories to craft containers of homogeneity.

While diverse vernaculars concurrently exist throughout many global urban contexts, they typically appear as distinct territories. Personified through "ethnic enclaves" in public laneways such as Chinatown, we have created artificial architectural, cultural and social utopias that were historically derived from xenophobia and stigmatisation.[6] The result of these enclaves is an 'untangling' of the "complex conceptual knot" that defines aesthetic and social vernaculars embedded within urbanised public space.[7] Moreover, in many ways, this untangling undermines contemporary discourse surrounding the success of diverse cities — if multiculturalism, for example, can only be achieved through assimilation to a dominant culture or perspective, the diversity embedded within it is inherently lost.[8] Thus, contemporary urban public space is in a state of disrepair as our spatial vernaculars have not reconciled with social realities; put plainly, the design intent of public urban precincts is at odds with those who are occupying these spaces. This is reflected architecturally through a language of placelessness — the removal of vernacular that enriches place through cultural, social and temporal storytelling — as a result of hegemonic design.

So, with everything neatly in its place, the general ethos of the urban fabric that sits in between cultural silos and private thresholds maintains a sense of sterility. This sentiment is only marginally subjugated by the miscellany that its social participants inject into their surroundings. As global lockdowns reduced the need for travel beyond one's place of residence, much of the urban became isolated; therefore, now more than ever, the city has been framed as a place of innate transience.[9] Continuous efforts to encourage white collar workers to return to the office as society re-adjusts to life as it was, has indicated that dense urban precincts maintain few clear continuous occupants. Instead, these spaces are defined and supported by the experiences of those transiting through it on a daily basis. As a result, these precincts are subject to persistent instability (Fig. 2). Overlaid with spatial data that represents instances of public space as defined by the Victorian Planning Authority, patterns of continuous transition across the threshold of urban and rural come to light. As the public infrastructure of the Victorian region itself directs our attention to the urban, we can conclude that there is no standardised representation of the urban citizen. Its primary users extend beyond the imposed urban growth boundary line. Moreover, as the white lines in figure two denote opportunity for human intersection within the realm of the public through public transport networks and parkland, it becomes clear that the urban serves as the praxis for sociocultural negotiations of space. The urban ethos then primarily functions as a complex network of unique meeting places composed, directed and personified by "diverse social actors" whose interactions are fleeting and seemingly arbitrary.[10]

Fig. 1 (opposite): Hegemonic space. Reflective of a contemporary vernacular of hegemonic space, global cities with varying cultural contexts have increasingly similar urban architectural vernaculars
1 Doncaster East, Victoria, Australia. Image Source: Lendi, 2019.
2 Ekoda, Nerima Ward, Japan. Image Source: Pixta. 2020.
3 Tokyo, Japan. Image Source: Smart Cities World. 2018.
4 London, United Kingdom. Image Source: Wikipedia. 2020.
5 Melbourne, Australia. Image Source: Wikipedia. 2019.

Consequently, in establishing the notion that the urban is best described by its transience, it is innately appropriate to redefine the way we design western urban contexts. If the urban is for everyone, it must respond to and represent its participants in all their complexity. However, this has historically been difficult to achieve due to the imposition of singularly penned prophecies of utopia.

Utopia

Utopian visions of space have barred manifestations of cultural inclusion due to its mode of authorship. Historically, city making and planning principles have long been defined by a continuous pursuit of the ideal city through the cultivation of, as Ingrid Bock describes, a "coherent community vision."[11] David Wachsmuth and Neil Brenner's discussions suggest that this coherence has been materialised through the "homogenisation, fragmentation and hierarchisation" of space as a means of controlling urban expressions.[12] Consequently, when this goal of spatial organisation and compartmentalisation is overlayed with the transient nature of contemporary public space, the notion of what Francoise Chaoy has dubbed the

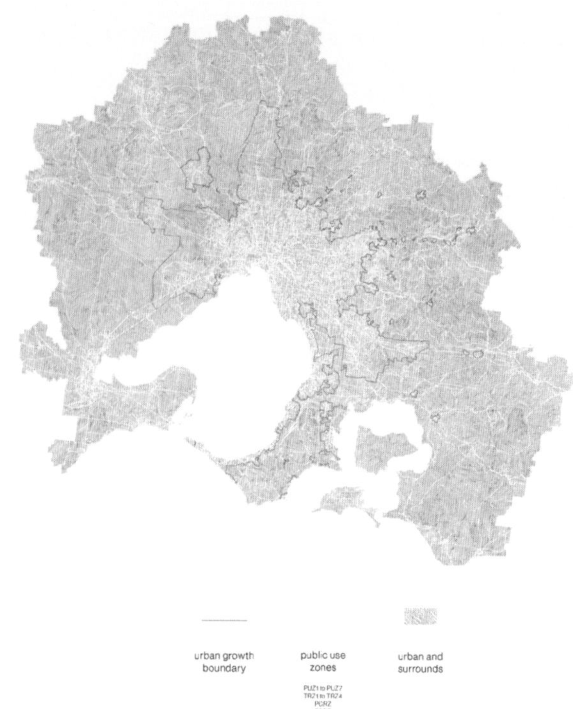

"colonial checkerboard" ensues; space becomes conquered by a dominant sociocultural group as opposed to shared.[13] The result is divided and segmented silos of space. This dismemberment of society distorts spatial vernaculars by prescribing underrepresented sociocultural narratives to peripheral urban segments.

Despite the action of repair implying an activity of the present in an attempt to amend the past, the concept of the urban utopia is seemingly embedded within the conversation of the 'next.' Jane Jacobs explains that "[p]lanners have been typically preoccupied with ideal models instead of understanding and addressing real-life cities."[14] To build on this sentiment, we can conclude that a part of the problem with a pre-occupation of pursuing an urban ideal is that it is typically conceived by a singular author, whether that be the designer, the client or legislator. Thus, the goal of a utopia, irrespective of how virtuous, is to apply a social framework which has been devised by a limited set of authors upon diverse actors of space. Figure three highlights the true extent of sociocultural diversity embedded within Victoria's urban boundary. In noting that much of the state's urban context houses migrant populations in excess of thirty per cent, the reality of singularly authored space becomes particularly problematic.

Sociocultural diversity itself is borne from relinquishing independent control over social interactions that dictate spatial realities. However, it seems as though we have only relinquished this control to a specified point. The utopian vision of a city has initiated a pre-emptive procurement of public space. Having been conditioned to pre-plan,

Fig.2 (above): Public opportunity
Demonstrates public zones of use as defined by the Victorian Planning Authority. As the white lines denote opportunity for human intersection within the realm of the public, it becomes clear that the urban serves as the praxis for sociocultural negotiations of space
Data Sources:
DELWP Planning Scheme Zones, 2020. https://mapshare.vic.gov.au/
DELWP Urban Growth Boundary. 2021. https://data.aurin.org.au/dataset/vic-govt-delwp-datavic-vmplan-plan-ugb-na

Fig. 3 (above): Melting pot
Analysis of migrant populations within urban zones. Notably, a large proportion (in excess of thirty per cent) of Victoria's region within the urban growth boundary have statused themselves as migrants
Data Sources:
NATSEM Social and Economic Indicators - Migration Rate SA2. 2016.
DEE Indicative Australian Urban Development Risk. 2016 - 2026.
DELWP Urban Growth Boundary. 2021. https://data.aurin.org.au/dataset/vic-govt-delwp-datavic-vmplan-plan-ugb-na

pre-program and pre-define spaces is embedded within a means to control, but moreover, an innate desire to strive for a utopia of social coherence. Nevertheless, the notion of a utopia implies impossibility. A model for spatial repair calls for an equilibrium between function and disorder to generate a messy yet equitably dictated urban vision.[15] Thus, urban precincts should focus on the cultivation of an architectural framework that facilitates the co-habitation of varying, and in some cases, opposing incidental activities by diverse urban actors.

Diversity breeds spatial richness through sociocultural contrasts and complexities, including the ones that have been disregarded by the self-elected authors of the urban. Drawing on the finding that migrants and refugees are typically much more concerned with the behaviour of others towards them within the context of metropolitan public space, the conversation around why this is the case could stem from the notion of underrepresentation.[16] Public space, the urban and site are hybrid entities that can be easily skewed as they are driven predominately by social visibility. In suggesting that authors of a utopian vision will always be limited in their expression by their own cultural and social pretences, urban expressions will inadvertently speak to the experiences of its author. This presents itself as an issue, as poor sociocultural representation in transient spaces muddies perceptions surrounding safety as being represented in space is core to feeling safe in space.

In recognising that architecture itself functions as a kind of 'framework for living,' ultimately dictating how we as actors of space occupy and engage with the designed world around us, we have to contend with the largely monocultural lenses that direct this framework. Architecture serves as an implicit materialisation of our relationships with space, but this generally relates to how that space is used and appropriated by its intended occupants. If monocultures are investing in built form, that singular relationship with or perception of space is amplified materially through a structure or scheme which excludes participants from public space. Thus layered authorship of space, irrespective of its 'messy' outcomes, frames itself as a genuine method for repairing exclusionary realities in design practices.

Quasi-Public

Beyond multi-authorship, equitable applications of space are closely linked with sociocultural and economic factors. Rem Koolhaas defines "quasi-public substance" as a carefully crafted atmosphere that permeates the public domain but subjugates the idea of inclusion in which the term 'public space' inherently implies.[17] The establishment of parklets and other functions of tactical urbanism have generated unique adaptations of what could be referred to in many ways as user-enabled design — a re-appropriation of space as dictated by communities themselves. While many have been granted the opportunity to enjoy this appropriation of space, we must always consider who these spaces inadvertently exclude from its narrative.

Beyond COVID-19 clarifying the socioeconomic inequity crisis at hand, spaces such as parklets and other urban interventions imply that your participation within this realm of publicly accessible space is dependent on your ability and to financially participate within that context. Dubbed colloquially as the coffee-tax, the resultant spatial output is skewed; the 'mess' that typically enlivens the city, driven by diverse cascades of interactions between bodies within void are nulled, leaving the urban in a state of disrepair.[18] Thus, messiness itself implies an absence of discrimination which spaces that are quasi-public tend to react against implicitly.

Further to this sentiment, it has long been established that the beginnings of contemporary place making sat solely within the frame of reference of a select minority; thus, a "colonial checkerboard" has been carefully constructed, overwriting diverse experiences of space through the hands of a self-elected writer and prototypical participant in communal space.[19] Figure four highlights the exclusionary nature that is borne from quasi-public developments. Constructed using median household income data by postal area, the image represents a selection of regions within the urban that are bolstered by quasi-public interventions while depicting those which have been left behind. Further, this narrative of socially segmented space and abandoned narrative comes to life. Nevertheless, this 'checkerboard' of pieces has arguably served as the framework that has long defined contemporary urban space. Its narrowness in approach has inevitably left experiences and their subsequent expressions behind, clarifying the need for urban repair. With the question of how to action repair remaining, an exemplar of of genuine contemporary civic space which can be used as a model for repair persists; the public library.

Library

Defined by Koolhaas as the "last repository of the free and the public," the typology of the public library serves as the ultimate Western precedent for messy and inclusive space.[20]

The contemporary library provides an active precedent for what mess and architecture look like in tandem with one another. Libraries inherently champion accessibility by providing free internet access, housing social events, as well as making concessions for language accessibility. Thus, this architectural typology is characteristically democratic, with access superseding the priority of essentially every other intention behind its existence in the urban realm.[21] Defined by its multi-functionality, this sense of quasi-public which permeates through many other public areas is in many ways eliminated. The typological public library is inherently citizen programmed. Often acting as an intersection between diverging sociocultural participants, the library not only invites various actors of the public to participate and co-exist in space, but cultivates enough flexibility within itself to encourage self-determined ownership over its program. Within the miscellany of the library's participants lies diversity in its programmatic function between these groups, inherently forcing them to negotiate the space and its resources.

Hence, this typology successfully "generate[s] conditions for non-specific events," aligning with the notion that mess itself is a cascade of conditions that program for everything and nothing simultaneously.[22] By creating a stage "where internal actions [between social actors] soar beyond control" the public library responds architecturally and materially to the praxis of facilitating social 'mess.'[23] Perhaps a key driver of the library as a messy urban subset lies within the idea that beyond changing relative perceptions of public space, we need to engender change within the way public space is experienced. While practical and tangible urban interventions all work to improve perceptions of the urbanised public realm, one could argue that these elements are not factors which define experience – the experience of space is felt through cumulative interactions between social actors while concurrently engaging with their own social subgroup. Thus as previously discussed, visibility and representation in space play a key role in allowing all to feel empowered with the right to access a variety of urban spaces, especially within the realm of publicly-accessible but private proliferations of space. As a result, the notion of repair through mess ensues, as creating concessions for sociocultural miscellany generates an urban landscape of empowerment through social visibility.

Kits / Canvases

Building on the precedent provided by the typological urban civic library, it is clear that genuine public space – that is, space intended for and directly responsive to the needs of a diverse population – cannot be authored by a select few. With varieties of social microcosms existing within expansive urban morphologies, it is uncontentious to suggest that if you tasked each of these subgroups with the same design brief, their respective spatial outcomes would be different. In an interview with Kim Trogal, Katherine Gibson discusses how diverse cultural economies and groups exist in essentially every building typology, irrespective of the number of authors a space has been designed by. She explains however that once you catalogue each of these unique economies, it becomes clear that "[there is] an opportunity to think [about] which parts [of designed space and legislation] we might do differently" to better cater to a multiplicity of societal needs.[24] In applying this thinking to the public realm, these individual economies which Gibson has recognised would each come up with their own 'kit of parts' or, simply put, 'vehicles of expression' that could dictate the way spaces are designed, articulating an idealised social framework for them to exist in.

This mode of repair is reliant on allowing differing social sectors to curate their own design kit of parts that could be used to generate a spatial utopian ideal. In a bid to allow sociocultural 'mess' to proliferate, these kits and their respective authors could be called together to co-design and negotiate a citizen-authored rendition of multi-modal urban public space. The result would be convoluted, littered with instances of compromise from ad-hoc negotiations, conceptual overlaps and duplicate parts. However, it could be said that this "collection of superimposing contradictions" is the ultimate mode of democratic space cultivation.[25] Looking beyond this proposition, what would happen if these kits of parts and modes of negotiation within the public realm had the ability to be continually re-interpreted, re-imagined and re-visited as dictated by the rightful owners of the urbanised public? As designed spaces will ultimately be inherited by social ecologies even more diverse than what we currently co-exist within, reframing these kit of parts as a cascade of blank spaces which can be inherited, built on top of and repurposed embraces the instability embedded within messy sociocultural realities. Ultimately, we can allow public spaces to operate in a constant state of repair as opposed to destruction and recreation.

Concessions

The intent of allowing for messy cities through tools such as a kit of parts or blank canvas approach is not to over code existing expressions, but to facilitate the expression of experiences within the urban. Arguably, equitable access to tools that cater for self-representation could act as a primary driver to repair the identity politics that currently divides urban and public space. In allowing mess to manifest through 'vehicles of expression' to repair urban vernaculars, we can bring forth the vibrancy of urban space. Succinctly, the first way to achieve this includes dismantling systems that propagate singularly authored utopian visions and interrogating the inequity driven by quasi-public space. These speculative tools of kits and canvases frame themselves primarily around agency in individual expression across urban fabrics in a way that emulates the social complexity of the public library. Stemming from agency in design through the adoption of citizen centred design approaches, or 'the citizen practitioner' which allow for informality and temporality to act as a means of increasing accessibility through visibility.[26] Consequently, the 'repair' of the social urban fabric could be generated through equitable representation and, perhaps more importantly, self-prescribed representation from marginalised groups through the implementation for a designated 'vehicle of expression.'

The urban, in some respects, is wholly capable of repairing itself if we are to let it be; we just need to give it the flexibility to do so. Hence, these vehicles for expression bear no expectation of explicit change but instead call for the implementation of platforms, spaces and products that provide all with the agency to equitably create, challenge and engage with space as a mode of urban self-repair.

Fig.4 (below): Checkerboard. By extracting spatial data by postal code with respect to median household incomes, we can begin to draw conclusions about the way public space is procured, who it benefits and who it excludes from its cultural narrative.
Data sources: Australian Bureau of Statistics. Census. 2020

01 Australian Human Rights Commission, Face the Facts: Cultural Diversity, (Sydney, NSW, 2014), 2, https://humanrights.gov.au/education/face-fact

02 Abidin Kusno. The Order of Messiness: Notes from an Indonesian City in Messy Urbanism: Understanding the "Other" Cities of Asia, edited by Manish Chalana and Jeffrey Hou. Hong Kong: Hong Kong University Press. 2016. 40

03 Phillip Goad and Julie Wills. Encyclopedia of Australian Architecture. Cambridge: Cambridge University Press. 2012, 288

04 Helene Frichot. Creative Ecologies: Theorising the Practice of Architecture. Bloomsbury: Bloomsbury Visual Arts. 2018. 20

05 Vikram Pakash. Messy Urbanism with Jeff Hou and Manish Chalana (2020), Architecture Talk. Interview / Podcast, 47:15. https://www.architecturetalk.org/home/10

06 "How 1800s Racism Birthed Chinatown, Japantown and other Ethnic Enclaves". NBC News, 2019. https://www.nbcnews.com/news/asian-america/how-1800s-racism-birthed-chinatown-japantown-other-ethnic-enclaves-n997296

07 Frichot. Creative Ecologies: Theorising the Practice of Architecture. 22

08 Geoffrey Brahm Levey. "The Turnbull Government's Post-Multicultural City". Australian Journal of Political Science Volume 54, Issue 4 (2019): 456, https://doi.org/10.1080/10361146.2019.1634675

09 Australian Bureau of Statistics, Impact of Lockdowns on Household Consumption: Insights from Alternative Data Sources. (Canberra, ACT, 2021). https://www.abs.gov.au/articles/impact-lockdowns-household-consumption-insights-alternative-data-sources

10 Jeffrey Hou and Manish Chalana. Untangling the "Messy" Asian City in Messy Urbanism: Understanding the "Other" Cities of Asia, edited by Manish Chalana and Jeffrey Hou. Hong Kong: Hong Kong University Press. 2016. 4

11 Ingrid Bock. Six Canonical Projects by Rem Koolhaas: Essays on the History of Ideas. Berlin: Jovis. 2015. 275

12 David Wachsmuth and Neil Brenner, "Introduction to Henri Lefebvre's 'Dissolving City, Planetary Metamorphosis", Environmental and Planning Division: Society and Space, Volume 32 (2014): 201, https://doi.org/10.1068/d3202int

13 Francoise Chaoy. The Modern City: Planning in the 21st Century. London: Studio Vista. 1970. 14

14 Jane Jacobs. The Death and Life of Great American Cities: The Failure of Town Planning. Harmondsworth: Penguin Press. 1984. 32

15 Bock. Six Canonical Projects by Rem Koolhaas: Essays on the History of Ideas. 275

16 "Your Ground Victoria Report". XYX Lab and CrowdSpot. 2021. Melbourne: Monash University XYX Lab. yourground.org

17 Rem Koolhaas. Junkspace. Quodlibet: Rome. 2006. 162

18 Feargus O'Sullivan. What Happens to Public Space When Everything Moves Outside? Bloomberg CityLab, 2020. https://www.bloomberg.com/news/features/2020-06-29/what-happens-to-public-space-when-everything-moves-outside

19 Chaoy. The Modern City: Planning in the 21st Century. 14

20 Rem Koolhaas and AMOMA et al. Content. TASCHEN: Cologne. 2004. 139 - 140

21 Bock. Six Canonical Projects by Rem Koolhaas: Essays on the History of Ideas. 263

22 Ibid, 266

23 Ibid, 267

24 Doina Petrescu and Kim Trogal. The Social (Re) Production of Architecture: Politics, Values and Actions in Contemporary Practices. Taylor & Francis: Milton Park. 2017. 149

25 Ibid, 151

26 Basil Schaban-Maurer. The Rise of the Citizen Practitioner. Newcastle: Scholars Press, 2013. 14

CODING THE GARDEN METROPOLIS

RESTRUCTURING MELBOURNE'S SUBURBAN ENVIRONMENTS

Leire Asensio-Villoria & David Mah
Assisted by Candela de Bortoli

Melbourne's early speculative urbanization was intricately tied to the promotion of, what was then, a fashionable ideal of a tranquil and healthy suburban lifestyle. The promotion of a 'Melbourne retreat' was one of the engines that established the suburb as the long-standing template for the city.

While the suburbs still dominate the public and cultural imagination and still constitute the vast majority of the city's sprawling footprint, a compact and infilled urbanism has gained a foothold in some of the city's suburbs. Differences between the inner-city and 'middle' suburbs have been established for a long time and can be seen to have been shaped by the differing motivations of its early communities. These variations in density have persisted to date where the centrifugal sprawl is propelled by a compulsion for the single-family detached home while the inner-city suburbs are tightly compacted. These two forces of outward expansion and inner densification have only accelerated in recent years.

In a counter-movement away from the urge of a socially distanced suburban lifestyle, livability has come to be associated with the animation of crowded and caffeinated laneways as well as the congested inner-city. The recent turn towards the compact city has been supported by a sea-change in lifestyle priorities coupled with the search for a more manageable urbanization. Two different sensibilities of the metropolitan lifestyle drive the city's polarized suburbanization.

Gardens have been largely jettisoned from the inner city neighborhoods and any resonance with Villa Suburban or Garden cities has also withered. On the other hand, the far-flung suburbs on the metropolitan periphery negate the gains of backyard gardens with slow congested commutes together with stretched amenities and infrastructure. At both extremities, the suburban promise has either been squeezed out or levies a high cost on the lifestyles of its communities. Today, the intricate mosaic of landownership frustrates a bolder engagement with these concerns. However, the

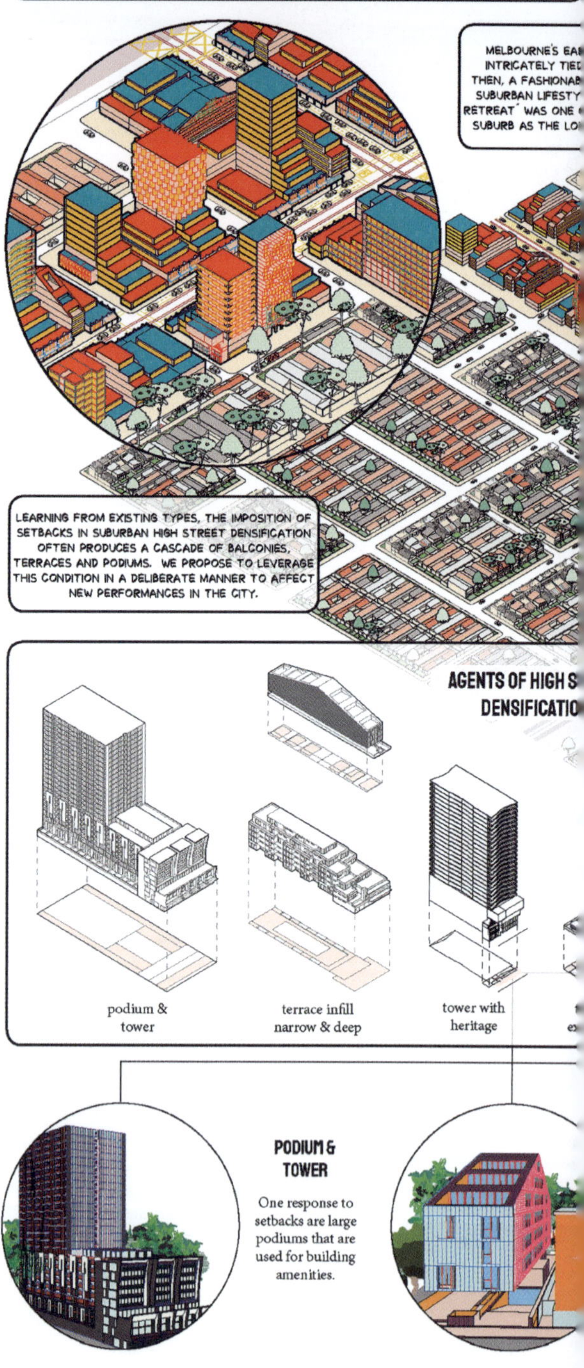

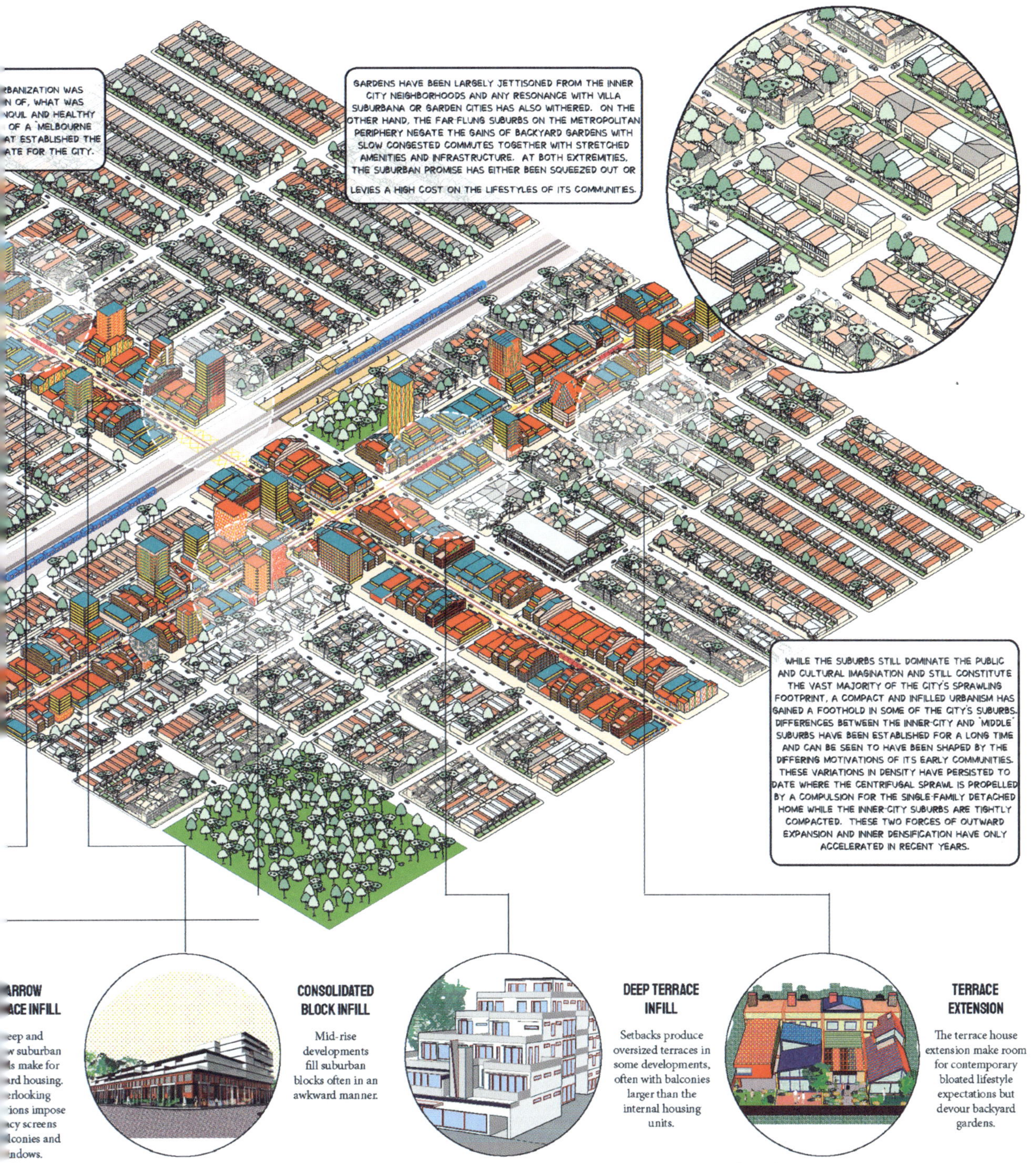
RBANIZATION WAS
N OF, WHAT WAS
NQUIL AND HEALTHY
OF A 'MELBOURNE
AT ESTABLISHED THE
ATE FOR THE CITY.
GARDENS HAVE BEEN LARGELY JETTISONED FROM THE INNER CITY NEIGHBORHOODS AND ANY RESONANCE WITH VILLA SUBURBANA OR GARDEN CITIES HAS ALSO WITHERED. ON THE OTHER HAND, THE FAR-FLUNG SUBURBS ON THE METROPOLITAN PERIPHERY NEGATE THE GAINS OF BACKYARD GARDENS WITH SLOW CONGESTED COMMUTES TOGETHER WITH STRETCHED AMENITIES AND INFRASTRUCTURE. AT BOTH EXTREMITIES, THE SUBURBAN PROMISE HAS EITHER BEEN SQUEEZED OUT OR LEVIES A HIGH COST ON THE LIFESTYLES OF ITS COMMUNITIES.
WHILE THE SUBURBS STILL DOMINATE THE PUBLIC AND CULTURAL IMAGINATION AND STILL CONSTITUTE THE VAST MAJORITY OF THE CITY'S SPRAWLING FOOTPRINT, A COMPACT AND INFILLED URBANISM HAS GAINED A FOOTHOLD IN SOME OF THE CITY'S SUBURBS. DIFFERENCES BETWEEN THE INNER-CITY AND 'MIDDLE' SUBURBS HAVE BEEN ESTABLISHED FOR A LONG TIME AND CAN BE SEEN TO HAVE BEEN SHAPED BY THE DIFFERING MOTIVATIONS OF ITS EARLY COMMUNITIES. THESE VARIATIONS IN DENSITY HAVE PERSISTED TO DATE WHERE THE CENTRIFUGAL SPRAWL IS PROPELLED BY A COMPULSION FOR THE SINGLE-FAMILY DETACHED HOME WHILE THE INNER-CITY SUBURBS ARE TIGHTLY COMPACTED. THESE TWO FORCES OF OUTWARD EXPANSION AND INNER DENSIFICATION HAVE ONLY ACCELERATED IN RECENT YEARS.
ARROW
ACE INFILL
eep and
w suburban
ds make for
rd housing.
erlooking
ions impose
cy screens
lconies and
ndows.
CONSOLIDATED BLOCK INFILL
Mid-rise developments fill suburban blocks often in an awkward manner.
DEEP TERRACE INFILL
Setbacks produce oversized terraces in some developments, often with balconies larger than the internal housing units.
TERRACE EXTENSION
The terrace house extension make room for contemporary bloated lifestyle expectations but devour backyard gardens.

densification and compaction of the inner city suburbs and the revitalisation of the city's CBD can be seen to have been exercised in a coordinated yet incremental transformation. Drawing encouragement and inspiration from individual examples of small yet highly concentrated private ecologies scattered throughout the city, we propose to affect an incremental yet systemic recovery of the garden in our suburbs. We propose to reinsert the garden as a structural element through the use of guidelines and regulations that delivers density but in another form. The 'high-street' and the 'garden-suburb' are shaped by a trade-off between height and ground coverage. The dreaded high-rise is given a new form at different scales to enable different garden cultivating microclimates to thrive.

The volumetric formation of high-rises at the architectural scale is determined by a pairing of a relaxation of height regulation along transport corridors with a second consideration for solar fan rights attached to smaller public gardens strategically located at a rhythm along high-streets. By punctuating these high-streets with small public gardens, the adjacent high-rises would be constrained by triangular envelope volumes, encouraging high-rise building profiles that would be characterised by cascading terraces: introducing gardens across a full range of levels.

Along north-south oriented corridors, the resulting skyline would be noticeably taller with a more dramatic expression of terraces, creating an undulating silhouette akin to a saw tooth or mountain range of balconies. For the east-west facing high-streets, this results in lower, mid-rise fabrics, where minimising overshadowing the adjacent street and blocks produce solar envelopes that support terraces flowing perpendicular to the streets. These new vertical grounds offer outdoor spaces, gardens and a latent social landscape for high-rise apartment lifestyles. The code is orchestrated to allow for the construction of these spaces as emergent and intentional urban patterns which multiply the garden and ground for its new constituencies of apartment dwellers.

In the areas spanning between the high-streets, a restructuring of the fabric is proposed to balance the densification of the transport corridors with a thinning of the ground coverage. A corresponding decluttering of the ground in these areas is orchestrated through building codes which trade building footprint reduction for height. This expresses a reversal in priorities where a reopening of the urban ground to larger garden footprints are traded off with taller houses. Allowing for the same gross floor area (GFA) allowable in these neighbourhoods, any new construction would be required to reduce its footprint while making up for this lost area by allowing taller (three to four stories) volumes. The solar fan regulations ensure that solar access is safeguarded in these enlarged gardens, helping to shape new envelopes and an emergent fabric that redistribute built form to produce a more open series of ground planes. In this case, an urban thinning emphasises a re-organisation of the figure ground balance of these blocks.

The restructuring of the typical types found in the suburbs offers a number of specific ways in which a new substrate of gardens may be opened up or grafted onto the grid. These are all transformations that operate at the individual parcel level but are also paired with other codes that help to generate a new urban pattern aimed at re-introducing gardens at a range of scales. These individual operations collectively contribute towards a larger systemic shift, where environmental continuities are defined, creating a patch matrix of landscapes that boost the urban ecology and recalibrate its microclimates. These cultivated landscapes instigate new strata of social spaces and offer an expressive shift of the streetscape from a manifestation of individual properties to a constellation of shared garden spaces. As a political diagram, this echoes a change from the notion of a society of individuals to one where larger patterns emerge from collective buy-in to action. It is an expression of the hope for a viral acceptance of certain trends or values which then contribute to a larger systemic shift. In Melbourne, the increment for systemic change is at the level of individual property. Any collective behavior needs to be adopted and managed rather than mandated.

Reflecting a shifting policy, the proposal for new suburban configurations also moves away from a singular template and cultivates a range of different patterns. The dense and urban coexisting with the thin and sparse to accommodate the new lifestyles desired by its diversifying constituencies. While aiming for a wider transformation, the strategy presented by the project also acknowledges its temporality. Transformation will occur over time, rendering the suburb in hybrid conditions during its transition. In the interim, these sites will be in perpetual states of renovation and incompleteness, vividly reflecting a kaleidoscope of its citizens' different capacities and values.

A new constellation of social spaces may enable an urbanism that reinstates an ecological substrate to our suburbs while providing a flexible social infrastructures capable of hosting different social and socially-distanced densities. A widely distributed network of garden spaces reconditions the city's grounds to better modulate our microclimates as well as better support the ecological and hydrological cycles. The garden metropolis supports compact and idyllic metropolitan sensibilities.

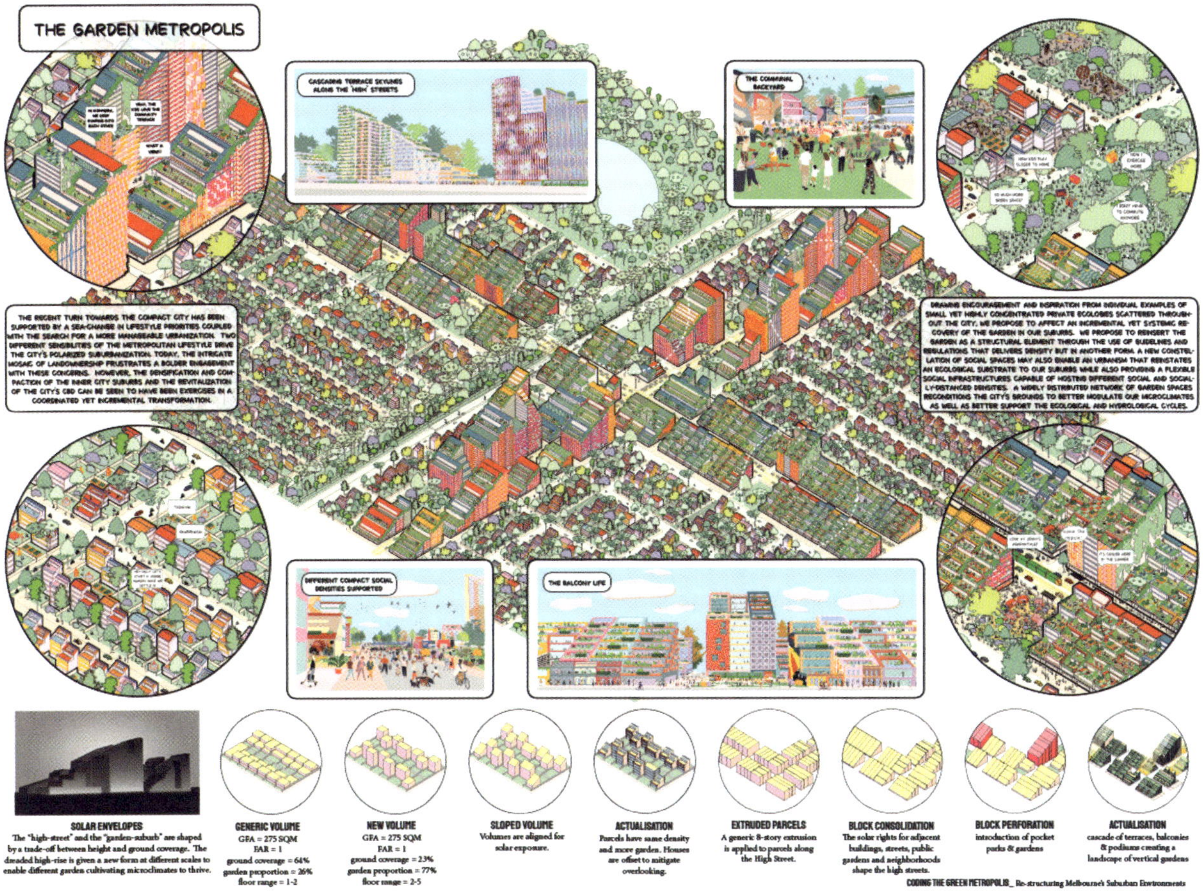

THE GARDEN METROPOLIS

CASCADING TERRACE SKYLINES ALONG THE 'HIGH' STREETS

THE COMMUNAL BACKYARD

THE RECENT TURN TOWARDS THE COMPACT CITY HAS BEEN SUPPORTED BY A SEA-CHANGE IN LIFESTYLE PRIORITIES COUPLED WITH THE SEARCH FOR A MORE MANAGEABLE URBANIZATION. TWO DIFFERENT SENSIBILITIES OF THE METROPOLITAN LIFESTYLE DRIVE THE CITY'S POLARIZED SUBURBANIZATION. TODAY, THE INTRIGATE MOSAIC OF LANDOWNERSHIP FRUSTRATES A BOLDER ENGAGEMENT WITH THESE CONCERNS. HOWEVER, THE DENSIFICATION AND COMPACTION OF THE INNER CITY SUBURBS AND THE REVITALIZATION OF THE CITY'S CBD CAN BE SEEN TO HAVE BEEN EXERCISES IN A COORDINATED YET INCREMENTAL TRANSFORMATION.

DRAWING ENCOURAGEMENT AND INSPIRATION FROM INDIVIDUAL EXAMPLES OF SMALL YET HIGHLY CONCENTRATED PRIVATE ECOLOGIES SCATTERED THROUGHOUT THE CITY, WE PROPOSE TO AFFECT AN INCREMENTAL YET SYSTEMIC RECOVERY OF THE GARDEN IN OUR SUBURBS. WE PROPOSE TO REINSERT THE GARDEN AS A STRUCTURAL ELEMENT THROUGH THE USE OF GUIDELINES AND REGULATIONS THAT DELIVERS DENSITY BUT IN ANOTHER FORM. A NEW CONSTELLATION OF SOCIAL SPACES MAY ALSO ENABLE AN URBANISM THAT REINSTATES AN ECOLOGICAL SUBSTRATE TO OUR SUBURBS WHILE ALSO PROVIDING A FLEXIBLE SOCIAL INFRASTRUCTURES CAPABLE OF HOSTING DIFFERENT SOCIAL AND SOCIALLY-DISTANCED DENSITIES. A WIDELY DISTRIBUTED NETWORK OF GARDEN SPACES RECONDITIONS THE CITY'S GROUNDS TO BETTER MODULATE OUR MICROCLIMATES AS WELL AS BETTER SUPPORT THE ECOLOGICAL AND HYDROLOGICAL CYCLES.

DIFFERENT COMPACT SOCIAL DENSITIES SUPPORTED

THE BALCONY LIFE

SOLAR ENVELOPES
The "high-street" and the "garden-suburb" are shaped by a trade-off between height and ground coverage. The dreaded high-rise is given a new form at different scales to enable different garden cultivating microclimates to thrive.

GENERIC VOLUME
GFA = 275 SQM
FAR = 1
ground coverage = 64%
garden proportion = 26%
floor range = 1-2

NEW VOLUME
GFA = 275 SQM
FAR = 1
ground coverage = 23%
garden proportion = 77%
floor range = 2-5

SLOPED VOLUME
Volumes are aligned for solar exposure.

ACTUALISATION
Parcels have same density and more garden. Houses are offset to mitigate overlooking.

EXTRUDED PARCELS
A generic 8-story extrusion is applied to parcels along the High Street.

BLOCK CONSOLIDATION
The solar rights for adjacent buildings, streets, public gardens and neighborhoods shape the high streets.

BLOCK PERFORATION
introduction of pocket parks & gardens

ACTUALISATION
cascade of terraces, balconies & podiums creating a landscape of vertical gardens

CODING THE GREEN METROPOLIS_ Re-structuring Melbourne's Suburban Environments

All Images by author.

AN ARCHITECTURE OF ART

TIMOR-LESTE AND THE FORCED CLOSURE OF ARTE MORIS

Chris Parkinson

An Observation

Imagine standing at a pause from the day's heat.

Darkened clouds gather along the mountains across the city's elevated spine, preparing to douse and cool the earth from the monsoonal heat, baking and breaking the alchemy of surrounding sounds; ribbons of trebled, tiny chords and melodies from kiosks, shops, ambling cars and homes splice the air. The cackled flow of running children echoes at your feet one moment, then courses through the city's winding lanes, bearing no attention to formal structure, re-routing the gridded vision of order, privileging a knowledge built upon concealment and the local.

Through this cartwheeling audio and elasticity to order, the pant of sales, the din of livestock — chickens, pigs, roosters, dogs — the chiming bells and horns of mobile vendors of soups, fruits and pastries snap through, alongside, before and after each layer of sound — momentary signifiers of a particular passing of time. Large trees flank the entry to one of the city's treasured spaces, housing people pointing, whispering, wondering. As more people gather on the street, the incongruous vision of painted portraits of the country's political and resistance heroes are strewn along the curbside, a heap of historical sentiment, recuperation and valour rendered as rubbish.

The red roofs making up the entry to the space are set off against a deepening charcoal blue sky, masking the famed red dome of the central building that welcomes visitors set slightly back from an expansive concrete courtyard. Wrapping around the courtyard is the verdant overgrowth of the tropics, its lilt a breath of vitality waiting for rain.

Large yellow trucks snake their way from the front of the venue to the back, roaring over the cracked concrete entranceway. They split an enduring palimpsest of caked paint, rendering upon painted rendering of a lineage of habitation and peaceful ideology; cultures and subcultures from around the world, referenced in colour, quote, or figurative representation. A bulldozer spitefully scatters dust and debris into the thick afternoon air, mincing the earth. Attention is averted by the swift movements of lithe bodies through thickening air, eager to follow the energy of collective catharsis. A line of canvases on easels, a stage, guitars, drums, speakers and a microphone manufacture the most practical example of the space's name — Arte Moris, or Living Art.

As the unruly reality of a government reducing a country's longest-serving informal educational space dedicated to the contemporary expression of art and culture materialises, minds swollen by heat, hunger and history actively galvanise around the activities that the school's inhabitants and alums know only to enact: repairing destruction with the force of art, imbuing art with the energy of life; living art.

Dated 1 December 2021, this is an account of the ransacking of Arte Moris, as witnessed through a hand-held WhatsApp video call facilitated by Melchior (Mely) Dias Fernandes. In 2012, Fernandes participated in a series of conversations between filmmaker Chris Phillips and myself, conducted in Timor-Leste, probing the impact of art in the country.

"So we are going to build a bridge to connect this generation, with that generation," Fernandes implored. "If we keep creating art and unite the youth, then I think we will minimise the problem, the troubles, in our country."[1] His words, paired with his recently observed comparison of the government's political decision-making regarding Arte Moris to abstract art, rung in my ears as his vision wandered, then pulled focus on Osme Goncalves.[2] Sat at the front of a cavalry of artists behind easels, documenting the unfolding of events with paintings; allegorical representations of the gathered audience, of the scene of waste at hand, marks made in spontaneous tones and themes as the embodied experience propelled reaction.

Within the context of Timor's contemporary creative expression, life as a substrate for making is pronounced.

Title Page: Maria Madeira, *Silence at What Price?* Installation image as part of Hasoru-malu, 16 May 2022. Image: Author.

Above: Art Work thrown in front of Arte Moris by authorities conducting the eviction. 1 December 2021. Image: Allone Twosix.

Established in Dili in February 2003 by Iliwatu Danebere, Tony Amaral, Gabi Gansser and Luca Gansser, Arte Moris (Lit: Living Art) is the first fine arts school, cultural centre and artists' association in East Timor. It is based in the capital, Dili, founded following the violent Indonesian occupation. Its primary aim was to turn art into a building block of the psychological and social reconstruction of a country devastated by violence, with emphasis on helping its young citizens.

As Arte Moris reappropriated the space that held their history from the forced removal of their possessions, they opened up spaces of congregation and learning. The demonstration of this collective of students and alums' response to this event created spontaneous slipstreams of space to negotiate the reality of their situation, reflecting the ideologies of sociologist Henri Lefebvre. As Claire Revol puts it in her analysis:

> Lefebvre proposes rhythmanalysis to construct an appropriate spacetime, including the ability to transform urban society and reconfigure the 'total body' so that the urban can be considered a work of art instead.[3]

Rhythmanalysis transforms praxis into poiesis, merging the creation of lifestyles with experimental utopias. Arte Moris's vigil transformed a contested space into a sphere of new imaginings, sculpting an embodied and collective aesthetic of activism and resistance, repair and recuperation. In countering the preposterous with providence, spatial reconciliation through artistic engagement emerges.
This is part of the architecture of Timor-Leste's contemporary art; an ethic of repair, cultivated in the spirit of Arte Moris.

Left: Mural by Arte Moris alumni Tony Amaral for Hasoru-malu, 14 May 2022. Image: Ali Baba.

Right: Artist Osme Goncalves, clowning on the makeshift stage in front of Arte Moris, 1 December 2021. Image: Allone Twosix.

"With Blood We Write" came the hastily marked canvas courtesy of Osme, linking this act of creative resistance to a lineage of history that coils itself around the country's identity, built upon the blood, soil and suffering of the resistance to Indonesia's furious occupation.

An Architecture

The architecture of contemporary art in Timor-Leste is an aesthetic venture that weaves the country's spiritual, social, traditional and political contexts around reconstructive, historical, affective and conceptual expressions. As a collective of identities working with this constellation of influence, Arte Moris, since their inception in 2003, embodies a collective rendering of this architecture. In Arte Moris, a collective identity emerged within the context of Timor-Leste's nation-building that re-routed tropes of a collective, national identity fuelled by the country's resistance.

In shifting the narrative towards the aspiration of peace and reconciliation, gleaned through the lens of artistic practice, Arte Moris's collective expressions challenged the consensus of the country's imagined identity by demonstrating art's interface with everyday life. Consistent with the waves of graffiti and street interventions that emerged from the school from 2003 onwards, it has enabled artists to "identify with and simultaneously critique, the dominant culture of the post-independence state established by the older generation."[4] Through painting, photography, graffiti, film, theatre and sculpture, the work of Arte Moris is marked by its gestation through significant social and political change in a post-conflict and post-colonial setting. Learning, activism, advocacy, making and living overlap in this space as artists negotiate the legacy of tumult in the country. This significance is gleaned through the understanding of the English translation of Arte Moris's name — living art — and the cultural affiliations and relations that have spawned from it demonstrate the key, collective value as a fundamental understanding of art in Timor-Leste today.

In an eloquent comparative analysis of creative learning spaces in Cambodia (Tiny Toones) and Timor-Leste (Arte Moris), Nuraini Juliastuti concludes with this recognition of the inherent life focus of Arte Moris:

> Studying together provides an avenue for learning about how to live together. Developing a free art school paves the way for creating mechanisms for living together. Arte Moris students are trained to be productive through doing art. The most important lesson, it seems, for being an artist, is to learn how to survive.[5]

The creative practice and aspirations of a generation of creatives born in the early years of the country's occupation under Indonesia is a crucial contributor to understanding Timorese artists' current-day compulsions and aesthetics. The *Geração Foun*,[6] or New Generation, is a generation of Timorese blighted by the struggle for resistance, teetering at the edge of the contemporary national narrative, "detached from the solidarity experiences of East Timor's resistance era, largely founded on the struggle for independence."[7] Artist Etson Caminha reminds us:

> It's important to keep the old traditions alive and in the present. They are embedded in our identity. Our generation, however, doesn't have another narrative to engage with from the past. Art presents a particular and peaceful way for our generation to have a voice in our history.[8]

Jaqueline Siapno encompasses the ethic that Caminha draws us towards through what she refers to as "repertoire's of resilience" as they manifest in response to violence, summarised by Siapno as, "cultivating a different 'nature.'"[9]

> The second response is to re-write, expand and increase repertoires of resilience and include the histories of the 'other,' hybrid, travelling nation-makers (not just dwelling in one fixed site) but in multi-sited positionalities of creative production and reproduction.[10]

This is important in the context of Timor-Leste and the role Arte Moris has played in nurturing repertoires of resilience and how artists innately engender their work with this repertoire — creating from experience to scaffold reparation of the future. Seminal Timorese contemporary artist Maria Madeira, through a commitment to engaging "fragments of traditions" as a cornerstone of her practice, ushers an understanding of the creative reclamation of tradition and cultural practices of the past in contemporary art in the country.[11]

Madeira's practice is indebted to exploring her Timoreseness as a diasporic artist. The deft representation and re-routing of artifacts — particularly the Timorese textile, *Tais* — within her work celebrates the role of women within traditional creative practices and sign-posts the centrality of this tradition flowing into contemporary, creative expression, oftentimes enacted by the overwhelmingly male constituency of Arte Moris, current and alumni students alike. Historical stories are interwoven into Madeira's work, where she often draws from an archive of historical events and moments with a visceral response.

The taxonomy *Movimentu Kultura* coined by academic Leonor Veiga in 2015 to encapsulate how Madeira applies the aforementioned 'fragments of traditions,' was also broadly applied to a suite of artistic practices in other artists, marked by their gestation through political change, demonstrating performances of citizenship that recuperate a legacy of tumult in the country.[12] Citing an integration with everyday life as one of three components of the definition of Movimentu Kultura, Veiga proposes that the "approximation between art and everyday life, through the integration of art's social functions" plays an important role.[13]

In the case of Arte Moris and the ethos of their practice, this integration between art and everyday life is something of a mission statement, a way of being. This practice is in accord with Veiga's observation but, by design of deeper integration, a living through — not merely an approximation to — life demonstrates an accentuation upon Veiga's taxonomy. To illuminate this accentuation, Jill Bennett's argument for practical aesthetics suggests a disposition towards an expression that focuses on being 'in' rather than 'about' an event — "an aesthetic continuum connected to the practices of everyday life."[14] This holds significant weight for the flow of Arte Moris's mission. The spiritual, social, traditional and political links are amplified through a collective undertaking that echoes Bennett's further proposal that the "linking [of] aesthetics to the continuum of everyday sensoriaffective interactions shape psychosocial life."[15]

A Rhythm

"The street is chaos and out of the chaos, comes art," Tony Amaral said during an interview in 2019, where the focus of our conversation about both his street and his studio practice; the private and the public if you will.[16] "It's not for us to invent stories," he continued. "It is for us to engage with what has happened and present that. What I witness, I present."[17] From 2002, the restoration of Timor-Leste's independence privileged Dili, the country's capital, with assumptions of the delivery of humanitarian aid predicated on "systems and institutions that function best [being] those created in the image of those

dominant in Western countries."[18] Concurrently, the twin ambitions of independence and state-building, constituent parts of a broader nation-building ambition, also converged in the city, housing a "complex mix of forces: from the reconstruction industry and its associated boom to those escaping conflict."[19]

Amaral's urban interventions operate in dialogue with the country's uneven modernity, engaged, as he is, with replenishing the urban environment with reminders of ways of being in Timor-Leste that the post-independence thrust towards modernity has rendered peripheral. Beginning by painting banners for clandestine acts of resistance in the early 1990's, Amaral's vitality for art crystallised on 12 November 1991, when the media merged with the horror of an assault on life that would propel the trauma and tenacity of the East Timorese resistance narrative internationally. Several thousand mourners marched from the Moatel church in Dili to the Santa Cruz cemetery in honour of slain student Sebastião Gomes. The Indonesian military herded the group of mourners inside the cemetery and opened fire.

Popular history sees this event, and the ensuing documentation of the tragedy by British journalist Max Stahl, as a catalyst in informing the world of East Timor's suffering. For Amaral, the trend for using art to tether his voice to the collective sustenance took root at this time. He describes giving something beautiful to people for them to see through it to find their own story to tell.[20] He is intimately concerned with the reproduction of and reminders inherent in, urban space; Amaral's large-scale compositions riff off the country's traditional textile — *Tais* — semiotic nods to the past and a fervent aspiration for a just and balanced future. Indeed, an ethic of Amaral's understanding and integration of tradition might be how he views *Tais* as an enduring connector of the relational and narrative both inside Timor-Leste and beyond. "The *Tais*, in our traditional culture, is to bring people together…To bring people to see what is Timor."[21]

With this rhythm of the past ringing in the present, Amaral negotiates the substance of social relationships and of artistic manifestations. What makes a work inspiring is not just the idea, the vision, the information or the insight. It is how these things and these interactions unexpectedly click in, come apart, meet halfway, build and un-build one another in their diversified movements. Painting on the streets enables Amaral to connect with people and allows them to connect with social and political themes and representations of themselves, fostering a rhythmic sensibility that finds accord in Bennett's theory for its connection to the "generation of new spaces and terms of operation beyond the social identities already in place," whilst stressing a Lefebvrian maxim, that "everywhere where there is interaction between a place, a time and an expenditure of energy, there is rhythm." [22, 23]

"The research behind my works comes from the engagements I have with the people of my country on the streets,"[24] says Amaral. Much of the potency of his work nestles itself in

Above (from left to right): Photographic portraits of East-Timorese artists Tony Amaral, Lena Caminha and Alfe Perreira. 17 May 2022. Images: Author.

liminal spaces, where the assimilation of this knowledge is juxtaposed with resistance. Ruin and repair emerge as a cyclical ethos fostering transformation, engendering Amaral's patina with a social function indebted to the pursuit of temporal harmony and the rehabilitation of an urban architecture peeling with the palimpsests of a singed, pock-marked and gouged history and the slow process of repair and rebuild.

An Atmosphere

> 'Should I talk, draw, photograph, video?' These are not the questions. It is not about knowing in advance what kind of technique will allow you to go on and not knowing what the technique will help you do. It is about realising that the method that will eventually help you go on, allowing you to enter into a relationship with an emerging problem, might not yet have been.[25]

I consulted Lena Caminha about using a *Tais* for a photographic idea I wanted to pursue on the periphery of the Hasoru-malu exhibition held in Dili from 18 May 2022.[26] I proposed portraits of the gathered contemporary artists in three different exposures with an aesthetic continuity bound together with the *Tais*:

1. A womb-like wrapping of the Tais around each participant
2. A "future" view
3. A "letting-go"

I photographed thirty-two contemporary artists in the country with the *Tais*. In doing so, a relational field emerged between people, creativity and culture. Threads of things I was not looking for wove themselves into my field of experience. My engagement with the *Tais* expanded an attunement to the event. Its weave reached beyond its materiality to animate Hasoru-malu's curatorial concept of 'weaving connectedness.'

Caminha's conceptual overlay for Hasoru-malu was part ceremonial mimesis, part cultural renewal; the *Tais* manifested a link of repair, enabling the affirmation of cultural identity in the present. History, the roots and routes of story, family, kinship and the flow of connectedness were all held in its weave, reverbing the silence. Tightly held lines of coloured cotton, hung and draped configurations whispered forth a jagged communion between history and the contemporary.

Their geometry tumbled from spatial demarcation, imbuing space with the lull of story, bearing witness. In one room, *Tais* were arranged around buffalo skulls, folding and flowing through forms of sound and video; they lapped at the boundaries of ritual, improvisation and regeneration. Pulled across a bed of nails, I saw mountainous forms. I saw the flow of the ocean. Geographically, it is hardly a stretch to make this observation, given we were on an island renowned for its mountainous jungles and surrounding sea. What I did not see was more profound. The piercing of a human body and the reparative reclamation of a historical event of torture. A new function. A new criticality. A rendering of suffering conceptually transposed.

Had I not photographed the *Tais*, I would not have seen the *Tais* and I would not have been as exposed to what was woven together for Hasoru-malu and what was, indeed, weaving through me. The sharing of knowledge, re-ignited connections and the gentle repair of relationships wading through the evident collective trauma of the closure — and history — of Arte Moris and the battle of temporal harmony in reconciling the past, the present and the future. Here, the *Tais* was a practical aesthetic, threading "new collaborative spacetimes of experimental togetherness, new forms of association."[27]

When Caminha asked for the *Tais* I had borrowed back, the weave expanded.

Artist Alfe Perreira, the *Tais* adorning his lower body, held a three-month-old baby wrapped in the Timorese flag as he wove through the audience of the Hasoru-malu exhibition. Inching towards a large black framed canvas, propped up amongst woven and ceramic artifacts, he passed the baby to its waiting mother, then trained his focus upon the canvas. His energy ricocheted as he spat his opening incantation of betelnut upon the empty black canvas, challenging the next marks to follow the contours of this initial splatter.

In guiding this relatively newborn life from the shadows to the light of his centre stage, Perreira evoked a curiosity towards what Portuguese sociologist Boaventura de Sousa Santos refers to as the 'Not Yet'; "the way in which the future is inscribed in the present."[28] The baby was a new hope in this spacetime; an entanglement of partly realised aspirations realised through twenty years of independence connecting to an allegorical future of *naroman*, or light.

Meanwhile, the *Tais*, weaved this moment together with many other moments, embedding the ritualistic into its form. Bodies formed a crescent around Perreira, themselves also adorned in *Tais*. After twenty minutes of improvisation, Perreira planted a white painted palm at the top of his painting. Initially, this gesture was to be a star. Through his twenty minutes of performance, a message linked to the hand took over him. "Hope isn't realised fully. I realised that during the painting of this piece. So I put my hand there. If we want to realise hope, the star in our flag, then we have to *tau liman ba malu* (offer each other a hand)."[29] The *Tais* wrapped around Perreira's lower body breathed the weave of the socio-political, the reconstructive, the affective and the collective.

A Conclusion (?)

Part of Lefebvre's Rhythmanalysis explores a critical theory where counter-spaces are fueled by imagination, linking the urban to the idea of an oeuvre.[30] For Bennett and the proposal of Practical Aesthetics, "the value of art lies in its capacity to attune to subjectivity and to the emotional valence that inflects our relationships to people, places, and things."[31]

Through the examples of works by Perreira, Caminha and Amaral, the socio-political, the reconstructive, the affective and the collective philosophies of Arte Moris have been shared as they intersect with theories of Rhythmanalysis and Practical Aesthetics, expanding upon pre-existing insights into contemporary art in Timor-Leste today.

In 2010, former President of Timor-Leste, Dr Jose Ramos Horta, introduced this author's book, *Peace of Wall: Street Art from East Timor*, suggesting that the expression evidenced in the country's graffiti was always relevant because it provides, at the very least, a snapshot of current opinions and attitudes, of stored feelings and concerns from the past, and fears and hopes for the future. Of course, Amaral and Arte Moris were at the forefront of Timor-Leste's graffiti movement in 2003.

If we are to sustain the Lefebvrian logic of the city as an oeuvre, particularly as it pertains to the production of space and spatial justice, Arte Moris' forced closure reaches deeper than an act of violence and destruction of architectural and urban space. The sad irony of portraits of the country's leadership being slung to the curb by the very people portrayed in those portraits as they ransacked Arte Moris, is steeped in a dialogue with the destruction of their own mythology within that oeuvre.

The carousel of conflict that has rendered young people, at one point central to the clandestine and urban-based resistance struggles of the late 1980s and 1990s in the country, as a group now actively maligned through the limited imagination of the country's government. Now, it manifests itself as an assault upon a generation of thinkers seeking to repair their nation deeply disturbed by foreign occupation and violence, guided by the peaceful force of creative thinking and collective decision-making. Benefactors of struggle, certainly, but also active agents in the struggle to sustain the fruits of that resistance; independence, freedom and peace.

The rubric of art and struggle, and art raising national consciousness supporting Timorese claims to independence are nothing new in the country.[32] What is new in this narrative is that the forced closure of Arte Moris and subjugation of their collective philosophy represents a damning juxtaposition of value and pride invested in creativity between war and peace, rubble and regeneration, between becoming and being.

In the spirit of juxtaposition, might it be that an atmospheric aphorism of Ben Okri best considers what it means for art to be in conflict with the state in building a new nation?

> The oppressors become so inflated with their history, their apparent stability and their military power that they forget how to listen and how to see others…They forget that the world is one, and that the fates of oppressed and oppressor are bound up with one another for ever.[33]

Dedicated to Max Stahl and Luca Gansser. Rest in Power.

01 Chris Phillips, "Animatism: Artistic Action in East Timor," Vimeo video, June 30, 2014, 3:10, https://vimeo.com/99583684. At the end of this quote during the interview, Fernandes paused and then refined his reference to the 'troubles' in his country saying, "Actually, it's not a troubled country. It's only the media that goes out and says that East Timor is like Afghanistan. Bullshit." Be that as it may, Fernandes still sees art as an important part of the nation's development.

02 Goncalves is no stranger to being the focus point of people's attention. His embodiment of culture has been critically addressed in the past by Angie Bexley, whose paper, *Seeing, Hearing and Feeling Belonging: The Case of East Timorese Youth*, spoke of Goncalves "express[ing] through speech, song and bodily movements the postcolonial predicament that many younger East Timorese face in regard to belonging in independent East Timor."

03 Claire Revol, "Henri Lefebvre's Rhythmanalysis as a form of urban poetics," in *The Routledge Handbook of Henri Lefebvre,* eds. Michael E. Leary-Owhin and John P. McCarthy (London: Routledge, 2019).

04 Catherine Arthur, "Writing National Identity on the Wall: The Geração Foun, Street Art and Language Choices in Timor-Leste," *Cadernos de Arte e Antropologia* 4, 1 (2015): 1.

05 Nuraini Juliastuti, "Free Art Schools as Tools for Inclusion," In *Forces of Art: Perspectives from a Changing World*, eds. Carin Kuoni, Jordi Baltà Portolés, Nora N. Khan, and Serubiri Moses (Amsterdam: Valiz, 2020), 281.

06 Members of the new generation are distinguished by two factors: firstly, they were not part of the original nationalist leadership in Portuguese times which formed the political parties, Fretilin (ENG: Revolutionary Front for an Independent East Timor. PORT: Frente Revolucionária de Timor-Leste Independente) and UDT (ENG: Timorese Democratic Union. PORT: União Democrática Timorense) and fought a brief civil war in 1975. Secondly, they grew up under Indonesian occupation and were educated mostly under the Indonesian system.

07 Matthew Arnold, "Who is My Friend, Who is My Enemy? Youth and Statebuilding in Timor-Leste," *International Peacekeeping* 16, 3 (2009): 380.

08 "Etson Caminha in conversation with Chris Parkinson," as part of *The World in 24 Hours Conference, an Art History and Curatorship Conference,* Wednesday 16 February 2022, presented by the University of Melbourne.

09 Jaqueline Siapno, "A Society with Music is a Society with Hope: Musicians as Survivor-Visionaries in Post-War Timor-Leste," *South East Asia Research* 21, 3 (2013): 447.

10 Ibid, 447.

11 Leonor Veiga, "Movimentu Kultura in Timor-Leste: Maria Madeia's Agency," *Cadernos de Arte e Antropologia* 4, 1 (2015): 87.

12 Ibid.

13 Leonor Veiga, "Movimentu Kultura: Making Timor-Leste," in *Routledge Handbook of Contemporary Timor-Leste,* eds. Andrew McWilliam and Michael Leach (London and New York: Routledge, 2019), 268.

14 Jill Bennett, *Practical Aesthetics: Events, Affects and Art after 9/11* (London: I.B. Tauris, 2012), 3.

15 Ibid, 227.

16 Tony Amaral, in conversation with author, 28 June, 2019. Dili, Timor-Leste.

17 Ibid.

18 Ann Wigglesworth, "Partnership in Crisis: Lessons from East Timor," *Aid in Conflict,* ed. Matthew Clarke (New York: Nova Science Publishers, 2006), 174.

19 Ben Moxham, "State-Making And The Post-Conflict City: Integration In Dili, Disintegration In Timor-Leste," *Development Studies Institute, London School of Economics* 2, 32 (2008): 4.

20 Amaral, conversation.

21 Chris Phillips, "Gertrude Street Projection Festival Artist Interview," Vimeo video, October 26, 2014, 2:23, https://vimeo.com/110096621.

22 Jill Bennet, *Practical Aesthetics*, 5.

23 Henri Lefebvre, *Rhythmanalysis: Space, time and everyday life,* (London: Continuum, 2004), 15.

24 Amaral, conversation.

25 Derek P. McCormack, "Devices for Doing Atmospheric Things," in *Non-Representational Methodologies,* ed. Phillip Vannini (New York: Routledge, 2015), 100.

26 Hasoru-malu, a collective exhibition, brought together works by some of the foremost active Timorese visual artists to present an overview of contemporary art in Timor-Leste, and their vision - of society, culture, identity; past, present, and future - for the 20th anniversary of Timor-Leste, 20 May 2022. More than 50 works by 15 artists of different generations, styles, and languages, including painting, drawing, video art, installation, and photography, were selected by the curatorship of Maria Madeira, one of the most celebrated Timorese contemporary visual artists. My thanks to Joana Saraiva and Fundação Oriente for the opportunity to undertake an artistic residency as part of Hasoru-malu.

27 McCormack, "Devices for Doing Atmospheric Things," 105.

28 Boaventura de Sousa Santos, *Epistemologies of the South* (New York: Routledge, 2016), 183.

29 Alfe Perreira, in conversation with author, May 30, 2022.

30 Henri Lefebvre, *Writing on Cities,* trans. Eleonore Kofman and Elizabeth Lebas (Massachusetts and Oxford: Blackwell Publishers, 1996).

31 Jill Bennett, "Can Practical Aesthetics Change Lives?," in *Practical Aesthetics*, ed. Bernd Herzogenrath (London: Bloomsbury Academic, 2022), 234.

32 Anthony Soares, "The Poets Fight Back: East Timorese Poetry as Counterdiscourse to Colonial and Postcolonial Identities," *Romance Studies*, 24:1 (2016): 139.

33 Ben Okri, *A Way of Being Free*, (London: Phoenix House, 1997).

CONSUMERISM VS COFFEE WASTE

RECONSTRUCTING DAILY LIVING

Kristen Wang

As the world's second-most traded commodity, coffee is considered a significant beverage consumed in over 2.25 billion cups every day by billions of people across the globe. Approximately 19 million Australians, more than 75% of the entire population, drink coffee daily; this means that Australia alone consumes at least 37,000 tons of coffee a year.[1] Suppose we see the other side of the coin, with an estimated average of 11 grams of coffee ground going into each cup of espresso or latte drink. In that case, each cup of coffee produces a staggering eight times more waste than the drink, from wet dispensed coffee grounds and cups to coffee husks and hessian coffee bean bags in the coffee industry chain.[2] Despite governments and local groups trying to convert some of this waste into compost, most coffee waste (an estimated half-million tons in Australia or 18 million tons worldwide) sadly ends up in landfills. However, worse than that, they generate significant greenhouse gas emissions, such as methane—one of the primary causes of global warming, which is 25 times more potent than carbon dioxide.[3]

The global consumerism of coffee is significantly considerable, however the public are mostly unaware of the waste behind the coffee industry and its waste damage. Each gram of disposed café coffee grounds accumulates. Here, the spark of an experimental design exploration begins—*Re.Bean Coffee Projects*, which aims to repair the current ecosystem of coffee waste. Through creative design work, the problems of waste handling are analysed and the potential of organic coffee waste is realised. The project consequently aims to investigate the potential solutions to the coffee waste issue by utilising the natural biological substance of coffee grounds with a combination of other bio-substances (ideally waste, too) to produce a biodegradable material for further applications.

Biodegradable materials contain polymers that should be capable of being ultimately reabsorbed by the surrounding environment and degraded by microorganisms (bacteria, fungi and algae) through composting processes to produce natural breakdown compounds such as carbon dioxide, water, methane and biomass without causing any pollution.[4]

Above: Coffee and Coffee Re.Bean chair.

Additionally, most sustainable furniture products in the current market conventionally incorporate other traditional or non-sustainable materials for the need for structural functionality. In contrast, many so-called biodegradable products are not entirely biodegraded or even mixed with toxic chemicals for mass manufacturing, ultimately weakening their sustainability goal. Critically, *Re. Bean Coffee Projects* challenge this binary approach by creating a sense of singularity and unity from the same material.

With this goal in mind, *Re-Bean Coffee Projects* aims to recycle, reutilise and reconstruct coffee wastes to create sustainable and fully biodegradable design objects that will induce no other harm to our precious natural environment after their end life. It poses a significant challenge—the invention of such 100% biodegradable material from disposed coffee ground waste, fabrication from this unique new material and functionality and practicality in balance with the material's biodegradability.

Material Learning from Prototyping

A coffee bean is an organic substance; the surface of untreated coffee ground particles is jagged, crumpled, porous, and irregularly shaped. Making use of its unique three-dimensional structure, disposed coffee ground plays a role as the filler of the material mixture. On the other hand, a binder that holds coffee grounds to create a solid determines the new mixture's fundamental quality and property features. In other words, the binder should also be a non-toxic or non-chemical organic substance that can break down in natural environments to achieve the biodegradability of the new coffee material.

Countless research and prototypes of coffee ground mixture matching, small sampling and ratio findings were conducted to find the most suitable bonding agent and formula to produce a desired solid form. The explorative binder testing included sugar, milk, banana, starch, tea leaves, etc. However, the most successful outcome was achieved from bone waste.

Further experimental testing with the amount of binder as a control parameter found that the number of coffee grounds affects the volume, the shrinkage and the drying speed of the new coffee material. This experiment aimed to find the optimum mixture for casting and gaining volume against the number of coffee grounds. With the added coffee grounds increasing, the combination changed from a runny liquid texture to densified paste state, which means when reaching a certain point, the mixture will be too thick to manipulate for casting.

A solid prototype of the new coffee material was tested on a compressor with a pressure measurement sensor. The data result recorded a 408kg pressure, proving that this coffee mixture material has an incredible compression strength. The slow-motion video captures that the material prototype broke from the hole and cracked.

Above: testing samples of coffee ground and binding ratio on solidity.

Design through Learning from the Failure

The success of creating solid forms from the coffee ground mixtures was a milestone in the *Re. Bean Coffee Projects*, but it set a new challenge on design and fabrication as no reference or making method was available for this brand-new material. The development of designing and making took place simultaneously and intensively through the study of the new coffee material itself with the aid of digital analytic and simulation software and modern digital fabrication techniques such as laser cutting and CNC milling. Most importantly, the failures of each prototype guided and pushed the development testing. For instance, a flat casting resulted in a shrunk and warped shape, giving hints to the subsequent design, making the cast require shrinkage allowance. In contrast, the design needs to accommodate the warping action of the new material. In the drying process, the edges of a model curved up naturally, forming beautiful double curvatures as a design feature.

In the de-moulding stage, 10 minutes after the cast, the material was highly elastic and flexible into a bowed curvature arch. Inspired and learning from this behavior, the next step to utilise this feature was to build a framework for setting different curvatures. However, too much warping or bending leads to cracking, as coffee ground performs well in compression but not in tension. To overcome this problem, a fabric member of hessian coffee bean bags, which are not only coffee industry waste products but also biodegradable thanks to their 100% plant fiber, was implemented to provide the best tension-resistant ability.

Louis Kahn asked, "What do you want, brick?"
Here I asked, "How do you want to be shaped, coffee-mix?"

When designing with this coffee material, success will only come with how it will perform in a bottom-up manner instead of from the top-down, forcing it to do what designers predetermine.

Through such experimental design approaches, the outcome results in a functional, beautiful, innovative, unprecedented, and, most importantly, biodegradable stool piece. *Re. Bean Coffee Stool* is one of the first sustainable and biodegradable works created entirely from the same material. It is structurally sound through the actions of folding in structural formation.

Left: Warping action of coffee ground.

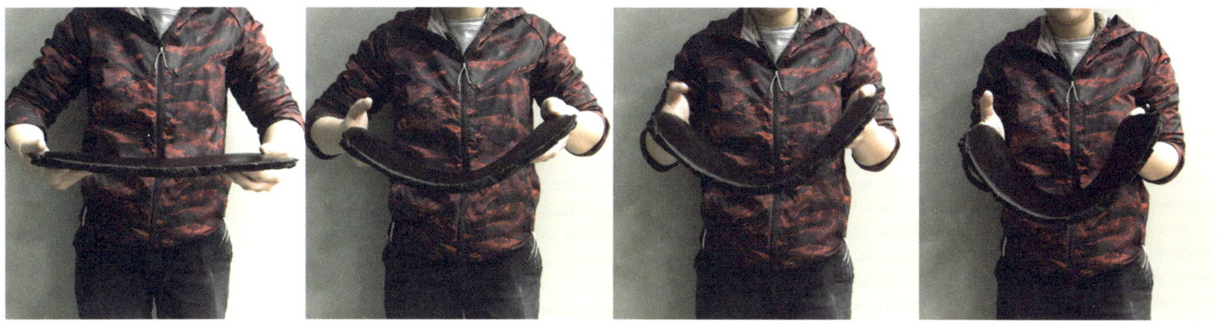

Warping action 10 minutes after de-moulding.

Above: Mixing process.

Above: Casting process.

Re.Bean Coffee Stool

Re. Bean Coffee Stool is the pioneering project among the *Re. Bean Coffee* design series. Aiming to develop innovative design solutions which reuse coffee waste and transform it into a sustainable and, more importantly, biodegradable design piece, a strong emphasis has been laid on intensive experimentations and research for both materiality and fabrication techniques throughout the development processes. The design utilises this unique coffee mixture as a completely homogeneous material to create an entirely self-supporting stool through the clever use of double curvature in its structural design.

Designed to function and be used in daily life, *Re. Bean Coffee Stool* has won several renowned Australian and international awards, including the Intesa Sanpaolo Special Award 'Food as Design Object' at the SaloneSatellite of Milan Salone del Mobile in 2019, against a tough crowd of emerging designers from around the globe.

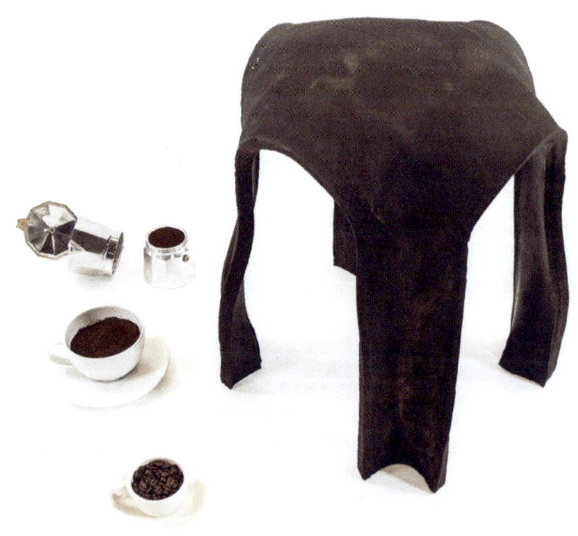

Re.Bean Coffee Stool.

Re.Bean Coffee Time - The Clock.

Re.Bean Coffee Time – The Clock

Time for a coffee?
Handcrafted from about 50 cups of coffee ground waste and other coffee industry waste, *Coffee Time – The Clock* continues the *Re. Bean Coffee Projects* as a timely reminder for your cup of coffee every day. Additionally, it is a question to remind us of how unnoticeable waste from our crazy love for and consumption of coffee can be transformed into an addition to our everyday domestic spaces, reconstructing the deformation and formation cycles of daily living.

Re.Bean Coffee Moment - The Lamp.

Re.Bean Coffee Moment – The Lamp

Is the mind enlightened during coffee moments? *Re.Bean Coffee Moment – The Lamp*, placed on any corner, lights up a moment of coziness during the night, redefines spaces against its organic forms during the day and returns to nature at the end of its life.

As initial steps in the broader vision for a sustainable product future, *Re. Bean Coffee Projects* seek to make a manifesto of creative design solutions on how designers can help to cope with waste problems in current global consumerism; it also tries to raise the public's awareness of the environmental issues of coffee industry waste and to promote coffee waste as the world's next sustainable design objects, furniture and building material.

Influenced by rawness in naturality and wabi-sabi aesthetic, *Re. Bean Coffee Projects* strives to return to its natural essence through originality, simplicity, materiality and sustainability. The brand-new coffee material of the series is handcrafted from locally collected coffee ground waste and other coffee industry wastes, completing the natural life cycles by being biodegradable in a genuine and entire sense—generating no waste to our eco-environment by the end of its life.

Through its coffee smell and unique sense of tactile and fabrication process, *Re. Bean Coffee Projects* reveal how our daily waste from coffee, one of the most globally popular beverages, can be transformed and reconstructed into new parts of our daily living beyond the morning espresso.

01 Thomas Hinton, *"Coffee market in Australia-Statistics & facts"*. Statista. 2021. https://www.statista.com/topics/4615/coffee-market-in-australiaBeom Yeol Yun et al. "Circular reutilization of coffee waste for sound absorbing panels: A perspective on material recycling". Environmental Research, 184, 109281. 2020. https://doi.org/10.1016/j.envres.2020.109281

02 Statistics, *"Waste Account, Australia, Experimental Estimates"*. Australian Bureau of Statistics. 2020. https://www.abs.gov.au/statistics/environment/environmental-management/waste-account-australia-experimental-estimates/latest-release

03 Catia Bastioli, *"Biodegradable materials - Present situation and future perspectives"*. Macromolecular Symposia. Volume 135. Issue 1.

04 Rebeckah Burke, *"Coffee Beans"*. The University of Rochester, Department of Chemistry. n.d. http://www2.optics.rochester.edu/workgroups/cml/opt307/spr16/beckah/index.htm

All images by the author.

(RE)COLLECTING RURAL

MEMORY, HERITAGE AND A RURAL IDENTITY UNDER THREAT

Jeremy Bonwick

Consider a small town on the very outskirts of Melbourne. The sort of place that might argue itself rural but through continual urban expansion is now at risk of being homogenised and absorbed into the urban condition.

This is the case for Warburton, nestled in the foothills of the Yarra Ranges on the banks of the audibly flowing Birrarung River, an hour away from its entry into Port Phillip Bay and Melbourne's GPO. The township's morphology embodies a tension between rural and urban symptomatic of its type. The main street, the Warburton Highway, holds its line, reluctant to bend save for steeper cliffs or slopes, driving a datum through the land. The spine of the settlement, the township's bakery, cafes and arts centre congregate and address this street in a formal, frontal manner. Behind all of this is the Birrarung River, or the Yarra River, takes its own way, winding along, without care but for the lowest path.

These parallel forces bound a site of forgotten significance, the former Sanitarium Health Foods Factory, an unashamedly Dutch-modernist-inspired cream brick building that stands north of the highway. To the south, the meandering Birrarung describes a curvilinear edge. Each is a datum in its own manner, the urban and the street, the relentless power and influence of nature and water. The building's presence and certainty are rare in its context. Formally, a composition of rectangular masses that pass over and through one another, punctuated by a strong vertical entry (complete with a civic gesture of a clock up the top of its central circulation core) and blue brick veins which enshroud horizontal bands of fenestration, reaching across the face of the otherwise uninterrupted cream bricks. There is a simplicity that demands attention from passers-by on the highway. Universality and pure representation were important ideas to its European modernist predecessors (in movements such as Neoplasticism and De Stijl), seeking a geometric abstraction of space that did not rely on a semiotic linkage with reality. Similarly, the composition is the foremost concern for this building. The factory was the site of Sanitarium's food production, including the manufacturing of Weet-Bix, until its closure in the mid-1990s. Constructed in 1936 and designed by prominent Melbourne architect Edward F. Billson, the structure has remained largely unaltered. A relic of an inter-war era somewhat at odds with its colonial context of an early settlement high street.

Above its formal significance, though, the factory holds a continual cultural value as an artefact of a time and modality which is quickly forgotten—a bygone era of local industry and production in the peri-urban and rural areas surrounding the city of Melbourne. The township of Warburton has always had a relationship with production. Its existence is owed to the discovery of gold and, as mining waned, found usefulness in timber milling, providing vast quantities of felled lumber to the city during the late 1800s and early federation era. With the arrival of the Adventist church around the same time, the town became home to the manufacture of 'health foods,' cereals which adhered to the Adventists' religious beliefs and Signs Publishing, the Adventists' own publishing house.[1] The place and its people were workers, producers and craftspeople. A primary reason for the Adventists' interest in Warburton as a base of operations was its positioning on the armature of the city—at intersections of the river, road and rail—the latter for connectivity and the former for power, tapping the river's water for reliable and cheap hydroelectricity. This is one way in which rural townships exist in equilibrium with the urban: a relationship of production and consumption, a symbiosis that manifests itself along the armature of the city, reaching out into the peri-urban and vastness of the rural hinterland. The nature of the rural is inherently work and craft of various types.

Understanding the Sanitarium Health Foods Factory and its role in a post-industrialised society of the present is formed by three key considerations, the first of which is the tensions mentioned above between urban and rural already expressed.

Top left: Entry through the Dutch modernist inspired fenestration.

Top right: Civic gesture of the clock on the circulation tower.

Bottom: The Sanitarium Health Foods Factory addressing the Warburton highway.

The second is methods and approaches for dealing with the existing architectural form and the understandings of heritage which are prevalent in contemporary discourse and in years gone—a debate around the importance of original material fabric and more intangible ideas of 'use' which reach a head in industrial heritage. Lastly, and on the issue of use, is the continuity and purpose of such a building in the twenty-first century. Through introducing programs such as community building and museology, places of industrial dereliction can be reimagined and reinvigorated, not as static remnants of defunct bygone practices but as new seats of 'useful' engagement and learning.

Heritage and industry

Heritage, as a broad practice and system of beliefs, faces an inherent tension; a grappling between significance and fabric. Value is attributed formally through the state, national and global bodies that stand to, broadly, protect the cultural inheritance of the built environment. Elements of these systems of attribution of value have long been contested discourses primarily because such values are constructed, not inherent. Heritage practice involves a process of attributing ideas of value to sites, buildings and (more intangibly) ideas from previous times. Often these buildings are found in a dilapidated state as a remnant of the past, often void of their original use, whether it is of 'value' or not. These buildings are shells onto which heritage systems project values and ideas.

Although some buildings enjoy enduring use and occupation, industrial heritage poses a particular problem when considering the issue of continual use. These structures date from a period in human history that necessitated "a forthright style of a building arising directly from the challenge of function."[2] Industrial architecture is often highly idiosyncratic and inseparably linked to a process or production. Surviving, if obsolete and abandoned, the original fabric represents the values of its operational heritage—any attributed heritage value tends to be tied up in technological innovations, discoveries and processes, as well as the people and communities involved and resultant. Additionally, remnant infrastructure is at greater risk of decay, not only through the ceasing of its continued use but also naturally through social misunderstandings and dereliction.[3] A ruin of physical fabric and purpose. Sites dating back to the early Industrial Revolution have commonly fallen into disuse as resources wane or technologies become obsolete.[4] This poses a problem and a serious threat to their continued existence and protection under heritage systems; these sites are no longer functional examples of processes and practices for which they are significant, yet neither are they of antiquity status nor have generally lacked recognition in world heritage listing. Continual authentic use is a key component of many national and global heritage systems. The forfeit or divergence of this continual use for adaptive reuse of now-abandoned industrial sites poses a risk to any heritage protections.

Until the early 2000s, industrial heritage was severely under-represented on UNESCO's world heritage list and only through advocacy from bodies such as The International

Top left: Composition of cream brick and De Sijl influence.

Bottom left: Concrete silos housed grain on the site.

Right: Original entry enshrouded with cream brick.

Committee for the Conservation of the Industrial Heritage (TICCIH), formed in 1973, began to shift.[5] This can be attributed in part to a natural process of reconciliation for industrial sites. In states of obsolescence and dereliction, these buildings are coded as negative symbols of social decline, exploitation and poor working conditions. However, the reframing of these sites sets in motion a transformation from "derelict functional structures to icons of an innovative industrial past."[6] Industrial sites that "offer archaeological evidence of past activities and technologies" rather than continual use can undergo a social reconciliation and revaluation through the lens of adaptive reuse.[7] However, such a repositioning of purpose stands to unsettle and threaten the heritage value, which is implicit in its original industrial operations and use. Despite renewed prosperity in adaptive reuse programs, there is an undeniable tension over authenticity in any regenerated state.

The sprawling UNESCO World Heritage-listed mining landscapes of Cornwall and West Devon in the south of England are evidence of this tension. The site was attributed value through its industrial and cultural significance as, at its height, the largest producer of tin and copper in the world and significant advancements in stream power technologies—particularly the Cornish Beam Engine, which became an idiosyncratic architectural feature of the landscape.[8] As the physical fabric of these stone engine houses, along with other surviving mining buildings, adjacent housing and townships, begins to deteriorate, local authorities naturally have turned to adaptive reuse practices. Although a significant element of the attributed value does not lie in the fabric itself (that is to say, it is an element of intangible heritage—the practices, inventions and societies of mining in Cornwall), heritage systems fixate on the fabric as a signifier of the past. Alterations to use which predicate adjustments to that fabric, or even radical insertions or addition, risks the loss of authenticity in heritage grading. In this example, developments at the North Quay port within the Cornwall and West Devon UNESCO site have been cited as serious risks to the continued listing of the site on the World Heritage register; with assessors arguing that the changes of use—which include new retail and housing developments—risked 'obliterating' the past, despite the renewed prosperity the residential developments would bring to the site.[9] Alterations in the pursuit of new use, therefore, must be carefully considered and mediated by respect for existing fabric.

This is not to say, however, that radical alterations and insertions into heritage sites predicate a definite sullying of value. Sverre Fehn's Hedmark Museum demonstrates architectural care when dealing with an existing condition despite sizable intervention. Glass is over-set in front of crumbling exterior walls, the decay left as a reminder of the temporal deterioration of the 13th-century castle-turned-barn. There is a delicacy to the moves Fehn makes throughout the site which belies the heaviness of the insertions and its materiality—thick concrete walkways and bridges traversing courtyards and internal voids hover illusionistically above the existing floor, coming to meet at a step which ensures a symbolic disconnection between new and existing. It is reminiscent of Peter Zumthor's Shelter for Roman Ruins, which similarly treats the ground and its archaeological significance with reverence. The visitor is cleansed from

Left: Dereliction on the facade of the Sanitarium Health Foods Factory.

Right: Framed by disuse.

Below: Recollecting the Sanitarium Health Foods Factory.

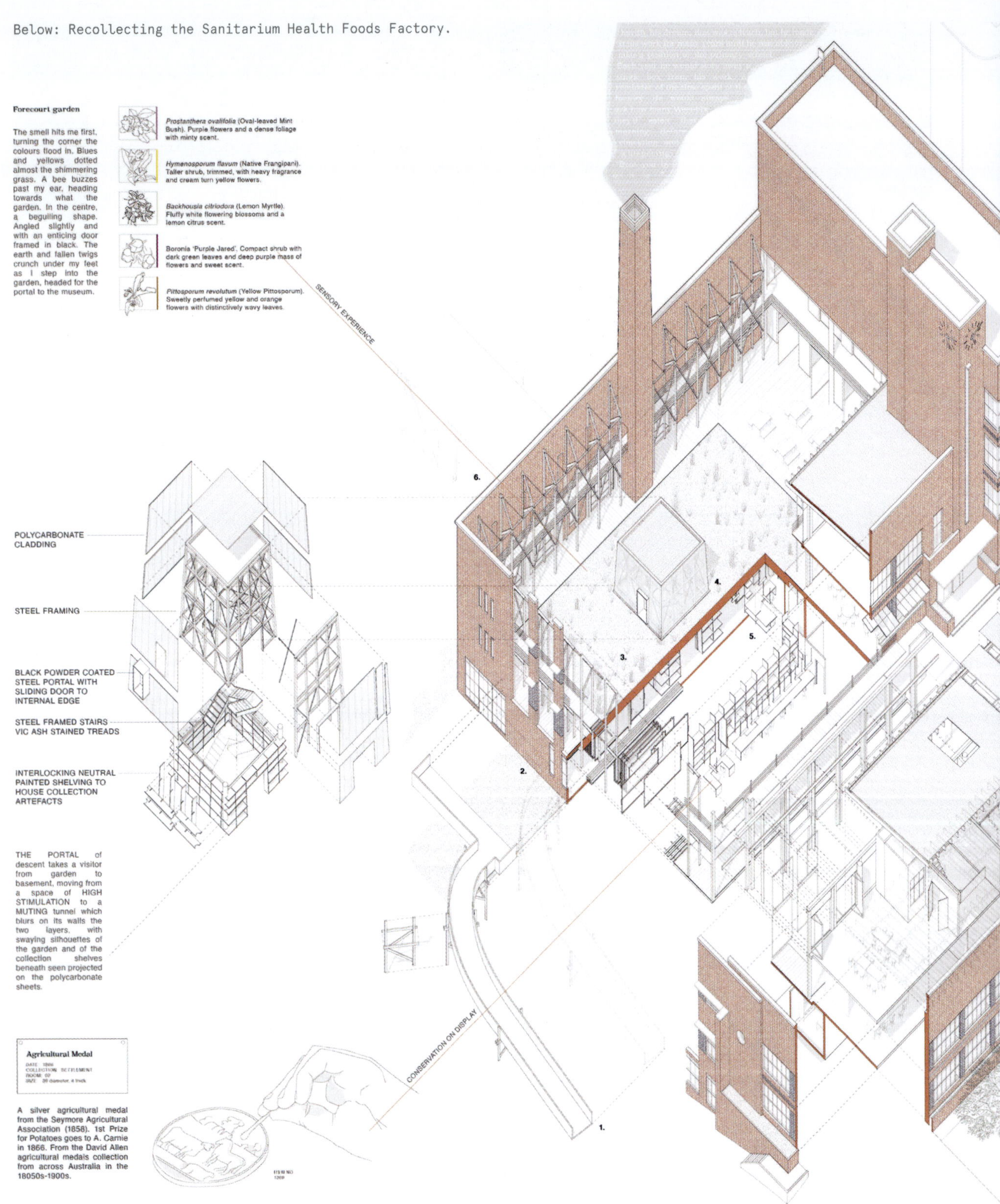

EXPLODED AXONOMETRIC
1:150

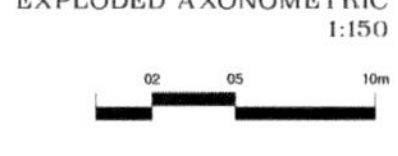

Sequence of entry
and experience

1. ENTRY RAMP FROM THE STREET
2. EXISTING FACADES RETAINED AS AN INDUSTRIAL SHROUD
3. OLFACTORY FORECOURT
4. POLYCARBONATE PORTAL
5. BASEMENT COLLECTION AS A PRECURSOR
6. MUSEUM TRANSEPT BRIDGE

the surrounding context through an extended portal door, which protrudes and cantilevers from the simple timber-slatted cubic form. Once inside, the visitor is first provided an omniscient view of the ruins from a suspended walkway over the ruins lying beneath, before a single staircase gives access to the ground plane and the displays. Similar to the entry portal, the final step levitates over the gravel and dirt of the existing ground. An attitude emerges here of sensitivity that takes a commonplace wall or crumbling footing and suggests a greater meaning—somewhere, in its being, is a significance of history, perhaps just its pure perseverance for continued existence. This is different from the attributed value seen in many heritage systems—here, the architecture retakes control of its own significance and the architect or practitioner exercises restraint and lets the remnant fabric tell its story through acts of framing or contrast.

Semiotically, the architectural surface becomes a sign; a signifier of past practices, inhibition and cultures. Rossi recognises this in *Architecture of the City*, stating that "buildings may be signs of events that have occurred on the specific site" and exist in a "relationship of site, event and sign."[10]

The surface of the wall in Fehn's Hedmark Museum is treated with care as it symbolises more than its physical state of crumbling stone; its assemblage, a trace of past construction techniques; the roughness of its hew a mark of a mason's chisel. There is value in these traces, however faint. A question of repair rears its head; rather than wiping away these traces and imperfections in order to return a building to some previous state of completeness, must tend towards preservation. Heritage systems have diverged on this assertion historically, pinwheeling on what level of intervention destroys the inherent value in the fabric or being of a place. In the 19th century, German academic Wilhelm Lübke wrote of a "restoration fever," lamenting the cleaning of ceremonial ash from burnt incense on chapel walls, 'obliterating' the "incomparable patina" of layered history.[11] These are the remnants and traces of 'forces' no longer present where "only the vestige remains" as "silent testimony."[12] Cracks in tiles, screw holes left from an old light fitting, the floorboard cut around a modern radiator. These traces of occupation are quite overtly expressed in Kerstin Thompson's interventions at the Abbotsford Convent in Melbourne. The architect has maintained the palimpsest of its internal walls, revealing and celebrating traces of a staircase that previously occupied the space as well as lines of services and changing wall finishes in wet areas. These traces begin to form a narrative of the site's actions and scarred surfaces become an imprinted substrate for its inhibition and now continual use.

Within heritage discourse, there appears to be a fetishisation of the original fabric and stasis of condition, which can counterintuitively threaten any buildings seeking to change or evolve their use. Where such a process almost mandates at least some level of alteration to the existing, impediments and encumbrances for a transition of use on these grounds risks further degradation. Ensuing disputes leave the building behind—in whatever state, it remains in the past, with no hope of redefining itself in the contemporary world. On the other hand, embracing the requisite changes to an industrial building, initiates a repositioning and decreases the danger of it passing into decay. The Sanitarium Health Foods Factory in Warburton is an example of the former; proposals to reinvigorate the site as a spa and resort have struck red tape (even given the extremely sympathetic nature of the design), and the building's state of decay has only accelerated as a result.[13] Clues should be taken from the work of European architects who have dealt with far greater numbers of industrial and general heritage sites, given the age and spread of their nations. For example, the Swiss firm Herzog & de Meuron's CaixaForum Madrid exemplifies a radical yet altogether cohesive and controlled approach to a disused power station. The early twentieth century brick form is, in a way, a reconstitution—a reimagining of the physical fabric in the form of collaging existing and new material. The architect makes this tectonic interplay abundantly clear through tactics such as windows that cut through the existing facade yet miss the original bricked-up fenestration and depression of the ground, revealing an external wall impossibly floating without foundations. These almost paradoxical relationships, which could almost be deemed careless in isolation, demonstrate consideration and architectural interest in the relationship between new and old, which occurs when a building undergoes a process of adaptive reuse. Moreover, the mere process of reinventing the building ensures its vestiges survive, and its use perseveres. Heritage value, although signified through the fabric and its patia or palimpsest, can just as easily be derived through ideas of continual use. In a state of decay, a building can be, at best, a relic of its significance. Injecting new life and continuity of inhabitation into a building of industrial heritage preserves more than its fabric but its importance as a place of human ingenuity, discovery and making.

Museums, memory and 'usefulness'

Industrial heritage, vacant and decaying in contemporary life, poses an opportunity for dual repair—both the place's usefulness and the usefulness of the local region. In a derelict state, such as the Factory in Warburton, such a shell can be recollected and used as a place of remembering and learning. Prior use is not forgotten and is considered beyond a facile reinstating of past practices. There is little point in glibly bringing, for example, smelting back to a smelting precinct or food manufacturing back to the Sanitarium Health Foods factory—such a move would belie the complexity of the place's relationship between occupation and use. Instead, industrial sites can be treated as "memory machines" with the opportunity to reframe "contaminated, well-worn, and tragic" appearances as reminders of past inhabitation and ingenuity.[14] The museum typology has exploited this state in recent decades—from the repurposing of space at the Tate Modern to the interventions at Fehn's Hedmark Museum—existing is appropriated and reused as a vehicle for remembering, its original purpose superseded by this new cultural function.[15] Such an intervention works on an interaction Pallasmaa notes between "perception, memory, and imagination" where "the domain of the present fuses into images of memory."[16] The built form becomes a device for recollection of the past. However, there is an uneasiness in this 'parasitic' relationship surfacing from the lingering questions around continual use and heritage value. To engage with a site's intangible heritage as a place of industry, the museum must, in some way, remediate its own existence through an engagement with the nature of manufacture and production. Broadly, these industrial sites were 'useful,' a fact which the museum should engage with to ensure it preserves the site's original purpose. As a result, the typology can expand to enact dual aspects of the repair – of the derelict industrial fabric and the surrounding post-industrial community; repairing society through reinstating vanishing values of usefulness and craft.

Hardly without precedent, these ideas echo back to Arts and Crafts luminary William Morris who, sensing a dismembering of the labour force under capitalism and industrialisation, advocated for a return to 'usefulness' and "hope of pleasure in the work itself."[17] The museum typology, already well equipped for modes of remembering and reframing, can expand beyond the static, white-walled "intensive care station" for artefacts and instead couple display with a sense of 'usefulness' in work.[18] Community and craft can be curated alongside exhibits, with programs which seek to reinvigorate industrial places by repositioning their significance as places of human advancement, community, production, and making. Museology as a form of adaptive reuse allows an industrial site's program to slip sideways. In our post-industrial society, use evolves from producing goods to producing culture, community, and fulfillment. Alistair Hudson has pioneered the idea of the "useful museum" and Arte Útil in the UK, a program which engages its community through the lens of

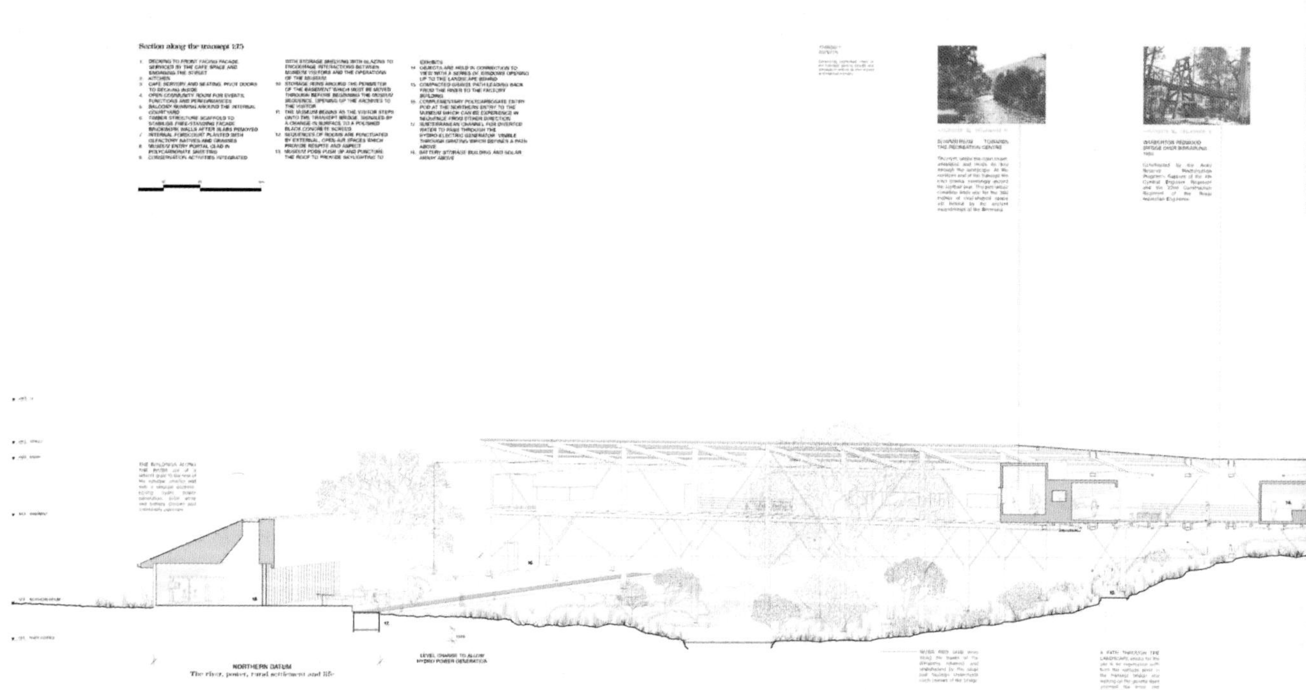

Previous top left: The scarred internal surface framed and supported by a new timber scaffold intervention.

Previous top right: Museum bridge stretches over the site away from the form of the factory building.

Previous bottom: Radical insertion; an internal courtyard displaces derelict factory program.

Above: A museological insertion bridging between the datums of the street and the river.

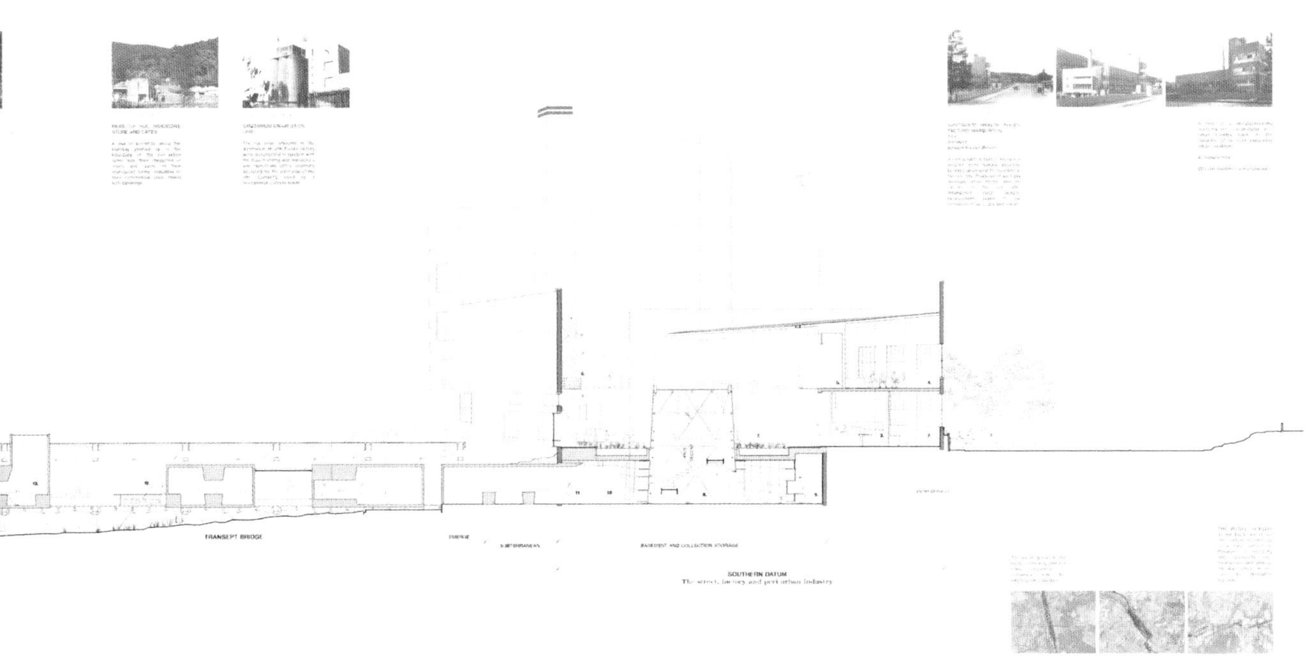
TRANSEPT BRIDGE
SUBTERRANEAN
BASEMENT AND COLLECTION STORAGE
SOUTHERN DATUM
The street, factory and peri urban industry

museology, utilising workshops and talks alongside display to foster engagement and encourage people to "learn how to make things [and, as a result] learn how to make society."[19] These places exist in the lineage of institutes such as the Mechanics Hall (of which an example exists on the Warburton highway, as with many other rural townships across Australia) and the Manchester Athenaeum, described as a "manufactory for working up the raw intelligence of the town."[20] With its scars and weathering, industrial buildings are apt for these insertions of 'usefulness.' The architectural surface, with its semiotic portrayal of past practices, craft and making, serves as a display and reminder of past exploits as well as a backdrop for new endeavors and learning. As the community is fostered through the injection of new use into former industrial sites, not only is the life of the built form extended and assured into the future but its former purpose and significance are reinvigorated and preserved.

The former Sanitarium Health Foods Factory stands as an opportunity to bring usefulness back to Warburton, a reminder of its heritage as a place of industry and production, and an opportunity to engage its townspeople. Through a museological intervention which pays homage to settlement and invention, rural enterprise and manufacture, a typology can be considered that mixes cultural and community engagement with reflection and active recollection of the past. Agricultural and Industrial artefacts are retooled as devices for reinterpreting modern problems, for approaching contemporary issues and relationships.

The factory transforms, its original purpose never forgotten—a place for the manufactory for Weet-bix no longer, but of identity and community for the rural township.

01 Earle Parkinson, *Warburton Ways* (Warburton: Signs Publishing, 1993).

02 Philip Cox, *The Australian Functional Tradition,* (Fitzroy: Five Mile Press, 1988).

03 Xu Yanfang and Cao Yinling, *"Cultural Industrialization: A Value Realizing Path for Industrial Heritage,"*Cross-Cultural Communication 8, no. 6 (2012): 105.

04 Marilyn Palmer and Hilary Orange, *"The archaeology of industry; people and places,"* post-Medieval Archaeology 50 (2016): 74.

05 Falser, *"Industrial Heritage Analysis"*, 8.

06 Hilary Orange, *"Industrial Archaeology: Its Place Within the Academic Discipline, the Public Realm and the Heritage Industry,"* Industrial Archaeology Review 30, no.2 (2008): 85, 87.

07 ICOMOS and TICCIH, *The Dublin Principles,* 1-3.

08 Ainsley Cocks and Nicholas Johnson, *"Cornwall's World Heritage bid and the beam engine,"* MunicipalEngineer 158, no. 3 (2005): 244.

09 Sharpe, Adam. *"Cornwall and West Devon Mining Landscapes World Heritage Site: Condition Survey2014".* Cornwall Council Historic Environment Service, 2014.

10 Aldo Rossi. *The Architecture of the City* (MIT Press. 1984).

11 Wilhelm Lübke, *"The Restoration Fever"*, Allgemeine Zeitung (Munich, 1861).

12 David Leatherbarrow, *"Tempered Terrain: Sverre Fehn's Villa Busk" in Building Time: Architecture, Event and Experience* (London: Bloomsbury Academic, 2020).

13 Darren Gray, *"Council pushes for rejuvenation of landmark Yarra Valley property"*, The Age, March 3rd2016.https://www.theage.com.au/national/victoria/council-pushes-for-rejuvenation-of-landmark-yarra-valley-property-20160303-gn9m3o.html

14 Antonello Marotta, *"Typology: Museum"*, The Architectural Review, published December 19 2012,www.architectural- review.com/essays/typology/typology-museums.

15 Marotta, *"Typology: Museum"*.

16 Juhani Pallasmaa, *The Eyes of the Skin: Architecture and the Senses* (West Sussex: John Wiley & Sons, 2005): 67.

17 William Morris, *Useful Work versus Useless Toil* (London: Hammsersmith Socialist Society, 1893): 2.

18 Harry Gugger, in Herzog and Herzog & de Meuron, *Natural History,* Philip Ursprung eds. (Lars MüllerPublishers, 2002).

19 Alistair Hudson, *"The Useful Museum"*, We Are Museums channel, July 2018, YouTube, 29:47.youtu.be/AmpCURA9nFw

20 Paul Pickering and Alex Tyrell, *The People's Bread: A History of the Anti-Corn Law League* (London:Leicester University Press, 2000): 226.

All images by the author.

(Re)collecting Rural is Bonwick's Master of Architecture independent thesis project supervised by Professor Rory Hyde, undertaken at the Melbourne School of Design.

Cream Brick

The sun dips,
reflecting off the relentlessly flowing water.
I can still hear the street,
dull now,
overlaid with a trickling and a rustling.
River red gums,
their canopy now at eye height,
coming to meet with a hand flour mill,
chipped and well used.
Next to it a railway sleeper,
timber greying and bolts brown with rust.
The football scoreboard peeks through
between the trees;
Warburton 5 goals 4, 34.
Bricks, layered with stories of labour.
The water runs on.

CARING ARCHITECTURE

Joan C. Tronto

What would caring architecture and urban design require? This question is not about the better design of so-called care institutions, about hospitals and homes for the aged. To follow the ways in which feminist scholars have reoriented the concept of care in the past generation requires an entirely new way of seeing the relationships among the built environment, nature and humans. Using care as a critical concept will require a fundamental reorientation of the disciplines of architecture and urban planning.

The starting point to making this shift is, in the first place, to see architecture as a reflection of power. Of course, architecture is a mode of artistic expression, a practical science to create built structures and environments; it is also an ultimate form of human power. When architects express ideas, they often do so in a way that draws upon and requires the deployment of vast material and human resources. Throughout human history and in civilisations around the world, architectural accomplishment has displayed such power. The device humans first seized upon to make themselves more god-like, according to the Torah and Old Testament, was a tower. In this case, their God took umbrage and confounded language so that humans would no longer be able to concentrate their collective power so effectively. That their God took the Tower of Babel as an affront to divine power tells us much about the permanence, solidity, and concentration of power that comes with the built environment that architects create.

Because their work usually requires vast resources, architects have often been in the service of the tastes and interests of the most powerful who command them. Whole epochs are captured in important buildings and structures, whether dams, city plans, cathedrals, castles, skyscrapers, football stadia, bridges, McMansions, public housing projects or gardens. Many times the goal is to overawe or control those who live in and around such structures. Capitalism, as an economic system that produces vast disparities in wealth, has rewarded architects and urban designers who have mirrored the values of capitalism: displays of great wealth, paeans to consumption, more efficient factories, and, in the neoliberal era, urban designs that attract the right sorts of people to the neighborhoods capital favors. Some decisions seem to be remarkable displays of brutish disregard: when a new American football stadium was built in Minneapolis, Minnesota in 2017, its beautiful glass structure posed an obvious hazard for migrating birds. Although the builders spent $1.1 billion, nearly $500 million of it in public funds, they declined to use a more bird-friendly glass that would have cost an additional $1 million.[1] On the other hand, architects and builders can also engage with their environment in ways that are friendlier to life forms: there is also the possibility of, and in some times even a keenness for, public squares, affordable housing, welcoming walkways, parks and public spaces.

The point is not that contemporary architects and planners are all uncaring; the point is that they are caring wrongly. They are caring about things, and, often, about the wrong things. When feminists began writing about care, they often started from the frames of caring that they knew best, about caring for (usually) vulnerable people such as children, people with illnesses, elderly people. But as scholarship has advanced, care theorists have begun to acknowledge that other sets of caring concerns are usually ascribed to men, and these are especially the caring tasks of protection and production.[2] So when men work and bring home a paycheck, they describe this activity as a form of care. The problem is that the paycheck money itself is not care; it needs to be transformed into clean clothing, food, a safe and pleasant place to live.[3] Doing so requires participating in the ongoing relations of those who are cared for. Buildings protect people from the elements. But by themselves, they do not provide care: what happens within the buildings? how the building fits within its location and context, how it was built, who it will house or displace; all of these aspects vitally affect the nature of the caring that the building does. Most frequently, then, architects and planners are caring about the world from the standpoint of using 'things' to give voice to particular sentiments, especially to power and capital. Consider how some modernist architects rued how the sleek look of their buildings would be ruined by the humans who used them: "Mies understood that the geometry of his building would be perfect until people got involved."[4]

Caring architecture will not be the same thing as sustainability, as important as that movement is.[5]

Sustainability began in the 1980s as an attempt to make architecture more sensitive to its environmental impact.[6] But as it was institutionalised, its standards became about things: it focused more on the materials used and it has been more successful in measuring what goes into a building than in monitoring the ongoing effects of sustainable building. Because care emphasises processes and relationships that extend back and forth through time, concerning all of the created relationships. Applying care theory to architecture would involve making a fundamental shift in perspective: care does not view the completed 'thing' — building, park, city zone, etc. — as its object. It starts instead from responsibilities to care, not only for this 'thing,' or its creator, builder, or patron, but for all who are engaged in contact through this thing. For example, what happened to the people, shops, goods, community, displaced to make room for this park? Who will occupy the space in the future? How were the building materials collected? (Do the LEED standards sometimes get 'gamed,' for example?) Who will clean and care for this building, street, infrastructure? Has it been built to last, or only built to last for as long as the builder remains responsible for manufacturing defects? While some scholars of architecture have begun to pay attention to such questions, what would it mean to have such an integrated, caring, approach to architecture? [7]

Here is where a feminist-inspired, relational, critical care approach begins to change our perspective entirely. Rather than thinking of buildings as things, thinking of them in relationships — with ongoing environments, people, flora and fauna — that exist through time as well as in space, changes the approach fundamentally.

Here is a modest claim that I offer to present and future architects: for our broken planet, we now need an architecture of care. Going beyond the ideas of 'what the client wants,' even beyond 'green' or 'sustainable' architecture, beyond the ideal of building a beautiful object, we now need an architecture that fulfills the basic tasks of sharing responsibilities for caring for our world, an architecture that is sensitive to the values of repair, of preservation, of maintaining all forms of life and the planet itself.

How then to arrive at a caring architecture? First we need to define care; then we need to see how it might begin to offer an alternative relational paradigm. Defining care is difficult; the term has many meanings. Some years ago, my colleague Berenice Fisher and I wrote:

> In the most general sense, care [is] a species activity that includes everything that we do to maintain, continue, and repair our 'world' so that we can live in it as well as possible. That world includes our bodies, our selves, and our environment, all of which we seek to interweave in a complex, life-sustaining web.[8]

This definition usually provokes frustration, because it is quite broad and does not well specify what should count as 'care' and what is outside of its purview. This definition is deliberately broad. Western thought has done a good job of thinking about production as the center of human life and of pushing the dimensions of care to the sidelines. Our goal in defining care so broadly was in part for us to see that care is a part of almost all aspects of our lives. Yet there are several ways to begin to discern where and what is care.

In the first place, most activities do not happen at this "most general level" of care, and so one needs to consider more specific care practices. Other care practices are 'nested' within other care practices to arrive at more general forms of care. Just as building requires assembling structural elements, plumbing, electrical lines, carpentry, etc., to make the entire building, and just as each of these activities must be done to its own standards in order to make the whole cohere, so too in the world of care many caring practices are woven together. Raising children is different from caring for one's adult self, which is different from caring for aged parents. Cleaning house is nested into these other types of care. Nevertheless, the point of care practice on this most general level is to make certain that these pieces all come together into a complex, life-sustaining web.

In the second place, care is always an activity, a practice. When people begin to think of caring practices, they often think of themselves as care givers, and as the receivers of care. But it is important for us to recognise that people, animals, plants, and other natural and artificial things are also enmeshed in practices of care. Given that care is an activity, it is sometimes difficult for people to switch and notice that care receiving is also a vital part of care.

In the third place, the definition sets a standard for judging care, "so that we may live in [the world] as well as possible." What this standard means, obviously, varies depending upon the decision of any community of 'we.' Every society engages in caring activities, and they do so according to their standards of living in the world 'as well as possible.' To evaluate whether care occurs well or badly, then, requires attention to the purpose of living well and to the purpose of care. This concern is highly political then. What we care about determines what kind of a society we are.

Beyond this definition of care, Fisher/Tronto specified four aspects of care to help explain the nature of care practices: caring about, caring for, care giving, and care receiving. In 2013, I added a fifth phase to these, caring with. These phases deserve some elaboration, and in doing so, we can get a starting sense of the importance of a relational way of thinking about care in architecture.

Before we do, we should note that care grows out of feminist thought for a particular reason. It may well seem as if, up until now, care is a soft and sentimental feminine activity. Indeed, throughout most of Western thought, discourses of care have been used to describe feminised processes of reproduction in the private, everyday lives of people. While some aspects of care do embody this set of sentiments, these care dimensions—what to care about, how to care for it, who will do the actual work of care, how to evaluate care, and how to make care into collective patterns and habits of care—are undeniably about power and political will. At this point, then, deciding who and what to care about and how to care for them, are highly contested. If care only means protecting the interests of the wealthy, it will result in a different architecture than one designed to repair the world. Caring to repair our broken world provides the political stakes of a caring architecture. Consider, then, a brief elaboration of these phases of care and how they might change architectural perspective.

Caring about means that we are attentive to the needs that need to be addressed. Before any caring process can begin, someone has to recognise the need for care. This is a more difficult task than it seems: some needs are made difficult to see or deliberately ignored. One of the ways that neoliberal spaces organise themselves is to separate people by class so that more wealthy people rarely encounter their poorer neighbors and their needs.[9] Even if caring needs are recognised, they are often in conflict with each other. Which needs should count more? Should the caring needs of wealthy clients, whose 'needs' for huge houses spread out on large parcels of landscaped suburban lawn, count more than the needs of farmers, less wealthy people, the earth itself?

Caring for is the phase of care that concerns the acceptance and allocation of responsibility. Once one has noticed a caring need, someone needs to step up and claim responsibility for it, or determine who else might be responsible. Stepping past a homeless person on the street in a city is a way to avoid responsibility. But what ought one to do? Throw some money in the cup? Take her home? Call the police? Support more housing for the poor? Deciding to act and to take on these unmet needs is another critical aspect of caring. For architects, we can ask that caring for involves taking responsibility for the entire process of building. Architects should take responsibility for how building materials are obtained, moved, and the environmental impact of those processes, of what has been displaced, and of how the building will be maintained. In building their football stadium, the Vikings ignored the impact of their glass building on migratory birds and, when the dangers were pointed out to them, refused to take responsibility for the situation. At what point do we excuse builders from the consequences of their decisions and processes? A more caring architecture would reach more deeply into these questions and allot responsibility for unintended effects.

Care giving requires attention to the actual acts of care giving. In the process of building, are the workers protected and cared for? Human Rights Watch in 2017 issued a critical report on the treatment of construction workers in Qatar, working on football stadia for the FIFA World Cup in 2022.[10] If a building is meant to provide shelter, for example, how does it do that? How do materials and workers get chosen, transported, used?

Care receiving. Once care giving is completed, what happens next? Because care processes go on, everyone and everything involved in the care process will be affected and transformed in some way by this process. How well were the needs that began the process met? Different participants in the process may decide that the process worked well, or poorly. In buildings and planned neighborhoods, ongoing monitoring is necessary. As time passes, how well does the building stand up? How easy or difficult is it to maintain the building? Who pays for ongoing repairs? What kinds of activities and responsibilities should users take on? At this point, care receiving requires that people notice what additional needs might be generated by having cared. And so the processes of caring begin again with determining needs, responsibilities and doing care.

Caring with. The recurring nature of care raises another set of concerns. Does care become reliable over time? When care needs are met reliably through time, people can develop an appreciation for those around them who provide such ongoing care. In such cases, care becomes a way to foster solidarity and trust among people.

Such solidarity and trust has a salutary effect: it makes it more likely that others will respond to the care that they have received in a reciprocal manner. In this way, despite the fact that care begins from asymmetrical needs, people may be able to see how participating in ongoing circles of care make them, over the course of time and through a life-cycle, somewhat more equal. Such reciprocity makes it more likely that people will recognise needs, take responsibility for the needs of others, participate in care giving and be honest about how well care is working. When people live in communities where such caring seems a part of their ongoing life together, they feel safer, pay more attention to their environment.

Of course, if some do not see or understand the care that they are receiving, or undervalue it, such caring with will not develop.

This leads us to a recognition of this key final point: just as architecture, as I argued at the opening of this essay, is about power, so too all forms of care are shot through with relations of power. Usually, those with needs are in positions of lesser power, but this is not always the case. But here is the looming question then. How might we direct our power towards caring for our broken world? Architects and urban planners will surely provide a critical part of the answer to this question, if they care enough to try.

Acknowledgements:
This piece is a facsimile of Joan C. Tronto's "Caring Architecture," originally published in *Critical Care: Architecture and Urbanism for a Broken Planet*, edited by A. Fitz, et. al. Cambridge, MA: MIT Press, 2019, with permission by the publisher.

01 Josh Peter, "Site of Super Bowl LII is a death trap for birds," *USA Today*, 11 January 2018, https://eu.usatoday.com/ story/sports/columnist/josh-peter/2018/01/30/sitesuper-bowl-2018-death-trap-birds-eagles-patriotsus-bank-stadium/1079934001/.

02 Joan C. Tronto, *Caring Democracy: Markets, Equality and Justice* (New York: NYU Press, 2013). 3 Batya Weinbaum and Amy Bridges, "The Other Side of the Paycheck: Monopoly Capital and the Structure of Consumption," in Capitalist Patriarchy and the Case for Socialist Feminism, ed. Zillah R. Eisenstein (New York and London: Monthly Review Press, 1979). 4 Andrew S. Dolkart,

03 Batya Weinbaum and Amy Bridges, "The Other Side of the Paycheck: Monopoly Capital and the Structure of Consumption," in *Capitalist Patriarchy and the Case for Socialist Feminism*, ed. Zillah R. Eisenstein (New York and London: Monthly Review Press, 1979).

04 Andrew S. Dolkart, "The Architecture and Development of New York City: The Birth of the Skyscraper," *Digital Knowledge Ventures*, Columbia University, 2003, http://nycarchitecture. columbia.edu/global/ 0141_1_media.html.

05 David Gissen, *Big and Green: Toward Sustainable Architecture in the 21st Century* (New York: Princeton Architectural Press, 2002).

06 Brian J. Barth, "The Past, Present, and Future of Sustainable Architecture," *Pacific Standard*, 13 June, 2018, https://psmag.com/environment/pastpresent-and-future-ofsustainable-architecture.

07 Nina Rappaport, "Real Time/Implication for Production Spaces," in *ACADIA Conference reForm ()-Building a Better Tomorrow*, Chicago, October 22-25, 2009 (Chicago: ACADIA, 1009); Nina Rappaport, "Preserving modern architecture in the US," in *Modern Movement Heritage, ed. Allen Cunningham* (London and New York: E & FN Spon, 1998).

08 Joan C. Tronto and Berenice Fisher, "Toward a Feminist Theory of Caring," in *Circles of Care, eds. Emily K. Abel and Margaret K. Nelson* (Albany, NY: SUNY Press, 1990).

09 Katherine Boo, *Behind the Beautiful Forevers: Life, Death, and Hope in a Mumbai Undercity* (New York: Random House, 2011).

10 David Conn, "Thousands of Qatar World Cup workers 'subjected to lifethreatening heat,'" *The Guardian*, September 17, 1017, https://www.theguardian.com/football/1017/sep/17/thousands-qatarworld-cup-workers-lifethreatening-heat.

To purchase this and other copies of *Inflection*,
please go to Melbourne Books at
https://www.melbournebooks.com.au